KU-523-268

The
Naked
Trader

FREE EBOOK EDITION!

Every owner of a physical copy of *The Naked Trader* 4th edition can download the eBook for free direct from us at Harriman House, in a DRM-free format that can be read on any eReader, tablet or smartphone – simply head to **ebooks.harriman-house.com/NT4** to get your copy now.

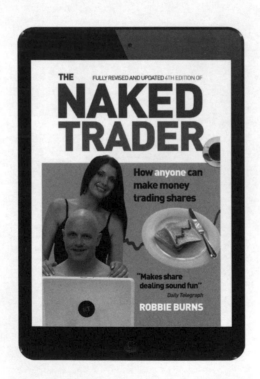

The
Naked
Trader

How anyone can make money trading shares

4th edition

by Robbie Burns

Hh

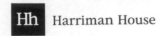 Harriman House

HARRIMAN HOUSE LTD

3A Penns Road
Petersfield
Hampshire
GU32 2EW
GREAT BRITAIN

Tel: +44 (0)1730 233870
Email: enquiries@harriman-house.com
Website: www.harriman-house.com

First edition published in Great Britain in 2005 by Harriman House. Second edition published in 2007. Third edition published in 2011. This fourth edition published in 2014.

Copyright © Harriman House 2014

Reprinted 2015, 2016

The right of Robbie Burns to be identified as the Author has been asserted in accordance with the Copyright, Design and Patents Act 1988.

ISBN: 978-0-85719-413-8

British Library Cataloguing in Publication Data

A CIP catalogue record for this book can be obtained from the British Library.

All rights reserved; no part of this publication may be reproduced, stored in a retrieval system, or transmitted in any form or by any means, electronic, mechanical, photocopying, recording, or otherwise without the prior written permission of the Publisher. This book may not be lent, resold, hired out or otherwise disposed of by way of trade in any form of binding or cover other than that in which it is published, without the prior written consent of the Publisher.

No responsibility for loss occasioned to any person or corporate body acting or refraining to act as a result of reading material in this book can be accepted by the Publisher, by the Author, or by the employer(s) of the Author.

Price chart images copyright © ShareScope.
Figure data, information and screenshots copyright © respective owners and sources.
Stock imagery copyright:

Rear cover and internal plain toast image ©iStockphoto.com/colevineyard
Front cover and spine toast image ©iStockphoto.com/courtneyk
Front and rear cover teacup image ©iStockphoto.com/PashaIgnatov
Toast pile image ©iStockphoto.com/gradisca
Tea mug image ©iStockphoto.com/lucielang
Headphones image ©iStockphoto.com/bluestocking
Paper plane image ©iStockphoto.com/peterglanville
Computer mouse image ©iStockphoto.com/malerapaso
Stacked mugs image ©iStockphoto.com/Anzelm
Traffic lights image ©iStockphoto.com/Aradan
3D glasses and camera image ©iStockphoto.com/mattjeacock
Laptop, cup and notebook image ©iStockphoto.com/ambrits

Cartoons copyright © Pete Dredge 2011, 2014 and Roy Mitchell 2005.

Author photos by Jim Marks.

Set in Plantin, Clarendon and DIN Pro.

Printed and bound by CPI Group (UK) Ltd, Croydon, CR0 4YY

Contents

About the Author

Robbie Burns has been a journalist and writer since he graduated in journalism from Harlow College in 1981. After starting life as a reporter and editor for various local newspapers, from 1988–1992 he was editor of ITV and Channel 4's teletext services. He also wrote ITV's daily teletext soap opera, 'Park Avenue', for five years.

He then went on to freelance for various newspapers, including the *Independent* and the *Sun*, and helped set up a financial news service for CNN. In 1997, he became editor of BSkyB's teletext services and set up their shares and finance service. While there he also set up various entertainment phone lines, including a *Buffy the Vampire Slayer* phone line that made him nearly £250,000.

He left full-time work in 2001 to trade as well as run a café in London, which he later sold – doubling his money on the initial purchase. While at BSkyB, Robbie broadcast a diary of his share trades, which became hugely popular. He transferred the diary to his website, **www.nakedtrader.co.uk**, which became one of the most-read financial websites in the UK. Between 2002 and 2005 he wrote a column for the *Sunday Times*, 'My DIY Pension', featuring share buys and sells made for his pension fund which he runs himself in a SIPP. He managed to double the money in his pension fund from £40,000 to £80,000 in under three years, as chronicled in these articles. By mid-2014 he had turned it into £350,000. Robbie now writes a weekly column for ADVFN and runs seminars using live markets to show how he trades.

Robbie has made a tax-free gain of well over £2 million from trading shares since 2001, becoming one of the UK's few ISA millionaires and achieving a profit every year, even during market downturns. His public trades alone – detailed on his website – have made more than £1.3m.

He owns a house in Barnes where he lives with his wife, Elizabeth, and young son Christopher. He also owns a riverside apartment on the Thames, where he sometimes works. But actually, he mainly plays pinball and table football there. His hobbies include chess, running, swimming, watching Fulham FC lose most home games, listening to terrible dance music, and trading shares from his bedroom, erm ... naked. After all, he wouldn't be seen dead in a thong ... (you might catch him in Speedos at the local pool).

Acknowledgements

Thanks to my wife Elizabeth for her support and putting up with me moaning constantly while I was writing (and rewriting) the book. Also, thanks to all the contributors to the real-life stories section.

Finally, thank you to my editor for his always valuable contributions (especially the boring chart stuff I'm too lazy to do myself) – and for making sure everything is as accurate as it can be. If there are any spelling misstakes they are his fault and not mine, okay?

Preface
Welcome to the Crazy World of Shares

Ever wondered whether you could make money by buying and selling shares? And maybe eventually quitting that damn job to do it? Being able to tell the boss to stuff it?

I think it's possible. I did it. And honestly, I am not a planet-brain, I'm not great at maths and I'm pretty lazy. So if I did it, maybe you can too!

But, of course, it's going to take time, and you need a disciplined mindset. Sorry to have to tell you … it takes plenty of hard work to get there! But it's a lot of fun. And once you've achieved it, there's nothing better.

This fourth edition of *The Naked Trader* will be your best friend along the way. It's for anyone who has ever wanted to learn how to make money from shares and it reveals all of the stock market knowledge that's taken me more than 14 years to learn. You can learn from the things I've got right – and even more from the things I've got wrong.

Not to mention things that other people have got right and wrong, too.

Oh, and don't worry – I speak plain English, not the financial gobbledegook others hide behind. You'll gain from my experiences without having to trawl through a lot of boring old financial twaddle found in so many other books about the market.

Is this book for you?

Who is this book aimed at? Well, anyone interested in making money from trading shares.

For starters, it's perfect for total beginners to the stock market – the first bits of the book, for instance, are all about exactly what your first steps should be, and all the core information you absolutely must know (but for once written in a way that won't give you concussion).

But it's also very much for those of you who are already trading and want to improve. It's packed to bursting with strategies and helpful hints that have all worked for me. I think that should also make it equally interesting to the more experienced investor, who perhaps wants to try out some new ideas.

If you've bought an earlier edition and are wondering whether to buy this edition: just buy it, you tight git! While some things are the same as last time, there is tons of new stuff to keep you happy.

And no matter your experience, if you have ever bought books about making money in the markets before but found yourself collapsing off your chair in boredom after five minutes, this book is for you. Trading isn't dull, so there's no reason for a trading guide to be a papery equivalent of Ovaltine. That's why I've tried very hard to make sure this one isn't!

The only trading topic this book doesn't cover in any great depth is technical analysis. So if double bottoms are your thing, I'm afraid you'll need to look elsewhere. [Oo-er, missus, etc. – Ed.] I'll touch on them briefly. [I bet you will. – Ed.] But that's all. [I'm out of innuendoes now. – Ed.]

Put simply, this book will teach you everything you need to know about how to make money from shares – and without giving you a headache. I've got a low concentration threshold myself. If I can write it, you can read it!

Robbie
London, 2014

Introduction
Trading Shares, Eating Toast, Making Money

When I wrote the original *Naked Trader* back in 2005 I thought it would be a one-off. I never expected it to sell many copies. I had felt there was a gap in the market for a simple-to-read book on how to make money from shares, written by someone who has really done it full-time, but I was stunned when it turned out that gap was pretty big and the book went on to be a bestseller.

Three years later I wrote the second edition, which sold even more than the first one. And then I did the third edition back in 2011, once more updating everything and adding lots of new content based on my more recent trading and what the markets had been up to in some very interesting/terrifying/opportunity-filled times after the Credit Crunch and Great Recession.

This fourth edition brings everything up to date once more. It also adds some really important changes I've made to my trading since the last edition – changes which have accelerated my profits.

I'm so pleased that my writing seems to help people. The emails from those who tell me they've never even bothered reading a whole book before, but have managed to finish *The Naked Trader*, are very satisfying indeed. Even better is when I get emails from people who tell me the book changed their lives.

This completely updated fourth edition is designed to be read from scratch, so there is no need to buy the previous three versions. In fact, if you bought one of those, I hope you will find this new edition worth getting too. It adds another three years of market experience to the core material of the earlier books, with tons of refinements and new stuff throughout.

Why a fourth edition?

Markets change and move fast. Since I wrote the last edition (2011), many things have happened in the world of shares, and I've learned a lot too. Like I said then, I only want to bring out new editions when I think I've got something genuinely new and valuable to add. The time definitely feels right now.

For example, just recently AIM shares have been allowed into tax-free ISAs for the first time. So I've changed my strategy on these types of shares a lot since the last edition.

This edition also contains plenty of other new strategies and ideas that have arisen out of the past three years of trading. In that time, my trades have actually become more profitable – significantly so. I've passed the £2 million profit mark for the first time. And I've been able to refine a number of new techniques that are definitely worth passing on.

So if you bought any of the previous editions and enjoyed them, I hope you will like this one just as much. Of course, there is some ground that has to be covered for new readers, and old hands may find some of this familiar, especially the first few chapters. If you are an improver and already know how to buy and sell shares you are allowed to skip the first few bits!

But I reckon this is still the one book you need to get started in trading, as well as a source of seriously decent strategies for making that trading worthwhile.

Jargon-free, common-sense advice

If you've never traded a share before it doesn't matter, as I'll guide you through every step of the process. And if you have traded for a while and have made losses, I am confident I can put you on the road to long-term stock market success by getting rid of your bad habits.

You won't find any inexplicable stock market jargon in this book – I write in plain English. You won't have to start scratching your head and think, 'Has he lapsed into Esperanto?' I'm going to explain how to buy and sell shares the easy way, and show you to the winners.

The fact is: stock market investment is easier than you think.

Brokers and tipsters love to spout jargon because it makes them look clever, and helps persuade you to part with your hard-earned money as a result of their 'advice'. But I'll take you past all that nonsense so that *you* can make your own decisions.

This is not a get-rich-quick book (sorry!)

One thing I certainly can't do is promise that if you have some spare money you will become a millionaire overnight as a result of reading this book.

Though I have technically become a multi-millionaire [It's true. He dresses like Mr Monopoly now. – Ed.], it has taken me many years. Building a fortune from trading takes time, and you will make more money by trying to grow your wealth slowly than by attempting to make a million in a year.

You know those ads:

> *"Make £400 a day from the markets … "*

> *"Become a stock market millionaire with our software … "*

Come on, you've always known in your heart of hearts that when something sounds too good to be true – it is!

This book is about building your wealth slowly and surely – with realistic targets and time frames. Using discipline, good stock-picking techniques and avoiding the mistakes new investors nearly always make, I believe I can make you richer. But you just aren't going to become a millionaire overnight.

I've made a couple of million, but believe me, it took loads and loads of nights!

Thrills and spills ahead

Trading shares is an exciting roller-coaster ride with plenty of thrills and spills. I really hope that excitement comes across in *The Naked Trader*.

Whether you have a small amount to trade, or you've inherited £100,000, I reckon that after reading this book you will be well-armed to enter the fray. I'm going to tell you everything I've learned over 14 active years of trading. You'll learn what makes shares move and what to watch for before pressing that buy button. I can also reveal how to make money by backing shares to go *down*. And I'll provide you with tons of useful info you just won't find anywhere else.

So, get a cup of tea, put your feet up and welcome to the crazy world of shares. Oh, and never forget the toast.

PART I
Getting Started

"Money can't buy friends, but you can get a better class of enemy."

– Spike Milligan

 # Escaping the Rat Race

My story

In 1998 I remember sitting in a grim office overlooking a dismal carpet warehouse on the A4 and thinking: "Is this how I want to spend my life?"[1]

I was earning quite a bit, but I wasn't happy. I didn't want to be in a horrible office working for a big company anymore. I knew what I wanted: freedom!

I quit the rat race in 2001 and have never looked back. I love my lifestyle. No moody bosses or targets. Just me! Of course, there are no office politics – but I can live without them! By 2014, lucky me had pretty much become financially independent forever. I bought a second property with some of my gains, so there is always a source of income there if I need it.

I now sit at home in my office overlooking the Thames, with my feet up, putting on a trade here and there and relaxing. My wealth continues to build in the markets over time.

---

1   Years later I actually made a lot of money betting on the shares of that carpet company going down. Which they did! Told you it was dismal.

Leabharlanna Poibli Chathair Bhaile Átha Cliath

Dublin City Public Libraries

Luckily for me, I realised working for someone else – unless you absolutely *love* what you do – is a mug's game. You're just there to pay the mortgage every month.

So while I worked for BSkyB, I also worked for myself. I had a shiny Reuters machine on my desk and (after the cleaner had been) I learned everything about the markets through practice.

I quickly realised I could make a lot more money trading than in my full-time job, and in 2001 I quit to trade more or less full time. Before this, though, I had to get some extra money to trade with.

The delectable Buffy

So while still employed I started to develop other income streams – one of which was a *Buffy the Vampire Slayer* information line. This made me £250,000 over four years! It simply involved me reading out the latest Buffy news on my phone at home – eager viewers would call the line to hear the recording and I made money out of each call. Sadly the series ended in 2000, and with it the line.

I started it for a bit of a laugh ... but on its first day the guy who owned the phone company called me and said: "Bugger me, it's just taken £400!"

Happiness is ... residual income

And I sold mobile phones and cut-price phone calls and energy for a company called Telecom Plus. And still do now, actually, from time to time via my website. I got – and still get – a cut of every phone call made or bit of energy used by customers who have signed up through me. It's called residual income and it pays all my bills even now. I still earn from customers I sold to in 1999!

Armed, therefore, with a huge pile of cash, I quit my job and decided to trade full-time. But I didn't go crazy. I started off by just putting £7,000 into a stocks-and-shares ISA and £10,000 into a spread betting account. I only added small amounts over the years (the government don't even let you add more than a certain amount annually to your ISA). *I did not want to lose my capital.*

I also wanted a bit of a fallback in case I wasn't such a great trader, so I bought a café near a tube station in Fulham. That proved a lot of fun and I made quite a bit of money. My wife and I improved it till it made £1,000 a day instead of £300 – it was very successful.

So successful, in fact, that it actually became a pain in the neck. More customers, which led to more staff, which led to more problems. Classic growing pains. Sometimes staff didn't turn up and I found myself making coffees at 7am! There were all kinds of things I didn't like doing: firing staff; dealing with customers complaining there was fish in their fish pie; and handling all the mess a café brings.

The worst incident I can remember was when all the staff were sick, and I was on my own behind the counter trying to serve a huge queue of people.

So I shouted out to the café: "I need help! Anyone want a short-term job? £10 an hour." And one of the customers came to my rescue and started serving. There was a lovely community spirit and I met a lot of great people.

But with my son arriving on the scene it became too much effort to run it, and enough was enough.

I had originally intended it to be the start of a chain, and I nearly bought a second café, but decided in the end I didn't want to be a retail mogul. Too much effort – I'd rather have less money and enjoy relaxing.

So I sold the café for roughly double what I paid for it. Interestingly, running the café helped my trading because a café business is quite complex, and learning the accounts helped me evaluate stock market businesses.

A lazy life

So now I just trade and run my website **www.nakedtrader.co.uk**.

I also hold five or six seminars a year, where I show readers my techniques using live markets on a large screen. I really enjoy them and they get me out of the house. It's also amazing how many share picks come out of these seminars that go on to make plenty of money.

It's also good fun to meet readers and have a drink with them. If you want to come to one, see the info on the seminars at the end of the book – or take a look at my website to check I'm still running them. Maybe we'll have a drink together sometime!

The markets have certainly made me very happy. There are plenty of other people like me around who have managed to quit their office jobs and trade. And they, like me, are nothing special. All it takes is some discipline, determination, and – I'm afraid – some trading capital (i.e. money). I can help you sort out the discipline and determination, but you have to come up with the capital.

I hope *The Naked Trader* will put you on the first rung of the escape ladder. Trading shares really is much simpler than you might imagine once you see past the jargon. And I promise you won't find any of that here.

What sort of trader am I?

I suppose I am more of a medium-term investor than a trader. Definitely not a day trader. Did you know that nearly everyone who tries day-trading loses at it? Maybe I should be called the Naked Investor. I expect you imagine a *trader* to be someone sitting at a desk all day feverishly buying and selling shares.

Well, that's not me at all. I don't want to be like that. I want to be, oohhh … drinking tea and eating toast. Having a snooze. Going to the gym. Watching the racing. Sitting in the garden with a good book (or a bad one – I always fall asleep, whatever the book is like. Especially if it is a financial one). And I enjoy playing with my son. And, okay, basically I'm a bit lazy (is it time for a nap yet?).

What I hope you'll learn is that **you don't need to spend 40 hours a week in front of a screen watching every move the market makes.** And it is even possible to trade or invest if you have a full-time job, as long as you can get some peace and quiet on the internet at some point during the day.

In fact, that may be the best way to start trading. Instead of spending all day emailing your friends, getting addicted to Facebook or Twitter, fiddling with your iThing – spend a bit of time learning how to invest. That way you can make some extra money and learn the tricks of the trade while you're working.

One of the things I really want to get across in this fourth edition is that you can actually trade *less* and make *more*.

Keep this book handy

I suggest you keep me handy, even when you think you've sussed out how to make money. Because, even if you've read the book once or twice, you may need me again if you fall into bad ways – and believe me, you will be tempted. And I will always be here for you to skim through ...

Anyway, I really hope you enjoy the book. You don't need to read it all in one sitting. Read it in bits and let it sink in. Take it on holiday and read it on the beach. Keep it handy when you're going through a bad trading patch.

Don't take it on a date, though. There just isn't room for three of us in the relationship.

A Day in the Life of a Naked Trader

Dear diary ...

6AM

It's *been three years since I wrote the last diary* and it's amazing how life changes. When you have kids it tends to revolve around them and how old they are. In the first book I was up at 6am watching *Teletubbies*. Po was my favourite. LaLa was a bit too ditzy for me.

Anyway, these days at 6am I'm in bed, of course! What on earth is 6am? I know people in the *Sunday Times'* 'A Life in the Day' column always wake up at 6am, go running for five miles, have power breakfasts, make executive decisions and are dressed and at their desks by 7am. But this day-in-the-life is an honest one. I will be sound asleep.

7AM

My 9-year-old son Christopher awakes on the dot of 7am. Luckily for me, my wife takes over getting the lad ready for school while I grab some tea and toast and head for my trading desk (well, it's just a desk with a computer on it).

Later on I might go and trade from the riverside flat I own. I don't have any debt and with two properties, if the stock market screws up and I lose everything I'll have rental income to fall back on. I feel very lucky.

Actually this hour is one of the most important parts of the day, because at 7am each day companies report their results and release announcements. First thing to do is to check whether there are any announcements on shares I own.

If there are, I try and quickly judge whether I need to take any action. Is a report looking a bit dicey ... have any question marks come up? How are profits looking? Should I sell and take my gains, or perhaps buy some more?

Likewise, if there's a bad news story on a share I own, I have to decide what to do. Cut it when the market opens or wait and see it out?

Often I see good news about a company whose shares I don't own, so I make a note to research it later.

Next I check the spread betting firms to see how the FTSE 100 is set to open. They tell me – and pretty accurately – whether it looks likely to be a good or bad opening, which often sets the tone for the first couple of hours. However, I tend to mainly hold smaller companies, so if the FTSE 100 is scheduled to open lower it doesn't necessarily mean I've got to worry: smaller companies aren't listed on it.

Recently I started doing one further important check at this time of the day. I now have a look before the market opens to see whether or not I need to move any stop-losses. These are instructions to brokers to get me out of a share if it goes down too much. When markets open, sell prices can do funny things and briefly be lower than they will actually be throughout the day (I'll explain why later), and I want to see whether or not I need to move a stop to keep it from accidentally closing a trade.

Also on 'ex-dividend' days – when a company pays out some of its profits to shareholders in the form of a dividend – shares often start lower by the amount of the dividend. So I just quickly check that no trade will close unnecessarily because of this.

7.56AM

Four minutes to make a fresh brew and some more toast before the market opens at 8am! Meanwhile, around about now the Mrs and Christopher head off for school.

8AM

The stock market opens at 8am and my monitors of various shares suddenly spring into life. It's always interesting to see how your shares are starting the day.

The first half an hour of the market is fairly important, and I whizz through all my positions to check nothing is tanking for any reason. However, one thing I have really learned since I wrote the last edition is not to worry so much about the opening prices.

It usually isn't worth trading during the first hour of the day, regardless of whether or not a share is racing up or down. That's because there is always an initial overreaction by the market to news, and this can be magnified early in the day when there are fewer people buying and selling.

It's easy to get caught out. So I always wait for the markets to settle and meanwhile simply watch with interest.

On the smaller shares, market makers will often mark a share up or down because the share has been tipped in the press. By the opening, a share will often already start higher or lower – you can never deal at last night's closing price!

8.30AM

Everything begins to calm down and the gaps between the buy and sell prices – the spreads – start to narrow. But I still rarely buy or sell at this time. So sometimes I get on the cross-trainer and exercise a bit while catching up with Sky News. After all, trading is a sedentary occupation and it's important to keep fit to keep the mind fit too.

9AM

Time for a look at the inbox. I get quite a few emails, sometimes more than 100 a day, and I answer them all, unless they are abusive or the person is obviously mad. [Finally, an explanation. Er, hang on a sec ... – Ed.]

Sometimes people become aggressive if I try and tell them it's their fault they've been losing money rather than the market's fault – a lot of people tend to blame everyone but themselves. But blaming the market is meaningless, and it's dangerous for a person's trading. I'd rather warn them, on the off-chance that the red mist won't descend, than send them a bland email agreeing with them just for a quiet life.

The hardest emails to answer are those with the subject line: 'Just a quick question'. Of course, that means it's an extremely long and complicated one! If an email is very long or complex it goes into a folder marked 'pending' and I answer it at the weekend. Otherwise I try to reply as fast as I can and keep the inbox clear.

The messages I hate are those asking whether or not to buy or sell a specific share. I have to reply that I can't give an answer – you have to be a regulated advisor. I wouldn't want to, in any case. If I tell someone to buy something and it goes down it will be my fault, and ditto if I tell them to sell and it goes up!

9.45AM

Mrs NT usually heads off to play tennis now. I have a look at the markets and see what's happening. This is about the time of day when I might consider a trade. Or not. Sometimes there isn't anything I need to do, sometimes there is. I never rush anything.

If it's a seminar day, at this point I'm getting ready to start, and chatting to those who've arrived. It's always a fascinating bunch of people who come along and I love doing them – there's something of a performer in me, and this is where it gets a chance to come out!

10AM

Time for another round of tea or coffee and toast. And a read of the paper. I'll then have a good look through my current portfolio. It is divided up into spread bets and shares held in an ISA – both of which enable me to avoid paying any tax on profits. Various governments make noises from time to time that either or both will be capped or some profits made taxable but it hasn't happened yet.

Is there anything bothering me, anything about to produce results? Anything I should take a profit on? If there is something that is on my mind to buy or sell I'll look at Level 2, which gives me a snapshot of how many buyers and sellers there are around. It gives me a good idea of whether my trade is sensible, and a final push to either make the trade or leave it till later.

These days I only push a buy or sell button if I really feel the time is right. The absolute worst thing to do is to make a boredom trade. A lot of people lose because they over-trade.

Things are generally busier for me if the markets are going down, as I might then have a shorter-term spread bet open, betting on the market to carry on falling, and that takes a bit more looking after.

If I feel like it, at this time of the day I'll also either do some research on anything that came up when I was looking at news stories earlier or do a bit of web surfing. I don't tweet and I'm not on Facebook, as both look too addictive. Sometimes people pretend to be me on Twitter and start actually answering questions. I usually set the Mrs on them and they are soon gone.

11AM

Markets tend to go quiet around 11ish, so I might nip to the health club close by for a swim, or pop to the shops. If the Mrs is back from tennis well … who knows … new balls, please!

11.45AM

Back to the markets. At about this time I look through my shortlist of potential buys I have previously researched and see if any are rising. Is it a good time to buy? I try and suss out the mood of the market and will trawl through Level 2 again to see if anything looks likely to rise. This is probably the best time of the day to buy.

12PM

Wednesdays I'll write up my website update, which I quite enjoy – though it takes some time to write. I blog about my life, a bit about things in the news that annoy me and then any trades I made in the last week. Often I've forgotten what I traded, so I have to go through my accounts.

On other days I'll reply to more emails. Again, it could be anything! Could be someone interested in a seminar, wanting some info about some aspect of the market, perhaps wanting me to make a speech (I never accept), or do an interview (I rarely do).

Often someone asks to advertise on my site. I refuse as I want the site to remain independent, and I wouldn't want to advertise tipsters or systems and similar, as I don't believe in them. I turn down some big sums but would rather that than get emails along the lines of, "I bought this via your website and now I live in cardboard".

12.30PM

Time for lunch. That might be a sandwich or something, or me and Mrs NT might meet up for lunch somewhere. Or I might meet a friend. Sometimes I just head off to the flat for a peaceful afternoon. The only exception is Wednesdays, when I am probably still writing stuff for my website update … the sacrifices I am willing to make for my loyal readers!

1.30PM

The market sometimes changes at 1.30pm. This is because it's 8.30am in New York, when they often release important economic data. The FTSE 100 as a whole, and individual shares, can suddenly move quickly in one direction or another, depending on what is announced.

It doesn't usually affect me that much, but if it's a down market and I am betting on the FTSE 100 to fall, I might quickly close that bet and take my profits if news from the US is good and likely to make the FTSE 100 pick up a bit.

1.45PM

If it's a nice sunny day I'll go for a sleep and a laze in the garden. Otherwise, a cup of tea and a KitKat, Twix or Yorkie bar! Told you I was honest – this is definitely not a diary c/o the *Sunday Times*!

Around about now I might also watch something I recorded last night. Preferably something with loads of violence and sex in it, like *Breaking Bad* or *Dad's Army*.

2.15PM

This is when I'll have a look at my shortlist of higher-risk shares. I buy some high-risk shares for my pension, which I run in a SIPP (self-invested personal pension). I'm sensible in my ISA and spread bet accounts, and so view my pension fund – or at least around half of it – as a place to open the throttle up a bit and try a few higher-risk ideas. Now I can put AIM shares in my ISA – which you couldn't do in the past – I look at a wider range of shares than before.

2.30PM

The Dow Jones opens across the pond, where it's now 9.30am in Manhattan – and where it goes, UK shares tend to follow. I check through the main portfolio again. The worst thing is when a share goes down quite a bit and I have to decide whether to get rid of it or not.

If the market is going well, it's unlikely I'll place any more trades for the day. If it is going very badly, I might consider buying a good share that seems to have dropped purely because of the market-wide panic-selling.

3PM

If it is a seminar day at this point in the afternoon we will be getting stuck into live markets and supply and demand and how to unemotionally judge if you should be buying or selling a share. I love it when I see light bulbs go off in people's eyes as we discuss this stuff.

On a Wednesday I'll check through my website update to see if it all makes sense and then publish it. If I make a terrible error, someone usually puts me right straightaway.

A new update generally means a whole lot of new emails to reply to after people read it. Sometimes I get a rude email if I mention I've sold a share that someone really likes. If it's close to a seminar I might read through some questionnaire responses from those coming, to start to judge what to cover on the day.

3.30PM

It's school-run time. Either me or Mrs NT does the honours. If it's a nice day and the market is quiet, I'll do it. I am usually the only dad doing pick up.

If the market is very quiet I might even call it a day at this point and go straight to the park with Christopher for a sit down and an ice cream. And definitely a game of football!

4PM

Time for a last look at the portfolio as the market shuts in half an hour. How have I done today? What did I miss? How much money did I make or lose? When you have a lot of money in the market (I have more than a million usually), it can be up or down by £10,000–£20,000 every day. It took some getting used to this. Over a month I could end up down or up by £50,000 plus!

4.30PM

That's it! The market's shut: hurrah! I have a final look through and close my web browser down and turn off the computer. This is time for playing with my son. We might go for a swim, or another game of football, or do his reading – anything we feel like.

5.00 PM

On Fridays, it's time for Fives football! My son plays for a team in Barnes and is the striker so it is up to him to score the goals. He's usually in the top five scorers for the season. (Proud dad alert.) I usually take him for a pizza after – a father-and-son's night out. Well, as long as he's scored at least three …

5.30PM

Time for tea. Mrs NT tends to do it, though I have a go twice a week or so. We try to eat healthily, but pizzas, chips and sausages do sneak in sometimes. We try and make sure Christopher has something decent, but he is always on the hunt for sugary things like his dad. Hey, where's my Twix gone?

7.30PM

Time for Christopher's bath and bedtime. It is so rewarding being with him all the time. Being a stay-at-home trader gives me precious time with my son that I would never have as a full-time worker. Some of the dads around here leave home at 5am and don't return till 9pm, never seeing their children. Not something I could do.

Once or twice a week, though, we get a babysitter in and Mrs NT and I go out for dinner with friends or to the cinema. We think it's important to get out for some 'us time' once a week at the very least.

8.30PM

Nothing on TV, so time for a cuddle with the Mrs! The next 5 ... I mean 30 minutes are censored. Then I watch *The Apprentice* if it's on, or *Dragons' Den*. I also like *Curb Your Enthusiasm* and *Have I Got News For You*. Sky Atlantic, which shows all the new HBO programmes, is good too. But there's so much old crap on these days that I find I'm watching less and less. And I really hate most UK sitcoms and soaps.

We watch lots of DVD box-sets – most recently *Breaking Bad*, which was amazing! Nearly as good as *The Sopranos*. We like comedies like *Girls* or the French programme *Hard*. If I am doing a seminar it's usually ending around about now and we're heading to the bar.

9PM

I check to see where the Dow Jones closed. This always has a big effect on how my shares start the day tomorrow. I also spend a little time doing research on companies flagged up from this morning's news stories, and check to see what's being launched on the market in the next few days. And I might look through some share lists and see if anything new comes up. More emails usually ping in and I get through some of them.

9.30PM

If there is a seminar coming up in a week or so, I do some preparation work. I never intended running seminars and I still don't do that many, maybe five a year, but people seem to really enjoy them and they are very rewarding personally. The feedback is always good and I'm glad to be able to help.

So many nice people come and we have great fun chatting over lunch and in the bar afterwards. I read through replies to questionnaires I have sent people in advance and they really help me plan the day – I try and give people what they want.

There is a lot of interest in Level 2 at the moment, which the professionals use to judge good entry and exit points. I explain Level 2 in depth and try and make what is complex simple. A lot of the day also depends on what's happening in the markets.

We've even struck up long-term friendships with people who've attended the seminars. A very nice couple who actually live near us have become great friends. I also made friends with someone who became my dentist, and a lovely couple who live in Switzerland.

The seminars came about by accident as a suggestion from a reader. I was really nervous doing the first one, but now I love the days and stay at the hotel where it's held the night before and after. I need recovery time afterwards – you just try and talk non-stop for ten hours and you'll see what I mean!

10PM

I have a check of the news and hope Robert Peston isn't on it – his presence usually indicates trouble! Sometimes we watch something we Sky-Plussed. Or even half a movie, which we'll finish off the next day. By now the computer is most definitely off again till the morning!

10.30PM

If we went out, we usually get back around now. The babysitter also does the ironing, which is rather handy, so now we just have a chat, a decaf something and then ...

11PM

... *It's off to bed and I'm asleep* the moment my head hits the pillo—zzzzzzz ...

3. Is Trading Right for You?

What do you want from your trading?

Before you launch yourself into the wild world of shares, you need to ask yourself why you're doing it. What sort of return are you after?

Are you a high-risk, high-return hotshot or do you just want a few extra quid? Are you looking to build wealth over a long period? Or do you just want a bit of fun?

Maybe you want to make a bit extra to buy a new car, or are hoping it will help pay school fees, or provide a better retirement.

Or do you want to become a full-time trader?

> Think about what you want from the market, because what you want (and how much you want it) will really affect how you trade.

Make more money by not relying on the markets

I believe it is easier to make money on the markets if it is **not** your main source (or would-be main source) of income.

If you're currently in a full-time job, you should do what I did and think about new income streams that will let you quit and trade but still have a fallback. I did a *Buffy* phone line and became a distributor for Telecom Plus, selling telephony and energy in my spare time. Think about things you could do, or find to do, to make extra cash alongside your trading.

Is there anything extra you could do at work to build up money for yourself? Or any contacts who might give you freelance work? See if you can find yourself some new income. It's one of the ways to eventually quit work.

> The reason I suggest more than one source of income is that you will be more relaxed when trading. If you are trying to make trading your only source of income you will be much more stressed – and therefore more likely to snatch at profits, not cut losses, and not make enough money.

How much money do I need to start trading?

The question of how much money you need to start trading comes up a lot. If you only have £500, there really isn't that much point because of dealing commissions. You also won't really be able to get yourself a balanced portfolio (AKA a broad range of shares). And you will want some balance in there.

With around £500, I reckon you're better off waiting till you've built a bigger pot. In the meantime, it's definitely worth 'paper trading'. In other words, give yourself (say) 50 grand in pretend money and play the markets on paper – keeping a record of buy prices for shares you go in for, and then how they perform, and what you sell for.

A lot of successful traders start this way, though it will never be a perfect replica of the real thing. (Extraordinarily, one can be a little calmer when risking a fictional fortune.)

Also, if paper trading, no return trips please to the Bank of Me, Myself and I, and its magic money-making biro when trades go the wrong way. Haven't you heard that credit is impossible to get these days?

So what's a reasonable figure? I would say that once you have around three grand or more, you have enough to start putting real money into the markets.

How much money do I need to become a full-time trader?

The amount of money you need to become a *full-time* trader depends on how much you think you need to live on and how much you think you can make from investing.

Realistically, I reckon full-time investors can and need to aim to be making 20–25% each year on the money they have invested. This is with dividends (the profits paid out by a company to its shareholders) paying for their trading costs.

This means that, if someone has trading money of £100,000, a full-time trader is someone who can get £25,000 out of it with the right discipline, and is happy living on that amount of money. If you need more to live on, you'll need to invest more.

It is possible to make more than 20–25%, of course, but you'd have to be really good or have a couple of lucky breaks.

The point is, you have to be realistic about it. I have people who email me to say they have started being full-time traders with just £10,000. I think they are bonkers. It won't happen.

Some people think they can do it by using leverage – in other words, debt on-demand that supersizes the amount they can buy and sell – in spread betting. However, what often happens is that instead of making more money they go bust. Spectacularly! Losing not just their own money, but money that isn't theirs … My view is: don't use the credit you can get. Use genuine money.

A reader writes: No margin for errors

"I tried a £50k day-trade using leverage, without having the money to settle. My position lost 10% and I had to sell other shares to cover the shortfall on a bad day for the FTSE 100. This was a memorable way to learn not to day-trade with someone else's money – they'll definitely want it back!"

A warning

I feel like a right boring old fart by having a warning so early in the book. After all, you bought this book because you wanted to make some money. And you *can* make money on the markets.

It's just that, over the years, I've met or read of people who have totally screwed up and instead of making money they lost it. In fact, later in the book you will read some terrible stories from traders who have had disasters.

Some lost nearly everything. One or two lost a fortune but then managed to get back on track. But some reckless traders have lost houses and even their marriages.

There have been various times in the markets when shares have slumped, taking people's money with them in spectacular fashion. Like 2000–2002. May/June 2006 was also pretty bad, as was August 2007. And let's not get into the Lehman implosion. Then Summer 2011? Horrible. In a week in August 2011 you could have lost a fortune. The point is, shares don't just go up – they can go down a lot too.

Don't think you'll get rich quick. It won't happen. But if you take things easy, are careful with the amount of money you put in, and learn from your mistakes, then I am happy to encourage you – because your chances are good.

(Of course, if you do get rich quick, go ahead and email me with the subject line 'Na-na-na-na-naaaah!' – and feel free to send me some cash as proof. Preferably used 20s.)

Can you afford to trade shares?

Before you buy a single share, I do urge you to look at your finances carefully and honestly. Ask yourself:

1. Where is the money coming from that I am going to use to trade?

2. Can I honestly and realistically afford to lose a lot of it?

3. Where the hell is the remote control?[2]

It's unlikely you will lose all the money you put into investing – if you are careful and follow the rules laid out in this book – but it's not impossible. It is quite possible that you could lose 20–30% if the market runs against you for a while.

Maybe you have £10,000 sitting in a building society account not earning much interest. Will you feel okay about it if you end up with £5,000 after six months of trading?

• If the answer is 'yes' to the above question, then go for it!

• If the loss of the money would devastate you, keep it in the nice safe account and just wait till you can realistically afford to trade with money you really can afford to lose.

Perhaps you've suddenly come into money unexpectedly – say, £50,000. Great! As you weren't expecting it and, presuming your financial status is okay, there's no reason why you shouldn't invest around £15,000 of it.

---

2   Under the second-to-left cushion on the sofa.

Let's presume you have the money to play with. One final thing to check: are you a compulsive gambler?

- Do you bet on the horses, buy scratch cards, go to the casino, play online betting games on a regular basis? And does that give you a feeling of excitement?

- Do you feel unable to stop doing these things because they are really enjoyable, even if you are losing?

- Do you hide your bets from your partner? (Under the sofa's a good place, but not the second-to-left cushion.)

If the answers to any of the above are yes, then give this book to someone else (or chuck it, so they have to buy a new one). Going into the markets will just be feeding your addiction – and losses on the markets can be difficult to control.

Your temperament is also wrong for trading. To trade, you need to be cold and unemotional like Mr Spock, but you will feel the same rush when buying a share as you do when backing a horse. So as an *EastEnders'* scriptwriter might say, "Leave it aaht!"

A reader writes: Trading on credit cards

"I lost a lot of money I could not afford to lose – I had been trading with cash borrowed from credit cards. I was heavily in debt before this, and wanted to use spread betting as a quick way out. Not good. But I know there's still a part of me that wants to make that money back through spread betting, and more."

In summary, then, don't trade if:

- you can't afford to lose some of the money

- you are likely to get emotionally involved

- you have, or could have, a gambling problem.

However, if you feel you are sensible, level-headed, have a few quid spare and want to give it a try, then go for it!

Okay, warnings over – let's get on with it!

The Trader's Toolkit

The nuts-and-bolts basics

This part of the book is really for beginners only – I give you full permission to skip the next few pages if you have already traded shares via the internet and know how to do it, or if you read the last edition of this book. This should mean you know how to buy shares online and are happy with how you do it. In which case, fine, move on, nothing to see here!

However, if you are a beginner or at all unsure of the best way to buy and sell shares online then I am afraid you are going to have to learn the nuts-and-bolts basics. It won't take long but it's important!

So, for those who know how to look up a real-time share price, have bought shares, have an online broker account and know a little bit about the markets, this is your last chance to get yourself some tea and toast and move directly to page 69.

If you have never, or hardly ever, or are not sure how to buy shares over the internet, then there is *no* escape. You need to read the next couple of chapters.

No skipping, right?

I promise you, it's not that boring. In fact, it's way easier than you might think to get started as a trader or investor. So you can start off by taking it easy. It really is quite straightforward.

The toolkit

Here's all you need to trade online:

- a computer or laptop or tablet with internet access (I know that might come as a shock!)

- an execution-only broker(s) (easy)

- access to share prices and market info (really easy)

- a notebook and pen (steal one from the bookies)

- lots of tea and toast and snacks (try Yorkshire Tea, it's the best!).

And that really is it – told you not to worry!

Let's quickly take each tool one by one …

1. Computer with broadband

The computer's the easy bit. You've probably already got one and it will almost certainly do. A standard desktop should be fine. Likewise a normal laptop, especially if you intend your trading desk to sometimes consist of your bed and several pillows.

iPads? Well, maybe. But personally I am not a fan of them for trading. I think the screens are too small and a bit too fiddly. I don't want to tap the wrong thing. It's up to you, but I would strongly suggest a PC or laptop and preferably one with a decent-sized screen.

I find having an additional laptop quite handy, so I can monitor share prices on one computer and trade on the other – but it's not necessary, especially if you are just starting out. You do not need loads of screens! If you do buy loads of screens you're just trying to show off and showing off ain't going to feed the kids.

2. Online stock broker

There are now countless ways to make money from trading without even having to open an account with an ordinary stock broker. There's spread betting, fixed-odds betting, CFDs, betting exchanges, binary betting, options and futures, and direct market access. It's never been easier to play the markets. However, even with all these exciting-sounding ways of trading, I still believe new investors should start with a basic online stock-broking account.

All the new ways of trading shares can be pretty dangerous if you don't know what you're doing, so I think the best way to begin is via one or two online execution-only stockbrokers. Once you are up and running with that you can move onto more advanced accounts like spread betting.

Why?

Because it's straightforward. And you can only lose whatever you put in. And it also means you can trade in an ISA and keep your profits tax-free.

With a conventional online broker account you can get used to investing or trading the markets for a while before getting into anything more complicated. I will get to the other methods later in the book, but for now don't worry about them.

So which kind of broker should you go for?

An execution-only one! This broker simply does what you ask and does not charge you for advice. Forget about *advisory brokers*. Those brokers will give you advice on what stocks to buy and sell, and even trade on your behalf if you want (this latter type are called *discretionary brokers*). **My view: some of them are absolute rubbish. And this book is all about doing it for yourself. So do it yourself.**

There are also other companies out there promising you all kind of riches if you let them trade CFDs for you. Not a good idea!

So back to *execution-only brokers*.

As the name suggests, no advice is given at all. You're on your own. They're just the means by which you buy and sell whatever shares you want whenever you want. And they're cheap. So from now on, when talking of brokers, I am writing about execution-only ones.

Selecting a broker

It's difficult to recommend specific brokers, as their services and charges are changing all the time. These days, though, the top ones are really much of a muchness.

Generally speaking they will all provide a similar service. Which is, quite simply, you choose to buy or sell a share over the internet, and they enact the trade for you. Your trade is usually recorded on your account which you can access anytime. And that's it. Some of them might send you 'contract notes', but on the whole everything is done online these days so you should find confirmation in your online account.

Occasionally, brokers' internet services freeze or don't work. In my experience it happens to them all at some point.

So in the end it comes down to the price you're charged per trade. The dreaded commission.

The average is about £12.50 per trade. You can get cheaper; if you trade a lot the price will be lowered. Watch out for firms offering anything lower than around £7, though, as they will try and get the money back off you in other ways – e.g. loads and loads of spam or just being a bit crap.

Go through a few brokers' sites (some are listed in a second) and check their price lists.

> Q. How many stockbrokers does it take to change a light bulb?
>
> A. Two. One to take out the bulb and drop it, and the other to try and sell it before it crashes.

Watch the small print. Some charge an 'inactivity fee' if you don't trade much.

I have accounts with two brokers and I don't find an awful lot of difference between them. They're both easy to use. My main share-trading account is with Barclays, and my pension is with TD Direct Investing. I have no complaints about them and they get me the same prices. I hardly ever have to contact them.

As it doesn't cost anything to set up an account, I would initially open two accounts. I'll explain a bit later why this can be a good tactic.

Be a bit wary if you find a very cheap deal with a company you've never heard of. If a broker goes bust, despite being supposed to have your money segregated, the bottom line of compensation rules means that you might only get a max of £80,000 back. I'd rather trade with the bigger names.

Broker checklist

A checklist when looking for a broker:

1. Check the broker's website.

2. Trades should cost no more than £12.50.

3. Watch out for hidden charges.

4. Consider opening multiple accounts with two or more brokers and compare their services directly.

5. Watch out for prices that are too good to be true.

Here is a list of some of the top online brokers. Check through their sites and see what they have to offer you:

- Barclays Stockbrokers – **www.barclaysstockbrokers.co.uk**

- Hargreaves Lansdown – **www.hl.co.uk**

- The Share Centre – **www.share.com**

- TD Direct Investing – **www.tddirectinvesting.co.uk**

Share certificates

Share certificates are a thing of the past – forget about them. Most online brokers use *nominee accounts*. This means you don't get a certificate; you are the electronic owner of the shares. In fact, getting certificates is next to impossible. So don't bother.

When you buy shares they simply go straight into your online account and when you sell them they leave your online account – wonderful! If you have any certificated shares you can transfer them into a nominee account with your broker. Call them for details of how to do this.

Show me the money

Sorry, but ... well, you need to put some money in your account or else you won't be able to buy any shares. D'oh!

The best and quickest way is simply to fund your account with a debit card, or you can send the broker a cheque. Sending cheques takes some time, so a debit card is best. Because of the new money-laundering rules (why people want to clean their cash is beyond me), some brokers may ask you to send proof of who you are, so you might need to send in a copy of a driving licence or passport.

Don't get annoyed with them. Blame the government or the money-launderers – take your pick, as they're both thieves!

Brokers do pay some interest on cash in your account, but not a lot. You generally should be using the money for trading. That's the way you'll make more money!

Which account should I open?

If you end up making loads of money, you don't want to pay capital gains tax (CGT) right? At the time of writing, if you make more than £11,000 trading a year, after costs, you start to pay this tax, and it's currently 18% or 28% depending on your income. A number of politicians have expressed ambitions to raise this to 40% in the future. Boo!

Why give away such a big chunk of your profits when you don't have to? Amongst the huge array of accounts and options on each stock broker's site, there's one in particular that protects your profits from all forms of tax. It's called an ISA.

> Look out for a link on brokers' sites to 'Self-select ISA', 'Investment ISA', 'Stocks and Shares ISA' or from 2015 perhaps just 'ISA', 'New ISA' or 'NISA'/'Nisa'. Anything like that.

Cash and stocks-and-shares ISAs used to be different things, but since July 2014 they've been merged and you can put in up to £15,000 a year for saving or trading. Usually they raise the amount you can contribute every year (roughly in line with inflation).

You can trade the money inside ISAs without *any* liability for capital gains tax. Every profit you make, you keep. You don't even need to tell the taxman about any profits.

Even better, since the last edition of the book *you can now put any share you like in an ISA*. Previously you weren't allowed to put in AIM shares. Now you can and you don't have to pay stamp duty on them either. More on this change later in the book.

I have saved thousands upon thousands of pounds in taxes that I would otherwise have had to pay if I hadn't put all my share money into an ISA.

As the years go by, and you build your portfolio, the ISA tax advantage becomes more and more apparent. For example, as I write I am sitting on over a million quid in my ISA – can you imagine how much capital gains tax I would have had to pay outside an ISA?

Let's say you have a few good years and manage to build up £150,000 of capital inside your ISA. All tax-free. Now say you have a *very* good year and turn that £150,000 into £250,000. That's a profit of £100,000.

Outside an ISA that profit could get nastily cut by over £25,000 in CGT. Inside, it's untouchable.

It is worth checking to see if your broker will make any standing charges to look after your ISA. Most do – expect to pay around £15 a quarter.

There is no maximum amount you can build in your ISA through stock market profits, only a limit on how much cash you can deposit in it from outside every year. Withdrawals from ISAs can be made anytime, but once cash is taken out, it cannot be replaced except within your annual allowance. But the great thing is there is *no limit* to profits you can make.

People do get confused about the benefits of ISAs, so here is a basic recap for anyone whose eyes have glazed over at all this HMRC-speak (I don't blame you):

- *They're brilliant.*

- You can add £15,000 of external cash into them in a year. (This is expected – but not guaranteed – to rise roughly in line with inflation each year.)

- You can make as much profit as you want inside them and everything you withdraw is tax-free. But once you take money out, you can only add back in the annual allowance each tax year. (Still no limit on profits, though.) If you've used that allowance, you have to wait till next year.

- You can buy and sell as many shares in them as often as you like.

- You don't have to report any of this to the taxman.

If you feel confused about ISAs even after that let me make it even more simple.

> ISAs let you make as much profit as you want, tax-free, and withdraw it whenever you want. But you can only add in a fixed amount of cash per tax year.

Easy, right?

3. Real-time prices (and some extra stuff)

A broker provides you with the ability to buy and sell shares. Once you have set up your account, you'll also need a website that provides live buy and sell prices, news and information. This is mainly because when a broker offers you a price it is generally delayed. Delayed prices are no good. You need to know what is happening NOW!

Plus you need to know some other stuff too:

- how to keep an eye on news about shares and what companies are announcing

- the dividends a company will pay

- when its next results are announced

- a chart of how a share price has been behaving

- what a company is worth

- how much profit it makes.

This is known as *research* and is something a lot of people can't be bothered with. But please be bothered. Because, really, you ought to keep yourself informed – especially once you are the proud owner of a few shares and can idly mention to your mates:

"I have a portfolio … "

On the other hand, maybe best not to mention it, as they may suddenly expect you to buy all the drinks.

Now, onto the sexy bit …

Real-time prices

Where do you find real-time prices and other stuff like news about shares?

Well, there are quite a few websites and the good news is most of the stuff you need is free. However, if you want 'always on' real-time prices you'll probably have to pay a small amount. In other words, while you can look up real-time prices for nothing, the 'real-time' service itself may only last a few seconds or so – you'll need to keep manually refreshing your screen!

I personally use a site called ADVFN (**www.advfn.com**). However, there are a number of similar sites you can use instead if you want to. I use the site simply because it was the first one and I have used it since 1999! I've got used to it and it works well for me.

For the purposes of this book, I'm going to use ADVFN as the basic information supplier. They've not paid me a bean to do this, by the way. It just makes it far easier for me to describe how to look for things if I use the one site. I write a column for them, but do so for a number of other sites too.

Once you've understood how to find what you need on ADVFN, you can easily move to another site if you want. You just need to know what you're looking for.

The following six sites are the main online sources for real-time prices and share-research tools:

- ADVFN – **www.advfn.com**
- Interactive Investor – **www.iii.co.uk**
- MoneyAM – **www.moneyam.com**
- Morningstar – **www.morningstar.co.uk**
- Proquote – **www.proquote.com**
- Digital Look – **www.digitallook.com**

When you're up and trading properly, it may be worth opening accounts with two or three real-time price companies as a back-up in case your favourite breaks down – it could prove cheaper than the therapy bills!

All these sites offer some free services, so you can get a good taster before paying for any extra services. Don't do any blind, blanket sign-ups.

Right – wakey, wakey, you beginners!

In case you've switched off, missed stuff or been sneaking looks at Twitter instead of paying attention … here's a summary of our trading journey so far:

1. Get some online broking accounts set up. Preferably with big names.

2. Think about sticking as much as you can/is allowed into an ISA to avoid tax.

3. Find a place where you can access real-time prices and other info.

In other words: a broker for buying and selling, and a separate information site for all the latest prices and so on.

Now, what other info do you need before you get cracking?

4. Finding information on share prices

How do you find the share price of a company, or monitor the share prices of a bunch of companies? It's easy! Let's dive in properly now to the ADVFN website. Remember, other websites will be quite similar – it's up to you which one you like best. They all have horrible flashing adverts, of course. But they have to make money or they wouldn't be there for us, so you'll get used to ignoring them (or you can just install AdBlock and zap the blighters into oblivion).

How to use ADVFN (and other similar sites)

Best place to start? I guess it's the home page. You'll need to register (it's free with ADVFN and most other sites).

ADVFN home page

The main thing you need to focus on is the navigation menu near the top of the page (see the screenshot above). I'll go through the sections you need to be interested in initially.

1. *Monitor:* this is the most useful page! This is the basic list of shares that you are interested in and may want to follow on a day-to-day basis. I'll explain how to add shares to this later in this chapter.

2. *Quote:* gets you a quote on the current price for any share.

3. *Trades:* brings up data on buys and sells that have taken place in the share of your choice.

4. *News:* obvious … it's, er, financial news!

5. *Financials:* info to help you research a share.

6. *Toplists:* one of my favourite pages. Contains rankings of stocks by all sorts of criteria, such as top movers of the day. Basically, a great place to find out where the action is happening.

7. *Free BB* and *P[remium]BB:* these are the bulletin boards that investors use to gossip.

You'll want to use the other buttons in time, but these should get you going.

Let's look at the information you get when you ask for a quote on a share using the quote page.

Stock codes

You'll quickly realise that everything on the ADVFN website (as with most other stock market websites) revolves around what are called *stock symbols*. These are short (three or four letter) symbols used to represent shares.

For example, the following table lists the symbols for the ten largest companies (by value) listed on the London Stock Exchange at the time of writing.

Top ten largest companies on the London Stock Exchange

Company	Code
Royal Dutch Shell	RDSB
HSBC Holdings	HSBA
BP	BP.
GlaxoSmithKline	GSK
Vodafone Group	VOD
British American Tobacco	BATS
Lloyds Banking Group	LLOY
AstraZeneca	AZN
Rio Tinto	RIO
Diageo	DGE

Note: Be careful, the code for BP is 'BP.' – including the full-stop!

These symbols are also – rather confusingly – sometimes called EPIC, or TIDM, or RIC codes. Or *tickers*. It doesn't really matter: throughout this book I'll refer to them simply as codes. (I hope you're not falling asleep at the back there – this is important stuff!)

Example – finding the stock code for a company

You've come across a company called Avon Rubber, and you want to find its current share price and start doing some research on the stock.

On the ADVFN website, click the 'Quote' button in the top menu bar:

The buttons at the top

On the next page, if you knew the stock's symbol already, you could at this point simply input it into the box (to the right of where it says 'Symbol:'), click the 'OK' button, and you'd be off:

The box where you type your stuff

However, if you don't know the symbol, type 'Avon Rubber' in the box. DON'T click 'Search or 'OK', though, just wait a second for the site to do its magic. You should find that suggested results appear below the box now:

Symbol:	Avon Rubber	OK	Search	Stocks A–Z
	AVON	Avon Rbr.		LSE
	AVP	Avon Products, Inc.		NYSE
	AVON.GB	Avon Rubber Ord		PLUS
	853836	Avon Prod. DL -,25		FWB
	AVZ	Avonlea Fpo		ASX

Suggested results appearing

Sometimes life is simple and you get just the one stock listed, or the correct one is obvious. In this case, there are a few Avons listed. Most times we'll be interested in the share listed on the London Stock Exchange (which is indicated by 'LSE'), for which we can see the code is 'AVON'.

At this point on ADVFN you can return to the main quote page and input 'AVON' as the symbol (ADVFN also make it easy for you, as clicking on the result itself jumps straight to the relevant quote page).

If you don't fancy using the search functions, you can, of course, just use the A–Z list to manually search for stock codes.

You'll see that there's quite a bit happening on the ADVFN quote page. It's worth spending some time finding your way around this page.

So let's have a look at the quote for AVON.

Name	Symbol	Market	Type	ISIN	Description
Avon Rbr.	LSE:AVON	London Stock Exchange	Equity	GB0000667013	ORD #1

	Change	% Chg	Cur	Bid	Offer	High	Low	Open	Volume	Chg Time	RN	NRN
↑	4.00	0.6%	659.50	654.50	660.00	660.00	659.50	660.00	112,008	16:35:19		

Sector	Turnover (m)	Profit (m)	EPS - Basic	PE ratio	Mkt Cap (m)
AEROSPACE & DEFENCE	124.9	9.6	32.7	20.168	204.6

ADVFN quote for Avon Rubber

Here you can see price information: the current sell price is 654.5p, and the buy price is 660p (the jargon for these, as you can see, is: *bid* and *offer*). So you can sell at about 654.5p and buy at about 660p.

The buy price is always more than the sell price, so remember you are already losing a little just by buying a share.

Interestingly, I used this Avon Rubber example in the last edition. Back then its price was 290p. So it's gone up by almost 130%! And it was chosen at random. Maybe market analysts need to start talking about the *Naked Trader* bump. [Isn't that what they call it when you've eaten too many slices of toast? – Ed.]

'Mkt Cap (m)' is an important piece of info on this page. It stands for *market capitalisation*, which means the value of the entire company in the market. (Worked out by multiplying the total number of shares of the company by the current share price – which gives, in this case, £204.6 million).

The latest price at which it traded is there too (under the label 'Cur', short for 'current').

A word of warning: don't necessarily trust the profit and turnover figures – under 'Turnover (m)' and 'Profit (m)'– as these can be out of date. Always check these directly from the company's latest results, which you can find down in the news stories listed below the quote.

Scroll down a bit further and you will see the share price chart for the last year.

If you want to find out things like their profit, loss, debt, etc., scroll down for the news stories, and find the last full-year or interim (half-year) figures.

Perhaps when you're next at your computer press 'Quote' on ADVFN to see the latest on Avon or another share, and check you understand this in the flesh. It's ridiculously simple, I swear.

Using the ADVFN monitor

You may decide you want to start watching Avon Rubber regularly. In this case, you should add it to your 'Monitor' page on ADVFN. You'll be able to track its real-time buy and sell prices, amounts traded, highs and lows of the day and the latest news stories about it.

To start this monitor or watchlist of shares, just click the 'Monitor' tab, then 'Edit monitor lists':

Edit monitor lists

Give a name to your monitor, then tap in "AVON", and click 'Create new monitor':

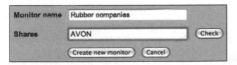

Creating a new monitor

You can add as many shares as you like to your monitor section. Remember, first find the code, then just add it in the same way. You can add a bunch all at once by separating the codes with a comma as you enter them in the box:

Monitor name	Possible buys	
Shares	AVON, BP., VOD, BARC	Check
	Create new monitor Cancel	

Adding multiple shares

Best of all, you can have any number of different monitor lists going, and this allows you to separately group and monitor shares of different kinds. For example, you could call one monitor 'FTSE 100' to keep an eye on

FTSE 100 companies, and call another 'Small companies' to track the smaller sector. You could lump your 'maybes' together in one list, and the shares you actually hold together in another.

Possibilities: endless. And much better than just reading off a single huge list. Access all this functionality through the magical 'Edit monitor lists' button. I use ten or so monitors for different areas of the market.

The cost of real-time prices

- When you look up a share price during market hours (0800–1630), ADVFN will quote you a real-time price for a few seconds before it times out. You can do that as often as you like.

- If you want always-on real-time prices, it costs around £10 to £15 a month via most sites. Money worth spending, I reckon. It's usually given to you for free if you pay for Level 2. On ADVFN, real-time prices come under its 'silver' service – and no, sadly it doesn't involve expertly trained butlers. But it is good. More on it soon.

---

5. Notebook

So, computer sorted? Broker account on the way? Access to real-time prices set up? Vaguely understand that quote page? Can you see where the news stories are? Still awake?

Good, we're nearly there. Final thing: I also recommend keeping a notebook handy. It's always good for jotting down ideas, share prices and bits of info. It's also obviously handy for jotting down phone numbers and losing them.

In fact, I strongly recommend you go one step further and keep a trading diary: write down everything you buy and sell, the prices transacted and *the reasons for buying or selling.* This will come in handy later on when you analyse why you made money or lost it.

If a notebook's just too Victorian for you, then note-taking apps like Evernote (**www.evernote.com**) and Simplenote (**www.simple note.com**) are well worth a look. If inspiration hits on the toilet, you will not be caught short. Though, erm, perhaps that goes without saying. [Come on, Robbie – that is *literally* toilet humour. – Ed.]

Similarly, next to each share on your monitor on ADVFN is a memo button. You can click on that and add notes about a share which you can come back to later.

Your trading environment

Stay clutter-free!

Keeping a clear head is very important when it comes to share trading – and it's just not possible if you're surrounded by clutter. I think it can seriously affect trading decisions if you're sitting in the midst of hundreds of old fag butts, empty bags of crisps, loads of bits of paper, newspapers and empty beer cans. [Hey, I let you into my office in the strictest confidence. – Ed.] Clutter will subconsciously put you under more pressure when making trading decisions.

Keep a clear desk and a tidy office and your head will feel clear too. And this will help your trading. Tea and toast are also vitally important to good trading. (Oh bugger, just spilled crumbs all over the desk. Fine example I set.)

KISS – Keep It Simple Stupid

Don't make trading too difficult for yourself. What I mean is: don't overburden yourself with dozens of trading monitors and a bank of TV screens in every corner of the room.

That's just to impress lovers/partners/friends, right?

Keep it simple. You don't need to be buying chart systems and complicated software to start trading. All you need is access to news stories, fundamentals, charts and real-time prices. You can get this from free websites, or you might need to pay a small amount to access them. That's fine.

You don't need to be buying multi-thousand-pound systems to display this information on. All that will do is confuse things. You need to keep your mind free to concentrate on just one thing: is a share a good buy or not? I promise you, your expensive systems are just dumb computers and won't be any help. Stick with the simple stuff. One day, when you've made your first million, by all means fill your office with impressive, flashing machines. But not for starters.

The other silly thing that might tempt you around about now is to drop a small fortune on a trading system. No! Anytime you catch yourself drooling over a glossy ad for a trading system promising to make you millions, walk away very fast. Just think of Baloo the bear from *The Jungle Book* – it's all about the 'bear necessities'!

What You Need to Know About Shares

Beginners: things you need to know about shares!

Let's look at some of the things you really need to know about shares. These are:

1. Spreads

2. Trading costs

3. Exchange market size

4. Trading hours

5. Why shares move up or down

6. Market makers and the crowd

7. Dividends

8. Different types of shares

I'll accept that some of this may not be immediately fascinating, and having read the above list you may well yawn and decide to stop reading for the moment.

Well, thanks a lot! I'm sitting here working hard (and definitely *not* watching *Deal or No Deal* at the same time) and all you can do is get bored.

But these bits and pieces are essential to understand before making that first trade. Many new traders lose money in the market because they don't understand what's going on. So you've got to get your head around these things!

And the exciting thing is … we'll end this chapter by showing you exactly how to make that first trade. It's pretty exciting stuff.

1. Spreads

When I say spreads I am *not* talking about those woolly things you buy to put over a sofa to hide the stains if someone is coming round. I'm talking about the difference between a sell price and a buy price, which is known as the *spread*.

Although you will often come across references to the 'share price', the idea of the price of a share is actually a little more complicated than that, and people new to the market can get confused over this. But actually, it's completely easy-peasy. First, we need to define some terms:

- *Bid price:* the price at which you can sell shares.

- *Offer price:* the price at which you can buy shares.

- *Spread:* the difference between sell and buy price (bid and offer).

- *Mid price:* the price halfway between the bid and offer prices.

A key point we can see from the above is that, at any one time, the price for buying a share and selling a share is always going to be different.

Let's look at an example:

ADVFN quote for Avon Rubber

In this screenshot we can see that Avon Rubber has a bid price of 654.5p and an offer price of 660p. That means if you want to sell the stock you'll get around 654.5p a share, and if you want to buy the stock you'll have to pay 660p.

Say you buy 1,000 shares at 660p, costing £6,600. If you changed your mind immediately having bought the shares and wanted to sell them, you'd have to sell at 654.5p. That's £6,545, so you would be down £55 (before even taking into account the commission cost and stamp duty). So add £12.50 for the buy, £12.50 to sell and stamp duty at 0.5% – that's another £40 or so.

> You now don't have to pay stamp duty on AIM-listed shares. Check **www.londonstockexchange.com**, which will tell you whether a share is AIM or not. (Click 'Quote' for the one you want and scroll down to 'Market'. This will reveal all.)

The *spread* is the difference between the offer and bid price and, as can be seen in this example, is a real and significant cost of trading. Why are spreads there? It's how the market makers take their cut (these are the people that make shares available for you to buy or sell – explained more later).

Be aware of the importance of the spread, and realise that as soon as you buy a share, you're down on the deal until (or unless) the sell price rises above what you bought the share for.

Spread size

You'll soon find spreads can be wide or narrow.

Obviously the narrower the spread, the better for us – the less work our investments have to do to get into profit. Spreads will be very narrow on heavily traded stocks, like those in the FTSE 100, and wider on the smaller stocks. On some stocks, especially in AIM, spreads can be ridiculously wide.

For example:

- Look at the bid–offer spread for a large company like Vodafone. The bid–offer prices quoted could be 227.95–228. That's a spread of next to nothing – 0.05p – it's tiny.

- But for a small stock on AIM, where much smaller companies are listed, the bid–offer price could be 10–12. That's a spread of 20%! If you bought at 12p, the shares would have to go up 20% just to break even!

A spread of 3% is about as much as I'll allow. Max 4%. If the spread is more than that, I would seriously have to consider not buying, even if I like the look of the company. Always work out what percentage of the price the spread is.

Spread headlines – the news tonight is:

- Remember: you're losing money as soon as you buy a share.

- Work out the percentage of the spread.

- Be cautious about trading a share with a spread over 3%, and never trade one with a spread over 4 or 5% unless it is a minor punt.

- The wider the spread, the bigger the risk.

2. Trading costs

The costs of buying and selling shares can add up quickly, so here's a rough guide to possible costs.

There are generally three elements to the cost of trading shares:

1. the **commission** charged by your broker, *plus*

2. (said through gritted teeth) a nasty and horrid tax on buying shares called **stamp duty** (currently 0.5% in the UK) *plus*

3. the **spread**.

> *Note:* You only pay stamp duty on a **buy**, not when you sell a share.

To illustrate the costs of all the elements together – the commission and the spread as well – let's take a look at a simple example.

Example – trading costs

You buy 1,000 shares in a company at 500p per share. Total value: £5,000.

Buying costs:

- Broker commission: £12.50 (average)

- Stamp duty: £25

Having bought the shares, you decide to sell them immediately, but because of the bid–offer spread, you may only be able to sell them at 495p. Total value: £4,950.

Selling costs:

- Broker commission: £12.50 (average)

- Stamp duty: £0 (only applies on buys)

So:

- Total direct costs (commission + stamp duty): £50

- Indirect cost (a result of the spread): £50

And a complete cost of:

£100

£100! That's 2% of your original investment. When you become a full-time trader, regularly dealing with substantial investments, you cannot afford to pretend costs don't matter. Let's not get all mopey, though, as there's a simple strategy for covering this. And we'll look at that when we look at dividends in a few pages.

Beginner investors sometimes forget to factor in the cost of the spread, but – please – don't. It is a real cost. Even if you were selling, in this case, with a luscious price rise to 800p, you'd still be down £50 from that original spread. There's no escaping it. You can never get away from it.

Of course, it could be worse – because it once was. Now we're in the age of the internet, discount brokerages and efficient trading platforms. Imagine what it was like before, when broker commissions were a cool £50 or more!

Over-trade at your peril

As you can see, the more you trade, the more the costs will stack up. In the previous example, trade five times, and you've knocked up total costs of £500. I probably pay around £6,000 a year to trade.

It means that if your mind is set on becoming a *day trader* – that is, buying and selling shares on the same day for lots of quick little profits – you have to be almost supernaturally good to cover the costs. And that's one of the reasons more than 90% of would-be day traders fail.

So don't over-trade. It means a lot of money wasted on costs.

3. Exchange market size

You may think you can buy as many shares as you like in any company, but it doesn't always work like that. It might be true for FTSE 100 stocks, as you're more likely to run out of available money before the market runs out of available shares, but you have to be very careful when buying a smaller company.

Exchange market size, or EMS, is the number of shares that market makers guarantee to sell or buy at quoted prices. If you want to buy or sell shares in a quantity above the EMS it can lead to problems. When you are more advanced, you can check Level 2 to see the number of shares you can readily buy or sell.

Till then, how do you check EMS for free? You need to head to **www.londonstockexchange.com**. Put the code of your share – say, AVON again – into the quotes search box at the top right. Click on the quote and then scroll down the box called 'Trading information' till you get to 'Exchange market size'. In this case it is 500. As I write Avon shares are six and a half quid. So that's about £3,250 worth you can deal in: 500 shares × 650p.

If you buy more, you take the risk you might be charged a bigger spread. However, in practice you can pretty much deal in three to four times the EMS without being charged extra.

If the market suddenly tanks, the market makers can shut down and only offer you quotes strictly in EMS size. And if you want to sell more than that they can charge you extra spread.

A particular danger is that, over time, you might build up a sizeable position in one company's shares – say 15,000 shares in Avon Rubber. If a time then came when you wanted to sell all those shares quickly, you would have a problem if the EMS was 500. You might only be able to sell some at the market price – and if you want rid of the lot, you might have to take a low price.

So bear this in mind before building up a really substantial number of shares in one company.

I am very careful and make sure the shares I buy have a decent EMS. I usually ensure the EMS is at least £2,000-worth of shares – though I prefer £5,000. To work out the EMS in cash terms, simply multiply the EMS by the share price.

If you are dealing in a FTSE 100 share, unless you are trading in millions, don't worry about the EMS. You can buy and sell as much as your heart desires. Same pretty much for FTSE 250 as well. When you are more experienced, Level 2 will tell you more exact amounts available on the market.

Summary

- Always check the EMS of a share before buying if it is a smaller company.

- You may pay more to deal in quantities larger than the EMS.

- Don't deal in shares with an EMS equivalent to less than £2,000.

4. Trading hours

The London Stock Exchange opens for trading shares between the hours of 08.00–16.30, Monday to Friday.

For a few minutes before the market opens and for a few minutes after it shuts, there are auctions of shares, but these are generally only for institutions. The opening auctions tend to decide the 8am opening price for most shares.

Be careful of dealing in the bigger stocks between 8am and 9am – the spreads can be huge because there is no depth to the market and you could get caught out.

You need to beware if you are looking at a share price *outside* market hours. The bid–offer spread may be much wider than normal because the market makers have gone home and there is only one left quoted. **Only believe prices you see during market hours.**

5. Why shares move up or down

Before we go any further, here's something you must get your head around:

What makes shares move up or down?

Not an unimportant question, no?

You might think that it would be easy to answer. But the factors affecting shares prices are quite complex. I get emails all the time from traders very puzzled by the movements of shares. They get frustrated when shares shift and they can't see the reason why.

A classic example is when a share price falls following the release of good news (perhaps strong annual results). What a perverse market, people wail. But the explanation, in this case, can be found in the old stock market maxim:

'*Buy on the rumour, sell on the news.*'

By the time the news is actually announced, all the information has *already* been factored into the price – just look at the share price behaviour in the short period leading up to the announcement. So when the news is actually announced, the smart money (having bought previously in the run-up) is looking to sell and bank profits. The price therefore promptly goes down.

There are many reasons why a share might move. I'll examine some of the reasons in greater depth later. But for now, and to show how difficult it can be to know why your shares are doing well or badly, here are some of the reasons:

Broker upgrade/downgrade

Brokers regularly put out recommendations to their clients, and a buy or sell recommendation can temporarily affect a share. You'll usually find your news feed will reveal which broker and what their recommendation is. Sometimes this can move the market a lot. In my experience the broker comment usually only affects the share for a day or two, sometimes only for an hour or two.

General market move

The whole market may move up or down – for whatever reason – and your share can move in line with the market. If it is a FTSE 100 share, it might be affected by, say, economic gloom from the US and move in tandem with other FTSE shares. Shares in small companies are less prone to a general move.

Sector move

Say your favourite stock is a telecoms share. A different telecoms company may have put out a profit warning, and your share could be dragged down along with all telecoms stocks.

Institution move

An institution has bought or sold stock. (Big trades – such as those made by large institutions – are usually notified on the newswires one or two days after the event.) Look for the phrase 'holdings in company' on the news service to check them.

Director buying/selling

Directors have bought or sold shares in their own company. Investors often follow movements by directors, so more shares may be bought or sold than normal, moving the price.

Results/news story

If the price is moving quickly, check the newswires for any story. It could be a price-moving statement from the company or another news story.

Dividend dates

The price will always move lower on a share's 'ex-dividend' date, i.e. the day the company pays out some of its profits to shareholders. These are usually twice-yearly, but do vary – some shares don't have dividends at all.

So if the dividend paid out to shareholders is 10p per share (and it's always done on a per-share basis), the share price will move down by around 10p.

Tipped

The share has been tipped by a newspaper, magazine or one of the many tipsters out there. Especially on weekend tips, the market marks up a share before the open in expectation of ready buyers.

Bulletin board manipulation

A tiny stock could soar because a group have got together to make it sound irresistible on the bulletin boards/internet forums.

Market-maker manipulation

Market makers are moving the price to encourage buyers or sellers, and are doing so just to suit their own ends.

Tree shake

Market makers push the price down quickly and drastically to encourage sellers, then move the price back up again. Often because they have a big buyer who will then take all those recently sold shares off their hands!

Surprise events

Something major happens like a terrorist attack – all shares could be hit. Or some political drama unfolds somewhere.

Rights issue

A company decides to raise money by offering more shares at a lower price. This usually lowers the existing price.

Takeover/merger

Companies announce a takeover or merger. Expect a big rise!

Stake-building

Someone is building a stake in the company.

> My brief summary shows just how on the ball you must be. Try and figure out why a share you might want to buy or sell is moving. There is more coming on why shares move later in the book.

6. Market makers and the crowd

We now need to talk about liquidity (no, this is nothing to do with what you fill a paddling pool with).

If you want to sell some shares on the stock market you need someone in the market willing to buy those shares. If there isn't anyone, you'd think it was a pretty rubbish market. But this can be a problem for small companies with few investors; at any one time (or even for a whole day) there may only be one or two investors interested in buying or selling the shares in a company. In these cases, the market in these small company shares is said to have *poor liquidity* (in other words, poor tradability).

For large companies (e.g. all FTSE 100 companies) this is not a problem. At any one moment there may be hundreds or thousands of investors wanting to buy or sell shares in, say, Vodafone. Anytime you want to buy (or sell) shares in Vodafone you can be sure there will be lots of people willing to sell to (or buy from) you. Therefore, the market for large company shares is said to have *good liquidity* (good tradability).

But we still have a problem with small companies – a problem of poor liquidity.

What can be done?

The answer the stock exchange came up with was to assign one or more financial companies to guarantee that they would always be willing to buy or sell shares. And this was done for all small companies. The financial companies that provide this guarantee are called *market makers*. In technical terms, market makers ensure that small company shares have liquidity (i.e. they can be traded anytime).

A quick glance at bulletin boards will reveal that market makers are not popular with traders. According to some traders, they are masters of spin – a kind of hideous lovechild of Gordon Gekko and Tony Blair.

Why is this?

Mainly due to the way they make their money. It can put them in direct opposition to traders. Here's how.

Remember, market makers make their money from a share's spread. The more that traders buy and sell, the more money that market makers make. Therefore, **it is in the interests of market makers to move their prices around a bit to encourage active buying and selling of shares.**

So, the market makers may move a price up to encourage you to sell your shares, or move it down to encourage you to buy. Or even the other way round. The result is that share prices can move in odd ways, sometimes with seeming relation to the actual situation of a company.

This can be very confusing to new traders who see a price moving but can't understand why it's moving. It drives a lot of investors crackers – especially if it makes you sell your shares at the wrong time.

Try and relax a bit with price movements and try not to watch every tiny penny move. **If you have a good company, value will out eventually.**

Tree-shaking

All sorts of 'tricks' are employed by the market makers. For example, when they drop a share for no reason, it's known by investors as a *tree shake*.

One morning you'll roll out of bed, switch on your computer and see your favourite share is down 2p, then 3p, 5p and 6p … ! You'll start to scream, sweat, swear and panic – that's exactly what they want you to do. In a panic, you'll sell immediately at any price because something terrible must be happening.

What's really happening is a tree shake.

It's designed to make you very afraid. Afraid enough to think that a share's going down further so you should get out. But once you and a few others have sold out, the price will gradually start to go back up. This will also make you scream and sweat, and probably swear. At least the panic will have gone!

You've been shaken out!

So why do they try and shake you out?

It may be because the market makers have a big buy order to fill and they need your shares to fill it. Or perhaps the company is doing well, results are due and they want to get some cheap shares into their 'bank'. They hope they will get your shares by dropping the price, especially by doing it one penny at a time.

Tree-shake antidote

Instead of panicking and swearing, here's what you do: check to see if there is anything on the newswires regarding the share. Maybe check the bulletin boards, too. If there is no obvious and well-publicised reason for the fall, it's 90% certain that it's a tree shake.

So instead of selling, go and make a cup of tea and some toast and relax. Later in the day you can pat yourself on the back – you weren't shaken!

A tree shake will also usually only last a few hours. If the share continues to go down over a day or two, it could be more than a shake. Click the 'Trades' button at the top of ADVFN and see if there has been any serious selling. Once you are more experienced and maybe using Level 2 you can make a clearer judgement.

A final point: if you do get shaken out of a share and it goes back up, sometimes it's best to swear a bit at the computer but then *leave it alone*. Otherwise you will go back in with a bit too much emotional involvement, and that can complicate things. It may make you less ruthless than you need to be in future. As we have discussed, you do need to be as cool and calm as possible.

There is always another share, another day.

The general point is, if you are happy with a share, there is no bad news about and it still looks cheap to you – and the main market itself is not in meltdown – it's best to sit tight and ride out a fall.

7. Dividends

Dividends are cash that you receive, usually twice a year, from a company in which you've invested. Most decent shares pay dividends.

The money comes from the company's profits, and the amount you get will depend on the number of shares you hold. It's always on a per-share basis.

Dividends may at first glance seem to be quite small amounts, but I can promise you that over the years they add up to an awful lot of money. A good number of companies pay out more in payments than you'd get in interest from a building society. So not only are you getting a capital gain (as the share price increases), but income too!

As interest rates are so low at the time of writing that they might as well not exist, and some companies' dividends will return you several per cent (a few as high as 5% or 6%) on your investment, this is rather attractive!

And remember the (up to) 2% or so that every trade costs? Dividends are a beautifully neat way of covering that, and that's what I use them for. A very good idea for full-time traders if you ask me.

So how do you find out when the company is likely to send you some money, and how much will it be?

Pretty easy. Just go to the last company full-year or interim report, and the amount of the dividend and the date is there. If you use my traffic lights system (see page 123) that will pick it out for you quickly.

And if you want a list of upcoming companies paying dividends, try **www.digitallook.com** and click *Research > Company Diary*. That gives you upcoming dividend payments. Magazines like *Investors Chronicle* and *Shares Magazine* have lists too.

Dividends are generally paid twice a year in varying amounts – the final dividend is usually bigger than the interim dividend. Once the dividend is paid out it arrives in your account as cash. Nice!

Ex-dates

Here's a question that must be in the top ten I get asked about shares:

When do you have to be holding a share to get its dividend?

It's quite easy. It's the day *before* what's called the 'ex-date'.

Say the ex-date is 21 March. This means that, on 21 March, the share will be trading 'ex' – or without – the dividend. So if you held the share up to and including the close of play on 20 March, *the day before the ex-date*, you would be entitled to the dividend.

But if you buy the shares on 21 March, which is the ex-date, you would *not* be entitled to it.

You may also come across something called the record date – just ignore this one, it doesn't really matter. The ex-date is the big one.

Now, often new investors say to themselves:

"Aha! I'll just buy a company late on the day before the ex-dividend date, and sell early on the ex-dividend date – picking up the dividend for nothing!"

Nice try, clever dick! Don't you think the market has thought of this not-so-cunning ploy?

Well, it has – so there goes your nice little earner.

Sadly, what happens **on the ex-date is that the share price will invariably start the day lower by the amount of the dividend.** So if you bought the day before 'ex', and sell the day after, what you make on the dividend payment you'll lose on the fall in the share price.

You should definitely know the ex-dividend dates for your shares. For example, if a dividend on your fave share is 10p per share, your share will start the ex-date 10p lower! If you aren't aware that it's the ex-date, you might panic and sell because you think the share is being sold off, or it has dropped through your stop loss. **So pay attention to these dates.**

Is it worth buying shares just for the dividends?

Is it worth buying shares just for the dividends? It really depends on your market strategy:

Low-risk investor

The answer is yes, if you are an older investor and are looking for very steady shares and prioritise income over capital gains. For example, utility companies pay big dividends, but their actual share prices don't move much, so you won't get quick capital growth. But say you're 60 years old, and want to grow your money slowly but surely and with minimum risk. You could just go for an income portfolio of high-yielding shares (the slightly agricultural name for shares with big juicy dividends).

Medium-risk investor

A medium-risk investor might look on dividends as just a bit of a bonus.

High-risk investor

The high-risk investor doesn't care about dividends because he only wants big growth, and the kinds of shares he invests in generally don't pay dividends.

What do I think?

I love dividends but don't worry too much about them. They are beautiful things indeed, and pay pretty much all my costs, but my trading isn't built around them. Nothing wrong with building your trading around them, of course, but don't expect to make a fortune from share price rises in the near term if you do so.

8. Different types of shares

One thing you must understand is that there are different types of shares and they all act in different ways. And of course, there are different sectors.

Shares tend to be classified like this:

- FTSE 100
- FTSE 250
- FTSE SmallCap
- FTSE Fledgling
- AIM shares.

The **FTSE 100** is, of course, the list of the 100 biggest public companies in the UK. You can buy and sell as many as shares in these companies as you want. They have tight spreads and move around constantly all day long because so many people trade them.

The **FTSE 250** has the next 250 biggest shares. They move around a bit less but are still actively traded and very liquid.

The **FTSE SmallCap** features companies with a market value from around the £100m mark up to the £650m level. These shares are less liquid and the spreads are a lot wider so it costs quite a bit to buy them. Their prices move quite a bit less.

The **FTSE Fledgling** features the smallest companies. Often many of these don't move at all during the day, unless a news story breaks, and spreads can be very wide.

All the above are known as *main market* shares.

Then there are **AIM** shares (the Alternative Investment Market). They can be of any capitalisation, from huge to tiny. There's much less regulation involved in being an AIM share, so they are riskier than main market shares and can go bust out of the blue. They can also be illiquid and volatile.

Remember, as mentioned earlier, **www.londonstockexchange.com** will tell you what market a share is listed on.

How should you approach these markets?

My view on them is: have less money in AIM and FTSE Fledgling shares. I like to put more money into FTSE 250 because at least you can definitely sell if problems arise.

In the last edition of the book I was very sniffy about AIM shares because you couldn't trade them tax-free in an ISA. Now the rules have changed and you can – so I am more interested. And I certainly buy them now.

But! I treat them with great caution and always have a very good look at their debt. I have seen many AIM shares go bust. They definitely need a bit more caution than main market ones.

How do you buy and sell a share?

How do you buy a share online?

Dead easy! Each broker's website is slightly different but generally they operate along similar lines.

After you've registered an account, logged into their website and put some money in (preferably into an ISA account) look for a tab or button labelled: 'Deal', 'Invest', 'Dealing' or 'Trade' – they usually use one of these words.

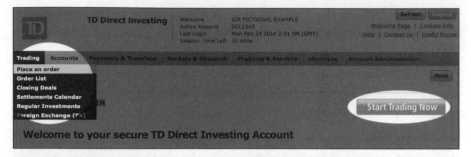

The 'Trading' buttons on TD Direct Investing's website

If the only button you can find is labelled something like 'Cha-ching!!' or 'Show me the money!!!', it's probably worth reconsidering your choice of broker.

The next page you'll see is the 'Place An Order' page. Lots going on here, but it's all quite logical. We'll go through it step by step, but you'll almost certainly find it pretty self-explanatory.

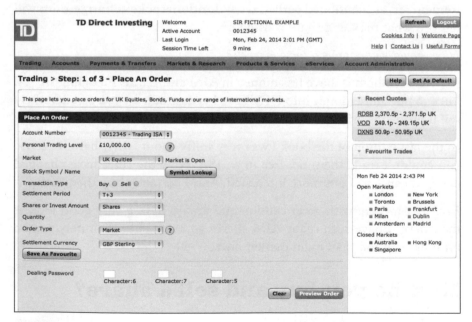

An example order page

Firstly, if you have multiple accounts with a broker, just check you've got the right one selected:

Selecting the correct account

Then, you'll want to make sure you're about to look up shares in the stock market you're interested in – by default this is set to UK Equities and that's fine for our purposes. The text next to this will also tell you if the market is open or not:

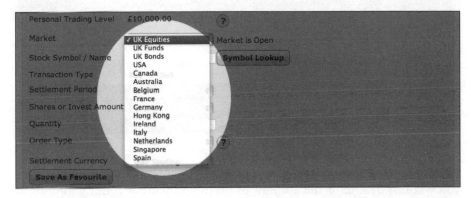

Choosing the market you're interested in

Next you type the code of the share you want to buy into the box below (e.g. 'RDSB' for Royal Dutch Shell). You can type a name and have it show you a list of results first if you've forgotten it, but do cross-reference with the code of the share you've researched as there are some very similarly named shares that are actually completely different:

Typing the share you want to trade

On TD Direct, a live quote will appear next to this box after a few seconds:

The live quote for your share

You then get a choice of whether to buy or sell:

It's buy or sell time

Ignore the settlement period. You'll be asked to enter the quantity of shares you want to deal in or the amount of money in your account you wish to use:

'Show me the money!' (or: 'Specify the number of shares!')

Finally – nearly there, honest! – you get a choice of the type of order you want to make:

The types of order

At the current best price

If you just want to buy it at the best current price then click 'Market'. On Barclays you'd click 'Quote and deal'.

Others have different names for it. Play around with your broker's site till you are confident you've found the right button for this!

'Limit' lets you place an order for a trade as soon as a share hits a certain price. The exciting sounding 'Fill or Kill' just means TD Direct will trade immediately for you if they can get your limit price or better. Otherwise they'll reject the trade. More on limit orders in a second!

Okay, so let's say we're going for the best current price. Next, we just have to hit 'Preview Order'. A summary will appear with a 15-second countdown showing how long you have to trade at this price. Don't worry – you haven't bought the shares till you finally press the 'Place Order' button.

Check you are happy with the price offered. And if you are, press the button:

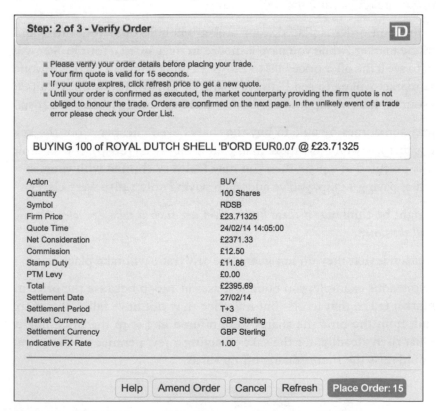

Tick-tock – the countdown and the 'Place Order' button on TD Direct

Don't worry about the 15-second countdown making you feel under pressure; you can always get a quote again if you let it expire!

Once the button is hit, the shares are yours!

At the price you want – if it becomes possible

If you want to be a clever clogs and try to get a lower price at some point, you could put in a 'limit order' by clicking 'Limit' or 'Fill or Kill' rather than 'Market'.

A *limit order* means you won't pay more than the price you want, as long as shares become available at the price you specify (if they don't, nothing gets exchanged).

For example, say the bid–offer price of Petrofac is 1472–1474. If you wanted to buy Petrofac shares immediately, at the current best price, you would pay 1474p. But perhaps you don't want to pay 1474p. Let's say you think 1465p is more reasonable. In this case, you would place a limit order with your broker, setting the limit at 1465p.

Once the limit order is placed, your broker will hold onto your order and watch the market (while you have a snooze in the garden). Your broker will watch to see if the offer price falls to 1465p (in other words, if there is anyone in the market willing to sell Petrofac shares at 1465p). If this does happen then your broker will nip into the market and buy you the shares at 1465p.

He may sometimes be able to buy the shares even cheaper – but the key thing is that you won't pay more than your limit price (1465p). If your limit order is executed at 1465p, then you may feel very chuffed with yourself – instead of paying 1474p, you've ended up paying only 1465p. Very clever.

You might be thinking: *if these limit orders are such a wheeze, why not use them all the time?*

The reason is that they do not guarantee any trade will take place.

In the previous example, you bought shares at 1465p because the price in the market fell to that level – but the price may not have fallen to 1465p. Instead, from the time the shares were offered at 1474p the price might have just risen steadily; for the sake of saving a few pennies on the price, you could miss the shares taking off upwards.

, All the above is also true when it comes to selling a share, except obviously you select sell not buy. (In the heat of the moment, it's easy to make a mistake here and select the wrong option – we've all done it. So be careful!)

If when buying or selling you don't get a 15-second countdown it means the share you want can't be dealt with online in the amount you want and the deal will have to go through a dealer. So instead of a countdown, your order goes through to a dealer. The site will shortly tell you if your buy or sell was successfully completed.

If this happens, you will not be sure of the price you are going to get. *So do set a limit price before pressing 'Send order to dealer'.* This is a price you do not want to pay more than. Otherwise if the share is fast-moving you could end up paying a silly price. So if you are buying a share which is 100 to buy, you might want to put a limit on of 102.

> If you're a complete beginner, practise a lot before you press the 'Place Order' button for real.

A bit later in the book we'll look at more complicated matters such as setting a stop loss when you place the trade.

THE NAKED TRADER GUIDE TO MARKET JARGON

- *Bull market* – A random upwards market movement causing an investor who is holding shares to mistake himself for a financial genius.

- *Market correction* – The day after you buy shares.

- *Stock split* – When your ex-wife and her lawyer split all your assets equally between them.

- *Stock analyst* – The twit who just downgraded your favourite share.

- *Momentum investing* – The fine art of buying high and selling low.

- *Value investing* – The art of buying low and selling lower.

- *Long-term investing* – The short-term trade that kept going down.

- *Head and shoulders formation* – That bloody dandruff is back.

- *Breakdown* – What you'll have when you hold onto one loser too many.

- *Profits* – What you used to make before you started share trading.

- *Moving averages* – You'll be moved all right, as they keep going down.

PART II
It's All in the Mind

"The safest way to double your money is to fold it over once and put it in your pocket."

– Kin Hubbard

Why People Lose At Trading

We're going to go into effective strategies, research tips and where to find shares worth looking at soon – in fact, it's probably the biggest part of the book. But before then, I think it's important to briefly cover two key areas that trip loads of traders up.

The next two parts of the book – II and III – are important, and will help lay a winning foundation for your trading. Get them right and you can make money from everything else we'll look at. Get them wrong and the rest really doesn't matter.

It's your brain, dum dum

Firstly I want to focus a little on the mental side of the markets.

The mind truly is the most powerful muscle. Unfortunately, for traders this is a blessing and a curse.

The good news is that the market will pay you for having cleverer or quicker ideas about companies and the future than other people. The bad news is that your brain is more prone to going rogue than a character in a John le Carré novel. It's a double agent, just waiting to stab you in the back and push you off London Bridge. You won't even see it coming.

Unless you're prepared.

More people lose than win at trading and psychology is a huge part of that. Understanding where they go wrong should help us not to be one of the losers.

I think I have a pretty good handle on market psychology, in large part thanks to the countless emails I've received from readers and fellow traders and the thousands of you I've met at seminars. I've seen it all. Fear, greed, stubbornness, self-destruction, gambling … sometimes all at once.

So what's the number one reason most people lose at trading?

Easy. It is **greed**. The desperate desire to make big money and to make it *now*!

Greed, for instance, leads to buying crazily risky companies in huge amounts. I once met someone who put £200,000 in *one* risky oil company. It was all the money he had. A bloke he met assured him this company was going to find tons of oil. It didn't. He is almost certainly still holding the shares. Which leads me to …

… **stubbornness**. This is the second great mental mistake losing traders make. 'I bought the share and I was right and I am only going to sell it once I've made a big profit, even if it's gone down 80% and the chief executive has just been led out of the building in plastic handcuffs.'

Stubbornness has a lot to answer for, but **fear** plays a big role; no one likes to feel they're over their head. And fear is the third big psychological reason for losses. Above all, fear surfaces in people being scared they'll *never make money* – and it becomes self-fulfilling, because once they make even a tiny bit of profit they take it, without allowing a trade time to breathe.

A quick final note here. You should try not to make any, or too many, trading decisions when you're tired. If you've had a few drinks the night before and you wake up with a sore head, watch what you do. Or if you feel generally in a bad mood, be wary of trading. If you don't have a clear head, don't expect to be able to stay unemotional and make good trades.

Who do you think you are kidding, Mr Market?

You might find it strange that I'm going to devote part of a chapter in a book on finance to a very old sit-com: *Dad's Army*.

I know, I know. 'What's going on, Burns? This book is big enough as it is. I'm off to the next chapter right now!'

Fair enough – you can just read the bits of the book you like. I don't mind. You bought it! Read none of it and use it as a doorstop – though obviously think twice about that if you're reading it on an iPad. (You may need to stack two of them.)

The thing about *Dad's Army* is that each of the characters in the series brilliantly represents a part of our psyche as we engage in the stock market. And we need to find a way to mute those bits of us that stop us making money.

So while you read this quick guide, think about which characters represent you (or part of you). Be honest with yourself. If you can recognise your defects (I have many, I promise) then you can avoid them bringing you down.

Being self-aware in the markets is hugely valuable and it's pretty much impossible to succeed long term without it.

Corporal "DON'T PANIC!" Jones: emotional

Jonesy is one of the best-loved characters in the series. He is also absolutely the worst possible candidate for a would-be investor or trader.

Can you imagine if one of his shares started to fall?

Panic is one emotion you definitely shouldn't give into. You need to be calm and focused and have a plan of what to do if things don't go as expected. *And this plan must not consist of panicking.*

'Oh, if the trade goes wrong, I'll just run for the exits and wait it out.' 'Oh, if the price goes up before I can get in, I'll just buy twice as many shares to get a similar profit on the price movement.'

That's not planning at all. That's Corporal Jones staying cool under pressure by running into a wall.

Your prepared responses need to be based on the same level of research, thinking and patience as got you into or out of a share in the first place.

If you are a bit of a panicker, you will lose money in the markets if you don't control it. Lots of people have sold something just because it went down a penny and they panicked. Trading costs mean this is never a free mistake.

So, never panic. Think about why you are panicking, calm down and think carefully about your best plan of action. Perhaps ensure you always have a stop loss in place to unemotionally cut a loss at a price you've decided in advance is unacceptable. (More on stops later!)

If you always feel like Corporal Jones and can't stop running around not panicking, maybe the market isn't for you.

The only time I ever panic? When I realise I've run out of marmalade.

Private Walker: greed

Walker is the spiv of the series. He always has something dodgy to sell on the black market. In stock market terms, of course, he represents our greed.

We want to make loads of money and we want it now, sometimes even if the means of making it are dodgier than a packet of delicious jam-filled snacks. If you are too much like Walker, you'll fail in the markets. Greed is the downfall of many a trader.

Someone at a spread bet firm once told me that one customer put in £10,000, made £250,000 within a couple of months, but three months later owed *the spread firm* £40,000. Why? He got too greedy. He took too many risks, borrowed too much money, started believing his own hype.

Greed makes us want to make money too quickly and when that happens we overreach ourselves.

Walker also represents the spiv element of the market. That is, tipsters, boiler-room salesmen, bulletin board rampers, system sellers ... well, the list is endless.

The moment you sign up for a trading account, expect any amount of spam and phone calls from various Walker-types.

Do not fall for Walker's tempting patter. "Fancy some exposure to diamonds, mate?" No, is always the answer. Just imagine all these fancy-looking firms with their whizzy websites and incredible promises of instant riches as a man in an alleyway asking if you want a cheeky peek inside his suitcase.

Private "We're all doomed!" Fraser: fear

Private Fraser, being Scottish and an undertaker, is of course the fearful one, always expecting the worst. He loves telling horror stories and is ultra-suspicious.

Fear is a huge enemy for traders. Fear makes you sell stuff way too early. Fear stops you trading. It takes over. If you are over fearful, you'll never make any money.

Fear is a hard one to get to grips with. That's why a plan (again) is important. What action are you going to take if a share of yours starts to plummet? And what constitutes plummeting? Fear should not be an issue, decisive action should be.

If you are too much like Fraser, you will definitely lose. Don't be afraid.

Sergeant Wilson: laziness

Sergeant Wilson, Captain Mainwaring's sidekick and Mrs Pike's bit on the side, represents laziness.

Wilson is so lazy and wishy washy. He can't command anyone and is only interested in shagging the next-door neighbour. If he was a trader he'd buy something because Walker had tipped it, then he'd forget about it and a year later realise he's lost all his money.

You cannot be lazy in trading. You are definitely doomed if you are. Don't get me wrong … I'm pretty lazy in life. But not in trading.

Laziness in trading means not doing your own research, copying trades from tipsters and bulletin boards, having no plan.

Oh, and losing a ton of money.

So do your homework. Read and keep learning. The lazy in the market have their money taken from them by the industrious. Keep on top of your trading and have a plan. Be one of the industrious!

Private Pike: stupid boys

Well, I guess Pike represents … stupid boys. And, by the way, they are always boys. Girls are too clever to lose all their money on the markets.

Stupid boys go into the markets thinking they are hotshots and pile into shares that make no money but promise a cure for cancer, or more usually gushing oil wells that end up producing a lot of … water.

Stupid boys also listen to the guy down the pub, online tipsters, and they love going on technical analysis courses.

Stupid boys believe they've just bought the next multi-bagger (a share that doubles, triples, quadruples in price) and can hardly believe it when a marvel penny stock plummets 50%. Stupid boys immediately buy more after a 50% fall. After all, if it goes up 25% they'll have broken even …

Captain Mainwaring: top trader

It's a bit of a surprise, but I actually think Captain Mainwaring would make a good trader. He has many attributes that a trader or investor should have.

Since he doesn't mind being boring, he would hold his good shares and keep holding them for the best gains. Since he's comically unflappable in the face of disaster, he wouldn't panic when things go crazy. Whether right or wrong, he knows how to make a decision – and he also knows how to change his mind if he makes a mistake (albeit, invariably making another mistake in the process).

Cautious yet courageous, Mainwaring would make a decent trader! Go Mainwaring!

Speaking of the good captain, the economy really started to go wrong 20 years ago when they replaced all the old-style Mainwaring bank managers with a bunch of Private Walkers. The Walkers screwed everything up for their own short-term gains. I say: ditch the Walkers and bring back the Mainwarings!

Private Godfrey

To end this piece on a bit of a down note, Godfrey just wants to know where the nearest loo is. And that's where we all end up. Sorry about that – but someone had to tell you.

My TV role model

Good as he might be at trading, Mainwaring isn't a perfect role model. There's actually someone much better from TV land. Someone whose example could make you a fortune.

Who is my TV role model for trading with the right mindset, then?

The one person you have to model yourself on is ... Mr Spock.

Spock would be a natural trader. That's because, of course, he has no emotion – and being emotionless is *exactly* what you need to be in the markets.

You can imagine him running his winners and cutting his losers without a worry. There would be no fear and no greed. He would make logical decisions at all times, Captain.

Indeed his Vulcan logic would make him exceptional, because trading is all about being logical, making sensible decisions. And he would never fall in love with a share.

Mind you, in one episode he did get high on a plant on some planet by mistake, and fell in love with a girl (apparently he went where no man had gone before). But apart from that, he has an unblemished unemotional record.

Want to be a good trader? Think like Spock would.

Not like Corporal Jones.

Confirmation Bias and the Most Important Lesson

Confirmation bias

Okay, so those are some of the more troublesome trading mindsets out of the way. Let's move on to another part of psychology that impacts our trading. In fact, I'd say it's the most vital to beat – it's called *confirmation bias*.

I came across a brilliant description of the problem of confirmation bias when reading an interview with Derren Brown, the hypnotist and showman, in a *Times* supplement.

I like Derren Brown. You should go to one of his shows; they're terrific entertainment. Anyway, here's the bit of the interview that made me sit up and take notice:

> "There is something called confirmation bias, where once you have an idea in your head it's hard not to look out for things that confirm it – whether it's that you believe someone doesn't like you or that you have a gambling system. It's a very human urge."

A lightbulb went off in my head. Yes, of course, I thought. This must be one of the major reasons so many people lose at trading shares.

When we go in and buy a share we think we are making the right choice. After all, we made an effort. We did our research, we did technical analysis, we looked at the charts. We were happy to wait to get our timing right.

Some may have even looked at the Bollinger Band Stochastics MACD crossover Elliott Wave dead-cross rice-pudding signals. And lots of other cobblers.

The trouble is: once the share took our fancy, it was too easy for everything else that followed – unless we were really, truly vigilant – to get twisted towards making us press the buy button.

And once we're 'in', we expect the share price to rise, because we are pretty good at stock-picking right? We look around and make sure our choice is validated by others. It's off to the bulletin boards to check everyone else agrees. And yah boo sucks to any moron who thinks differently.

We're right. The charts say so. And the fundamentals. And the tipster bloke. And anyway, there's going to be a takeover bid next week! That bulletin board chap knows his stuff.

And if the share price goes down and keeps going down, we will continue to scour the internet for more validation.

Sell it? Are you crazy? Time to buy more! Look how cheap it is now! The market always gets things wrong. The market is such a moron!

Now it's got even cheaper. Well that is GREAT news. Look at the price I can get it for now, it's like the sales. I'm in for MORE.

You know what I'm getting at.

What should we do instead of trying to validate a choice we've already made? We should do the opposite. It's the hardest thing in the world to do. We should seriously consider if we're wrong. We should thoroughly consider getting out (or not getting in). We should always look at the alternative argument.

If we're *right*, we have nothing to fear from this process.

A good way of doing this is to imagine a share you're interested in in six months' time. Imagine it has fallen 50%. Why did that happen – and could it happen again? How? What are the possible negatives? Try to find them all.

The most important lesson

The most important lesson I can teach you about trading is one quite closely related to confirmation bias. In fact, confirmation bias is probably its greatest enemy. That's fine, though, because it can help kill confirmation bias stone dead if you take it on board.

It is, quite simply: *make money by making losses!*

You heard what I said. Don't pretend you didn't.

Before you start trading, I want you to bear this in mind – taking lots of losses will make you a lot of money.

Sounds crazy, right? But really, taking losses will make you a lot of money.

In fact I should say it in capitals for emphasis. Why don't I?

TAKING LOTS OF LOSSES WILL MAKE YOU A LOT OF MONEY!

It really is true.

Let me expand on it a little. I should add the crucial word 'small' – taking lots of *small* losses will make you a lot of money.

And further to this I must add: take lots of small losses and one or two big gains and you will make a lot of money.

There. It's all about getting rid of losses while they're little, and holding onto profits while they grow. What I look to do is to take losses quickly if a share starts to go down soon after I bought it. But I try to hold on tight to the really good risers and look for 30% and upwards from those going into profit.

So a really good trader's banked losses and profits could look something like this:

Last ten closed trades
-7%
-5%
+25%
-10%
-3%
+40%
-7%
-6%
-9%
+32%

At first glance, this trader looks like he's losing money. He's taken a lot of losses: seven, in fact, and only three winners. *But!* He has made a lot of money.

In fact, if each trade had been £5,000 of shares, the trader would be up by £2,500.

So it's really a percentages game. It's not the number of wins or losses that matters.

If the trader above had taken his profits too quickly, despite cutting his losses, he wouldn't have made much. He may have been tempted to take profits at just 10% instead of the 25%, 40% and 32%. And that would have spelled disaster.

You need the courage to sell losers fast and hold winners for a while.

If the losers start to fall quickly, even by not that much (though more than just a penny or two – I'm no Corporal Jones!), I tend to cut them. And if a share is really tanking, no arguments, I am out. I never want to hold anything that's down more than 15%.

The art of treating gains correctly is an opposite one: you mustn't be ruthless with a gradually expanding number. Don't get giddy and grab them. I have let my winners run and run. The biggest percentages among the winners have been held for a couple of years. And I think they still have further to go.

Of course, I have picked some decent shares. However, I have also picked my fair share of losers but cut them before they started to eat away at the profits.

It is one of the hardest concepts in share trading – to sell at a loss. And blokes are really bad at it. Just as hard a concept as resisting taking profits too early.

Some traders find taking losses next to impossible. So you have to steel yourself into thinking that taking a loss is a *good* thing.

HE'S HAD A GOOD
DAY– SOLD SOME
SHARES AT
A LOSS...

Remember, if you're aiming for at least 30% as a reasonable gain, if a share starts going down by more than 10% and you're still holding, you'd have to think it will actually be a far better buy than you originally anticipated: now you're expecting at least a 40% gain! Even though it's done nothing so far but tank. Crazy! Especially if you let it tank by 20, 30, 40, 50% (and I know people who have). So you think that share you bought, and reckoned might give you a 30% gain, and which has done nothing but lose its value, is actually going to be an 80% gain?

It will be – around about the same time the devil has put his skis on.

I have met so many people who just can't take their losses. I did this a few times myself in my early trading career. The worst I remember was Hartstone, where I bought at 450p and allowed it to sink all the way to 250p before bailing out.

Another good example is Coffee Republic. When I bought the shares for 28p, if I had set a stop loss of 22p, and acted on it, I would have sold without emotion at 22p and lost only £500. As it was, with no stop loss (and after actually buying *more* shares), I eventually lost around £7,000.

Example – waiting for the comeback

"It's going to come back."

This is the perennial claim of traders who have a big losing position. In fact it was once said directly to me by someone who had bought a share. He'd bought it at 1200p. It had gone down and he'd then bought more at 800p. It kept going down.

"I've just bought some more at 400," he told me very confidently. "It's going to come back," he added.

"It might go down some more," I said. "Shouldn't you have set a stop loss with each trade? Then you wouldn't have lost so much money."

He got annoyed. "I haven't lost anything," he said. "I only lose if I sell. But I won't. This is a great company, it's just been caught out by the oversold market."

"How much have you got in it now?" I asked.

"About 20 grand," he said. "It'll go back up to 1200p and I'll have made a fortune!"

There was no point in me arguing that the fact it was down so much already meant that something was badly wrong. Nor was it worth telling him it wouldn't do his trading any good if, every time he opened his account he had to stare at a massive losing trade.

Or that he had made the classic mistake of letting a losing position run away with him.

He was fixated.

The thing is, you can always buy back lower if, in the long run, you think things will eventually turn round. **You don't need to be along for the expensive ride downwards for that.**

But it is amazing the number of shares that go down 15% and just carry on going down. And if you carry on holding them, you're risking some serious damage.

I've met people who STILL have a 70% loser and have had it for YEARS. They can't bear to sell it. I suspect they never will.

I ought to end by telling you what the company was my acquaintance had bought.

Northern Rock.

(And he never sold.)

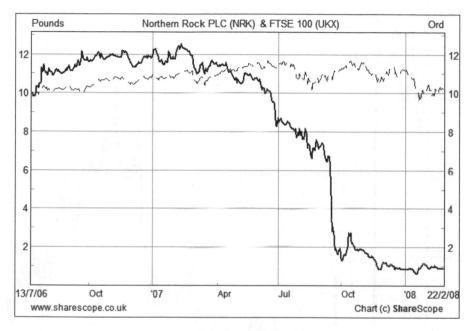

A cautionary duffer: Northern Rock (July 2006–February 2008)

It's all down to our emotions. If you can conquer those when you're trading, you'll be a winner. You need strength and courage to sell those losers and hold onto the winners. I used to find it difficult too – now I love it.

Mmmmm, taking a loss … delicious!

A typical few years in the life of a trader who never read my chapters on psychology

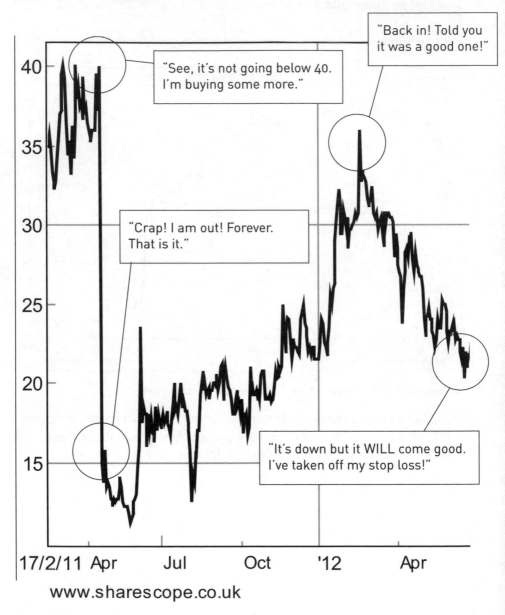

A mystery share! (February 2011–October 2013)

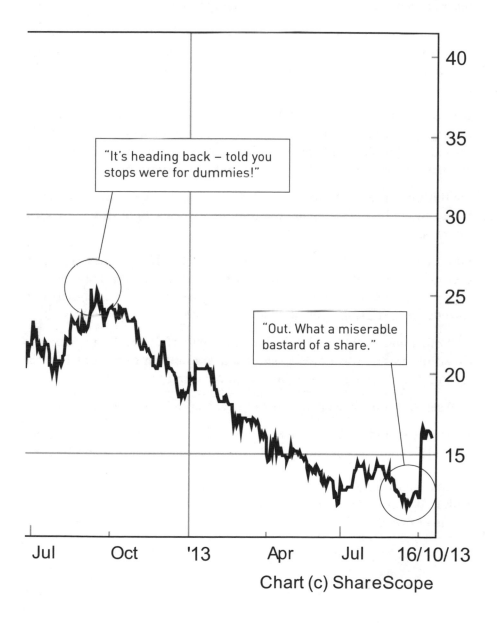

Chart (c) ShareScope

The share, by the way, was Desire Petroleum – and the five years of pain just described were a true tale for some traders. Desire was eventually put out of its misery in late 2013 when it was taken over at 16p.

I have met so many people that lost money on that one. It said it had found oil, and then announced that it was actually water.

The picture painted here is a bit dramatic, but it's true to life. You'd be surprised how easy it is to combine almost all of the worst trading habits in a single bout of out-of-control trading. It isn't inevitable, though: you just have to be disciplined.

If need be, don't just get out, but get out, close the laptop down, stop trading for a while and pledge to abandon forever a particular share that's caused you problems. There's no point obsessing over one when there are so many others out there that you can make money from.

On this point there are two traders I've met that stand out. Both sat in the front row at different seminars and told their stories. Both stories are very interesting.

One chap told us how he had nearly lost his house, marriage and everything by punting on just one oil share using CFDs. He was very happy to get his story off his chest – he was keen to warn newcomers not to get into the terrible state of mind he got into.

The other one was in a real state. He had a basketful of really awful penny dreadfuls and he was down a significant amount on them. But I had a feeling that, despite the losses, he was never going to sell them.

"I'll sell each one when it gets to, say, break even," he suggested.

I knew there and then he would never make it as a trader. Unless you can take a loss you really are doomed. I expect he will have the shares forever.

So that's all I have to say on psychology for now. Well done if you stuck with it. If you want to read up further on it, try *Your Money and Your Brain* by Jason Zweig.

PART III
Warning! Warning!

"Never invest in any idea you can't illustrate with a crayon."

– Peter Lynch

The Market Can See You Coming

If it seems too good to be true – it is

So, a dodgy mindset can seriously damage your trading. But your brain is not the only threat to your profits. From the moment you open your first broker account or register for any shares site, you will be bombarded by those who want to take your money. I promise you all the sexy stuff is not far away – Part IV is only just around the corner! – but along with trading psychology you really do need to have a good grasp of the dangers out there before you jump in.

I actually just got a call from someone who wanted to sell me diamonds. "Don't call this number again" was my reply ("No thanks, Blofeld" also works). I always stop them before they get into their script. Hanging up straightaway only delays the inevitable repeat call.

There is nothing the market likes more than a 'mug punter'. Sorry, but this could be you if you're not careful and suspicious. Hopefully after reading this book you'll be safe ... but just remember, all the great big silly mug punters started out like everyone else!

When you start trading shares, everyone loves you. Brokers get commissions. Spread bet firms make money on the spread. The more you trade, the better (for them).

Meanwhile system-sellers want to sell you their amazing systems, all guaranteed to make money (though guess who *actually* makes the money). Pumpers and dumpers on the bulletin boards are desperate for you to buy their red-hot penny tip to push it up a little more before they dump it. Tipsters want £100 off you to subscribe to their useless tipping service. (If the tipster is so good why is he still tipping shares and not retired to the Caribbean?)

CFD brokers want to 'trade for you'. Boiler rooms want to sell you companies that don't even exist. And lots of people want to sell you gold, diamonds, commodities or whatever they think you might fall for.

In fact, the market is full of nasty pieces of work. Complete and utter lowlifes who couldn't care less about you and want to rob you by any legal means possible. They are all over the place. They want to take your cash.

Please do not give it to them!

The one thing that you can be sure of in the markets is: *if it seems too good to be true – it sodding well is!*

I get emails all the time from people asking whether so and so system works, or whether a £3,000 seminar will help them to make millions. No, is the answer, in both cases! But it's scary that it should even occur as a question. Because the markets seem bafflingly complex to outsiders (they're not), beginners are all too willing to credit the most ludicrous, expensive advice or products in attempting to get on top of them. Don't!

Do not give out your real email address when you register for anything. Set up what I call a dump mail. For example, when I sign up for anything and have to register I use the mail address junkmaildump@etc, etc. It's a real address, but not one I ever use. It means the mailbox I do use doesn't get bunged up with spam.

Also, think carefully before you give out your real phone number to anyone connected to the financial world. Otherwise you will get inundated with phone calls. Check with whoever wants your number that it does not get sold on.

It sounds horrible, but think of everyone out there in the wonderful world of shares as your implacable enemy, unless over time you are convinced otherwise. The friendlier they appear, the more likely it is you will get led up the garden path (before being relieved of your wallet and pushed into the garden pond).

Of course, it is very tempting to believe a trading system works and you just have to follow it to make money, or someone will tip you the right shares. But ignore all offers and concentrate on learning about the markets slowly and cautiously – do not get side-tracked by the easy way out. It's invariably a trap door to somewhere nasty.

Here are some particular scams to watch out for. Once you know what's out there, you should be well-armed to avoid it all.

Scams

Phone calls/boiler rooms

Phone calls from 'boiler rooms' often come from America. A plausible-sounding bloke opens up with a question like: "You handle your own portfolio – how's it going?" When you mumble something like "It's going okay," he'll start his sales pitch. He has an incredible stock that is going to treble in a few weeks and he's offering *you* the chance to get in!

It could be one of a couple of scams.

This bloke will probably claim to be from a broker that can let you have this wonder stock cheaper than the current market price. What this *really* means is he, or even a reputable-sounding broker, has bought a shed-load of stock in a crap company and wants to offload some to you at a worse price, thereby making a guaranteed profit.

Or it could be worse. You could send your money off and not even get that pile of rubbish in return!

Alternatively, the call could come from a UK company offering tips or shares at a knockdown price. Again, the share is likely to be a small penny share and they are trying to make money out of you in the same way as above.

Ignore all these and just hang up. You are unlikely to get rich quick and are more likely to become considerably poorer.

Before hanging up, ask them where they got your phone number and try to get off the list.

If you want to see a boiler room in full operation, check out the movie *The Wolf of Wall Street* (though this recommendation comes with a content warning for those who don't like films with lots of sex, drugs, sex and sex in them).

When it comes to boiler room emails, a reader once passed along this very useful piece of info:

> "I have been called three times this month alone with boiler room scams. While I think you should just tell them you are not interested (if the share's so good why aren't they just busy buying it themselves?), if you really want to have a look at the stock then check out the details of the company and the firm pushing it to you. Here are a few tips for doing so:

> "1. Use **whois.domaintools.com** – this will tell you when their websites were created (normally, if it's a scam or fly-by-night, this will be recently).

> "2. Check the IP address of any email you've received by using **whatismyipaddress.com/trace-email**. If it's not in the country they say they are emailing from, you're usually dealing with a scam.

> "This should be sufficient to find the scammers."

And always remember: it is a lot better to say 'I wish I had put some money into that, it's doubled', than 'I wish I hadn't bothered with that one, I have lost all my cash.' There will always be other profitable shares. There will not always be other cash you can use to trade!

Newspaper/magazine get-rich ads

I'm sure you've seen these. They usually say something like:

"Learn stock market secrets … "

or:

"Make £400 a day from home … "

What happens is you get enticed to a free seminar. The guru will talk about things like spread betting and technical analysis and then spend the rest of the time trying to flog his work manuals, books, and another paid-for seminar or expensive software. Sometimes the sell can be very hard indeed. (*'Lock the doors, gentlemen, I have a proposition for these good people!'*)

The plain fact (again) is: if it seems too good to be true, it invariably is.

It is highly unlikely you'll make half a grand a day or other ridiculous figures that get bandied about. The guru will make money out of *you* by selling you his books, videos and courses. Again, all you have to do is ask yourself: if the guru is such a phenomenal genius why doesn't he sit at home with his systems, rack up the millions and just be happy?

Seminars

My seminars are brilliant (of course), but watch out for the ones that demand a lot of money, £3,000 and the like. They usually suck you in by offering a free seminar, which is where a heavy sell is used to get you to stump up for the expensive seminar, where they will reveal 'the true secrets' of the market. I'm pretty dubious about these and haven't heard from anyone who has genuinely benefited or thought they were worth the money.

What they usually do is spend hours teaching you market gobbledegook. One good trick: ask to see their trading accounts!

There's no substitute for learning to do your own research and gradually learning the ins and outs of trading.

Systems

Everywhere you look in the stock market, someone somewhere will be trying to sell you a system. Not just devious scammers. Even vaguely legitimate outfits. They're not quite as seedy as the scammers, but will be just as bad for your wallet.

These people promise you the world:

> *"Spend just five minutes a day and make big profits."*
>
> *"Our system picks all the trades for you."*
>
> *"Trade from home and make a living from the markets – with no experience."*

But just think about it.

Don't you think that if the people that came up with the systems had devised an easy way to make millions they'd keep it to themselves and end up in Barbados sunbathing? Don't be fooled by promises of big profits for no effort. And take anything they say, like their 'record of profits', with a giant pinch of salt.

The only dependable 'system' is to learn about trading slowly but surely through hard work and decent research. You get nothing for nothing. Ignore the ads and bin the junk mail.

Of course it is tempting: the system sellers are clever and they are playing on our inherent laziness (well I'm lazy, and I don't mind admitting it).

It sounds lovely: a computer will do all the work for you. Pure science fiction, I'm afraid.

A reader writes: An expensive system in more ways than one ...

"I do not believe in systems. In my opinion people who produce and sell them are very cynical creatures. Their customers believe if they pay a lot for a product it will work and bring them profit. My ex-partner attended a very expensive seminar, something about £4k for two days (they didn't even get a lunch). The price was ridiculous and I was curious if it would really work.

"It didn't. Like most systems it was based on technical analysis but the reality is not that simple. Fundamentals are important as well and you have to switch on your brain and spend some time researching."

Scams summary

- Don't buy shares offered over the phone.

- Be sceptical about 'get-rich' ads.

- Software is an expensive waste of money.

- Don't take the 'easy' way – take time to learn about the markets.

Tipsters – the bad

There are loads of share tipsters around, as you will very quickly find out. They usually charge a fee for access to tips, or they come in the form of a monthly newsletter. Like entertainers, they all have some kind of shtick to pull you in. Some claim to be maverick City insiders. Others 'read the charts and the signals'.

As I see it right now there are about five or six guys who are behind a massive number of tip sheets. A kind of share-tipping mafia if you will. You will probably get to know them as they are advertised everywhere. They want to get you on a nice yearly direct debit which they hope you will forget to cancel (most people do).

As well as tipping stocks they are just as likely to launch 'shorting raids', trying to drive a share price down (while betting on it happening) by bombarding their followers with reasons why a company is going bust.

Every single tipster will quote what seems like amazing performance figures:

"Our tips are up 40% this year!"

"Amazing profit every year!"

"Three penny shares that are about to rocket … !"

What they don't brag about is the ones they picked that halved in value or even went bust. So you won't see headlines like:

"We tipped a share and it went bust!"

"Everyone who followed our last tip lost thousands of pounds!"

There'll usually be a list of shares with percentage profits made against each one. Amazingly, you'll see hardly any losing shares. Obviously following these geniuses is a licence to print money!

Sadly, their claims are unlikely to be realistic. Some tipsters are very clever and use various manipulations of statistics to show performance that often just isn't true. And you'll often only see the winners highlighted. My cat could have picked some of those by sticking her paw at random on the share prices in the *Financial Times*!

Nearly all of the dodgy tipping organisations tip very small penny shares. You won't find them tipping many bigger companies. That's because in percentage terms they only have to hit on one or two big winners (out of the dozens of companies they tip) to look like geniuses.

Here are just some of the ways they create amazing performance figures.

Tipster tricks

Tipsters often use 'mid' prices. Never the real buy and sell prices. With the small company shares they tip, this means they are already up on the percentage game.

Let's take an example. A tipster tips a share that is 9p to sell and 10p to buy. So the tipster says his tip is at 9.5p – the mid price. No one can actually buy at this price, but never mind! The tip is published in a tip sheet at the weekend. On Monday, before the market opens, the market makers have seen the tip and raise the price to 10p to sell and 11p to buy (the mid price is now 10.5p). Subscribers buy in at 11p, but the tipster can now claim to have profits of an amazing 10%! (The difference between his mid-price tip at 9.5p, and the new mid price of 10.5p.)

What has actually happened is that those who bought the tip are already nursing *losses* of nearly 10%. They've bought in at the real buy price of 11p, but the selling price is only 10p!

What's worse is that the market makers know the mug punters have bought at 11p and during the next few days will drop the price, and those who bought will suffer even worse losses.

The tipster doesn't care: that now goes down as a 10% profit. On the table of winners it will show: tip 9.5p, high 10.5p, +10%!

But none of the subscribers could possibly have bought or sold at these prices.

Of course, most of the tipsters tip anything from 50 to 200 companies a year. There's no way subscribers could afford to buy that many of them.

So even when a tipster manages to tip a big winner, chances are the subscriber won't have bought it. It's Sod's Law, but they will probably buy the one that's gone bust!

None of it matters because, while people are cancelling subscriptions, there are always new mugs ready to start up subscriptions.

Tipsters – the good

Okay, of course, as with everything, there *are* some good tipsters out there. There are a very small number of names that are worth paying attention to. If you can find someone tipping who trades as well, that is an advantage. Alternatively, someone who specialises in certain shares, for example those listed on the FTSE 100 and 250.

But if you don't feel like finding your own shares, how can you find the good tipping services?

It'll be difficult, and is another reason why you shouldn't be so lazy! The clue is to ask around. Try the bulletin boards, put up a message: 'Is so-and-so's tipping service any good? Have you made money by following the tips?'

Bulletin board writers are notoriously difficult to please, so if you do read a number of plaudits for a tipping service, then maybe, just *maybe*, it's worth a look. (Make sure all of the users aren't freshly registered and suspiciously united in praise, though.)

If you do subscribe to a tipster service, don't just buy the tipped shares automatically. Do your own research. Look on the tips as a possible basis for further research (always check the debt!). Monitor the service carefully and write down the real prices you could have bought or sold at and judge performance yourself.

> If you subscribe to tip sheets, you must only use them to help you generate ideas.

Tips and market makers

And, whatever you do, don't buy a tip right away. **The market makers will have marked up the tips and if you buy right away the price will be far too high.** Wait for a few days for the share to settle down.

The other sort of tips you get are the free ones in investment magazines and newspapers. Again, beware of the market maker mark-up – these shares should not be bought (or sold) right away.

Be especially careful of buying tips in the Sunday papers, as on a quiet Monday morning these will already be higher and you will be paying far too much.

Example – tips affecting a share price

Here's an example of a tip affecting a share price. On 2 February 2014, the *Mail on Sunday* tipped hotel group Action Hotels. Before the tip the shares traded at 59 to sell, 63 to buy.

The market makers know they will get buyers at any price on Monday morning. So it opens at 65–68, already marked up heavily.

Within a few minutes, the buy price is 72 – nearly 15% higher than before the tip! *Mail* punters buy in heavily at this point.

After a while, the market makers simply start to drop the price. The paper's readers get scared and some sell for a loss … and the shares end the day at 64 to sell, 66 to buy.

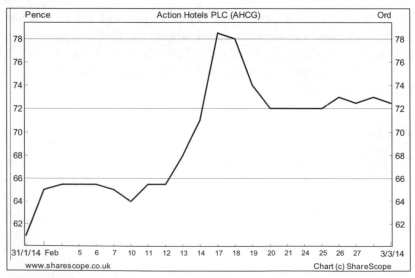

Action Hotels price action (31 January–3 February 2014)

In other words, you would have made a loss buying those shares *at any time* after the tip came out. The only winners: the market makers, who made a bundle.

Two weeks later the shares were 63p to sell. Those buying at the top of the tip were worse off by nearly 15%.

Moral of the story? **Don't buy a newspaper tip the day after.** If you want to buy it, wait a few days for the tip's effect to wear off.

In addition, remember these tips are being written by journalists. Many are probably only on £25,000 a year. If they were any good at picking shares they'd be trading full-time themselves! They are also under pressure to regularly come up with tips and ideas, so they are not necessarily going to be much good.

There are writers out there who are different, and do it for the love of investing (and even waive their fees). Take a closer look at them.

Tipsters summary

- Be sceptical of the performance figures quoted.

- Tips are marked up before you can buy.

- Do you really need a guru?

Bulletin Boards

It can be a lonely business buying and selling shares. But that's where the internet bulletin boards (BBs) come in.

The three most active and biggest bulletin boards are:

- ADVFN – **www.advfn.com** (click 'Free BB' or 'PBB' if you're a subscriber)

- MoneyAM – **www.moneyam.com** (click 'Investors' Room' and 'Traders' Room')

- Interactive Investor – **www.iii.co.uk** (click 'Community & Discussion').

All BB contributors have to choose a nickname, so you have no idea who they are. If you want to contribute, you just register on the site, pick your nickname and you are away.

On ADVFN and MoneyAM, each topic is called a 'thread', and they appear in order of the most recently updated. There are the main bulletin boards which are free, and both also have premium BBs which you pay a small amount to access. The premium boards attract a more serious investor and tend to be better.

BBs are like a big pub where blokes (generally) talk about shares in the same way they talk about football.

The main rule regarding the BBs is: treat them as light entertainment!

I used to be a contributor to the bulletin boards. But as my profile grew you can pretty much guess what happened. Every time I posted, some idiot would come on with something nasty about me.

I didn't mind at first – I figured I had put myself in the public eye so I could expect to be criticised. But I just got tired of it. There are only so many online custard pies a person can take. I know it was just one or two people, but it was exhausting – and in the end a little creepy, particularly with one guy who got so obsessive he wrote about me all the time.

Bear in mind that many BB contributors are trying to push a share they've just bought. So treat everything you read with some scepticism. Especially comments on very small companies.

- A **bad sign** is if there are dozens of posters all enthusiastically discussing every tiny movement of a share. Even worse, if there are posters claiming it'll be a ten-bagger (10× price rise) and the like, or posters saying they've bought some and are going to buy more etc. And worst of all is when there is loads of inside bitching and backbiting between posters!

- The **best sign** is a reasoned, quiet but informed thread. It means the share concerned is actually more likely to be a winner.

Some bulletin boards are good, some not so good, and others a complete waste of time. There is a good filter function on the ADVFN BB. If you find a particular poster a waste of time, you can filter that poster so their posts just disappear from your screen and never appear in future. Handy!

My view on using them?

Well, I think the BB on the company you've just decided to buy is worth a quick look in case there is some additional info you missed. You never know.

Sometimes you might find some handy research done for you. For example, if it's a retailer some posters may have visited stores and reported back their findings. Quite often with oil stocks you can find very informed posters who know their way around oil exploration and the like.

Sometimes, really good BB posters will make life easy for you and will cut and paste in company statements and reports, dividend dates, etc.

However, don't take everything you read as accurate! Remember you are just using the BB to put in place another piece of the jigsaw.

Rampers and other species

Rampers is a term applied to those on BBs who continually talk up a share they are holding in the hope others will buy in and so raise the price of the share in question. They then hope to quickly sell on the strength generated and make a profit.

They will say or write anything to make you buy. They will often claim to have inside information or say there's a 'bid coming' or there's an amazing 'chart breakout'. They pick on the smallest shares in the market and make clever remarks about them intended to suck you into buying.

Don't believe everything you read, especially if comments are made about an illiquid company with a small market cap.

There are different sorts of posters to bulletin boards:

1. **The complete idiots** who just like using naughty words or having fights with others.

2. **The really good posters** who are well-informed and come up with decent and well worked-out predictions.

3. **The wind-up merchants** who don't even trade and just like winding people up. Watch out for posters who don't post during the day. This is a big clue that they don't really trade much but want to appear authoritative.

4. **The in-and-out types.** They will breathlessly post their trades, one minute saying what a great share it is, then ten minutes later saying they sold because it wasn't moving. Best ignored.

5. **The gurus.** Often with their own blogs; they try to set themselves up as the wise ones. They will post trades but will quietly fail to mention the losers. Beware.

6. **Complete fantasists.** They really think they are the dog's proverbials even if they just have losers. Avoid.

7. **Approval seekers**. Will latch onto one poster and agree with everything they say for a bit, seeking their approval. It usually ends in tears.

Given time, you will work out which is which!

Do watch for those who claim to have inside information. Remember they are breaking the law if that's true.

And don't think you can hide behind a nickname. You can still get done for libel and if you deliberately post misinformation you can get hauled into court.

This has happened on a few occasions.

Summary

- BBs should be used mainly for entertainment purposes.

- Don't get conned into buying worthless shares.

- Treat everything you read as suspicious.

- It is worth reading a board before you buy a share.

PART IV
Getting Down to It

"Select stocks the way
porcupines make love –
very carefully."

– Bob Dinda

How Do I Find Shares Worth Looking At?

How do I find shares worth looking at? You want to know, do you? Oh, all right, if you insist.

The best way to explain this is to tell you how I look for them. Usually I try the kitchen first, then the living room but I typically find them under the bed. [Robbie! Shares, shares – not keys. Concentrate please. – Ed.]

Well. There are many ways to find shares worth buying. A good summary, I think, would be that I am looking for shares where *something seems to be happening*.

And preferably the shares are rising already.

My first stage is to simply try to find shares that *might* be of interest. I'm not saying I'll buy any of them right away – I'm on the hunt for shares I might buy soon, or I might buy next year.

Finding shares

Right, here's how I try to find shares at least worth adding to my daily watchlist. And I would say I am not looking to get involved with hundreds of different shares ... if I can find just one good one over a week then I count that as job done!

Where I don't look for ideas

These are the places I *avoid* looking at to get ideas:

- internet tipsters/tipsheets
- bulletin boards
- columns from gurus.

Where I look for ideas

These are my favourite places for looking for ideas:

- national newspaper round-ups
- investment publications
- newswires (especially at 7am)
- ADVFN Toplists.

Why do I use these particular sources?

Well, they have all served me well in the past, and shares usually appear in these sources because there is a story to tell or the share is moving. Of course, if you read about a share rising in a paper or a magazine it doesn't mean it'll carry on going up: it might well fall.

But when I say these are places that I look for ideas, I don't mean these are places I will just copy ideas from. **They provide good starting points for putting on the old deerstalker and playing detective.** This is where I start my research, Watson.

Let's look at these sources in more depth.

1. Newspapers

I get the *Times* every day and, erm, the *Sun*. Mrs NT gets the *Mail*.

I find the *Times* very good. I have a proper read through and see if any share is mentioned in there and make a note to research them if they sound interesting. The *Mail* is worth a gander, too.

It might sound strange, but I don't bother with the *Financial Times* – I find it too dry and heavy-going. It's more of an international, business-oriented paper. What I might buy is the weekend edition of the *FT*, which has some thoughtful coverage of shares.

Within the newspapers, I'll take a look at the daily stock market round-up – reporting on the shares that have gone up or down and why. I'll also have a scan of the news stories.

Once or twice a week I'll see something that looks interesting. I'll make a note of the share and why it might be one to buy.

2. Investment publications

There are two main magazines that I regularly check out:

Investors Chronicle

The *IC* is as sober as a judge and has a large circulation – it's been around for a long time. It has some good analysis of company results, some good trading input and some interesting in-depth pullouts which are well worth reading. I think it is worth getting. It does an online version too if you're a cool dude and into that sort of thing.

(Published: weekly, on Fridays.)

Shares

Shares appears to be aimed at a younger readership more inclined to the 'have-a-punt' approach. It's heavy on oil exploration and riskier stuff. But it has some sensible stuff too. Sometimes one or two ideas come up. So again, it's worth a look.

(Published: weekly, on Thursdays.)

I think both magazines do a reasonable job, so I rate both as 'buy'! [Shameful pun. – Ed.] **But I would NEVER be tempted to buy into the tips of either magazine (especially as these would already have been marked up by market makers on the morning of publication).** You should look at the comments made by the magazines as a guideline and not just buy something because a company is recommended.

Sometimes a story they've written about a company might intrigue me, so I'll have a look at it. I especially like the round-up both mags do of recent company results statements. It's interesting to read their comments; they get some right and some wrong. Occasionally I'll notice a company I haven't spotted before and pop it in my notebook to look at in detail.

A word of warning: don't get fooled by any magazine that boasts about producing winning tips. Some of their tips will turn out to be epic stinkers! Also, note that judging the performance of tips is not always straightforward:

- Was the broker's commission and stamp duty taken into account?

- Was it actually possible to deal in the market at the prices used in the calculation?

Often the aggregate tips performance will be heavily influenced by the stellar performance of one flukey share – if you'd missed buying that one share, the aggregate performance of the remaining tips might be nowhere near as good.

However, it is important to know which shares are being tipped (even if you don't buy them). Tipped shares will often increase in price before the market opens, and it's important to know why they rose (i.e. they were up on a tip). Otherwise you might buy them thinking there was more to the rise!

> My tip is: by all means buy good quality magazines, but use them for reference and as prompts for trading ideas, not as a source of sure-fire tips.

3. Company news from 7am

To get company news piping hot and fresh, you could use ADVFN, which has a streaming newswire (i.e. it continually refreshes itself, without you having to reload the page). There is also a nice and free site called **www.investegate.co.uk** which is simply a list of the latest company news.

Most company reports are published between 7am and 8am, so I usually pay more attention to the news then.

Again, sometimes I'll find a company worth looking at, especially if a company report looks very positive. I make a note of anything that catches my eye, from a company reporting to directors buying – often waiting till the evening to check out the company concerned.

There are plenty of other newswires and websites out there if you are interested in following the latest news.

The majority of the most interesting stuff is released just after 7am. I read through what the various companies are reporting and take notes if there are things I like the look of. Make sure you get up early if you don't want to miss this! (Hey, there's nothing wrong with going back to bed afterwards – if you're your own boss, you can make it company policy.) And of course you should keep an eye open for any news on any share you are holding.

4. ADVFN Toplists

ADVFN Toplists are a great way to look out for shares on the move. The lists are compiled by a computer that has been given certain criteria:

ADVFN Toplists menus

As you can see, on the left are the lists you can have for free and on the right are premium lists that cost £75 a year to access.

You can just go with the free lists if you want – I'm not here to pitch for ADVFN, and we've already covered tons of ways of finding shares for free. But I have found these Toplists really useful and it wouldn't be an honest book if I didn't say so.

If you're at all offended by offers in books, please look away for the next paragraph (I totally understand) …

… because I like these lists so much, I got ADVFN to offer *Naked Trader* readers access to the lists for £50 for the first year, saving £25. If you want to take up the offer, just email me at **robbiethetrader@aol.com** with 'Cheap Bronze' in the subject line and I will email you back with the details. Bronze also gives you access to the premium bulletin board on ADVFN, where serious investors discuss shares. Oh, and if you want bronze plus real-time prices, ADVFN offers a £30ish discount on that too. Email me with 'Cheap Silver' in the subject line.

The lists I particularly like are:

Percentage gainers and losers (free)

In other words: the biggest movers of the day. These lists give an excellent snapshot of what is moving.

To find out why a share is soaring up or plunging down, there may be a '1' or '2' by the share in the list's news column that you can click on to get a reasonable idea. It means there are one or two related news stories.

I'm interested in shares going both down and up, because the ones going down this year could be the recovery plays of next year. And the ones going up could have a lot further to climb.

Breakouts (premium)

Looking at breakouts is probably my favourite share-finding method. This lists the shares breaking out of previously established price ranges. A breakout is often significant.

ADVFN allows you to search for 52-week, 12-week and 4-week breakouts. My preference is for 52-week breakouts. A 52-week upward breakout often means a share is about to rise steadily higher.

Why is looking at breakouts potentially so rewarding?

Because you are finding share prices breaking out of previously established ranges, and this often points out something interesting happening with a share. Probably more people are buying in. Volumes will be up, something good may be going on and there are fewer sellers around.

When you click on the breakout list you will often find 20–30 shares on there to have a look at. I do my usual initial screening process at this stage.

I tend to favour shares that have a market cap of between £50m and £900m because they have a lot more room for growth than, say, a FTSE 100 share. These can be found on the FTSE 250 and FTSE Small Cap indices.

Most of the ones you will find on the ADVFN Premium TopLists will be similar. The computer is just telling you a share has gone up through an old resistance area. In other words we are actually doing a little bit of technical analysis via Toplists! (The strange old world of TA is covered in Chapter 23. You need to worry about it a lot less than you think.)

Once you've found a share that's broken out, of course, the real work begins: it is then time to do the research to check it's dependable.

Sometimes you will get what is termed a *false breakout*: the share breaks away for a short time and then goes back to where it was. So sometimes it is worth missing a point or two by not jumping in immediately, and checking it really is breaking out.

Tons of examples of profitable shares I found using a whole variety of methods are coming up a bit later in the book, in the bumper chapter on 20 trading strategies … but no skipping ahead just yet. I'm watching! How many shares you look at depends on the time you have. Just take the first ten maybe.

So those are just a few ideas on where to find interesting shares and how I go about doing it myself. You may find other ways and that's cool. There are lots of other publications out there. In the end it doesn't matter much and I guess there is a little bit of luck involved – all these are just nice ways of finding potential goodies.

How to Choose Good Shares

It's all about the research

So that's how you find interesting shares in the first place. Now we need to know how to tell whether any of these interesting shares are really worth buying. This is where research comes in.

Please don't rely on anyone else to select your shares for you. By all means investigate shares that others have brought to your attention. But don't be a lazy so-and-so and just expect a writer or journalist or tipster to have got it right. Take a good look for yourself.

My research involves finding out everything I can about a company before I consider buying in. And so should yours. The lazier you are about research, the less money you'll make. And really, it's not even that difficult.

I want *the whole story* about a share. *I want it* and *I want it now!* (Sorry – the last bit is a coded message to the Mrs.)

I look at everything I can, and much of the research involves trying to pick out the negative things (remember we looked at confirmation bias earlier in the book, whattya mean you skipped that cos it looked boring!). I guess I'm trying to put myself off! I use every scrap of info I have to come to a decision – and so should you.

> Good research means if you reach a decision to buy a share you are really sure it is worth buying.

A reader writes: Skipping research, losing money ...

"I bought £15k of African Eagle at 10p, and it's currently trading at 4.75p! Never ever buy a share on impulse because someone tells you it's going to rocket. Proper research beforehand is so important!"

What's the story?

What I do is build up the 'story' of a share.

Do I want to buy the story?

I want to share with you some of the questions that I try and answer in my research. And I don't buy a share until I have found the answers. What I'm trying to do is build a clear picture in my head about what a share is all about. Where's it been, what is it doing and does it hang around outside the fish-and-chip shop causing trouble?

First, let me highlight one major point:

> I am looking for a share that has everything going for it, with no question marks.

If I find myself frowning a lot when I'm doing my research this is not a good sign.

I am also trying to keep things simple. Perhaps what I'm trying to say is: you need to cut through the bullshit. I'm looking for good things and trying to avoid shares with the bad – or with question marks.

Keep it simple

Let me give you an example.

You've probably seen two TV shows that feature no-nonsense bosses: Lord/Baron/Sir/Darth Sugar ("You're fired!"), and millionaire (so he says) chef Gordon 'F*** I need more botox' Ramsay.

You haven't? Oh right, I forgot, you spend your time watching *EastEnders*, *Emmerdale* and *Neighbours*. Don't try to deny it – I've got your number!

Well, that Baron Alan is as sympathetic towards BS as he is tall: not very. Now imagine what he'd want to know if he was thinking about buying a share in a company. He'd cut through the crap like a lightsaber through ice cream, which is exactly what I try to do. I can imagine him collaring the chairman and barking:

> *"Don't give me no bloody crap about Fibonacci Bollinger hatstands, resistance stars, bleedin' double negatives and roving averages.*
>
> *"What I wanna know is: how much is your bleeding company worth, how much are the bloody profits, and how much do you owe? Don't give me nothing else, I don't need it."*

And if he got the reply:

> *"But Lord Sugar, the company has EBITDA of £5.3 million, our reorganisation is going well and we've hired some consultants … "*

The mighty Sugar would say:

> *"Right! I've bloody had enough. You talk and talk but don't give me no real answers – it's all complete rubbish, I can't make head or tails of it. You. Are. Fired!"*

This is exactly what is needed. And in this spirit, I always try to be a bit Sugarish when I'm looking at potential share purchases. I don't quite go to the length of making all my potential shares live in a house and perform weekly tasks in order to winnow them out. But I do keep it bloody simple.

Similarly, on one of his numerous shows, chef Gordon Ramsay goes into failing restaurants and tries to rescue them whilst swearing loudly. He generally finds out that everything they do is too complicated and that's why they're losing money. Their sauces are too over-thought, their menus don't make any sense unless you've got a PhD, they spend money on the wrong things. It's exactly the same with share traders who try and over-analyse situations. Simplicity is best.

I know just what he'd say if he visited a share trader losing money:

"F*** me!"

Yeah, I know he says that about everything. (From now on I'll just put (f) when he talks to represent his favourite word.)

> *"Look at all those (f) screens on your desk. What have you got all those (f) chart packages for? (f) me you've got hundreds of stock analyser tools – no wonder you're losing (f) money, you haven't even got (f) time to buy a (f) share."*

And I really believe both these successful people would approach share trading in the same way I have.

Lord S would be right. You just need to ask a few direct questions about a company to know if it is worth investing in or not. And Ramsay would be on the money too: you don't need to get bogged down in too much detail. You should find all the answers on ADVFN or an equivalent service.

There are so many traders out there with so many systems. Yet my simple methods have always worked and made me lots of money.

The questions

Okay, best thing for me to do here is take you through some of the simple steps I use to build up my research.

As Lord Sugar might say, the first two things I want to know are:

> *"What's your bloody company worth and what are your profits?"*

But here is the full list of questions I want to know the answers to when looking at a share.

These are the kind of questions you should be finding out the answers to as well. Write them down if you want and use them whenever you look at a share.

Questions to ask about a company

- What is it worth? (Market cap)

- What are its full-year pre-tax profits?

- Are profits rising?

- Are dividends rising?

- Is the outlook positive?

- Are there any negative things happening?

- What is the net debt?

- What kind of dividend does it pay?

- What does it do and what sector is it in?

- Are its markets likely to improve or get worse?

- When's the next statement due?

- Is the share price on the way up?

All the answers to these questions can be found online. I use the following places to get them:

1. The quote on the share to get the market cap.

2. Then the last full or half-year results to check the company's figures for myself.

I don't use ADVFN's 'Financials' tab or any financial website to check things like profit and debt because they can be wrong or out of date. The most recent officially published results are the place for that. So I click 'News' on ADVFN for the share and scroll down till I come to the last full or half-year results. This also means my highlighter system will work (coming later in this chapter!).

I want the answers to all these questions and only when I'm satisfied with all my answers will I be tempted to buy – then it's down to timing, which I'll discuss later (if I get my timing right).

Now, let's look at how to interpret any answers we get.

The answers

Perhaps a hazy mist is coming over you now and you're thinking:

> *'Yeah, yeah, research – all a bit boring, isn't it? Sod that, I know Robbie's right but I can't be bothered and I'll take a chance and trust to luck.'*

Well, not if you want to make good money and avoid losing it. It doesn't even take much time!

1. Market cap

Okay, market cap first. Remember, this is what the market thinks the company is worth. It's not a special hat that traders have to wear.

The cap stands for *capitalisation*, and it is worked out by multiplying the current share price by the number of shares a company has.

A quick guide:

- **Up to £80m:** is considered very small (FTSE Fledgling)

- **£80m to £650m:** small to medium (FTSE SmallCap)

- **£650m to £4bn:** the company is probably in the FTSE 250

- **Above £4bn:** the company is probably in the FTSE 100.

As we saw earlier, the market cap info can be found on the far right of the ADVFN quote page.

I personally prefer to look for companies in the £50m to £950m size range – they often have better growth prospects than, say, FTSE 100 stocks. But I do buy FTSE stocks sometimes too.

2. Company report

The next thing I want to do is find out the health of the company. So, as we looked at earlier, having brought up a company on ADVFN, click on the 'News' tab and then scroll down till you see 'Full year, preliminary or interim results'.

Two things in particular I'm after: finding out the negatives and looking for the positives.

Reading company reports

Every few months, companies have to put out a financial report. These sometimes come in the form of a full report, which includes in-depth figures. Sometimes it's a trading statement, which gives an indication of how things are going.

The statements are usually quite long and complicated. And it doesn't seem to matter how badly the company concerned is doing, there will almost always be some kind of positive spin – so knowing what it actually means is never completely straightforward.

If you're like me, you won't want to trawl through a company report: they're pretty boring. Fortunately, there are one or two key things to watch out for when reading a report that mean you don't have to sit there carefully weighing every sentence only to find out, four hours later, that the company's a duffer and you wasted your time.

I came up with a system which works through a company report in a few seconds and lets me know in a matter of moments whether it's worth getting into or not.

So, without further ado, let me present …

The Naked Trader traffic lights system!

I call it my 'traffic lights' system: red for sell, amber for hold and green for buy.

It enables me to quickly tell from a results report or an AGM (annual general meeting) statement what the state of play is. I can tell in just a few seconds whether to carry on looking at a company or to forget it immediately. Once you have set this little system up you will wonder how you ever did without it.

How does it work?

It uses a neat tool available at ADVFN. The tool can be set up by clicking on the 'News' tab in the top menu bar, and then clicking 'Highlight Phrases' on the next page:

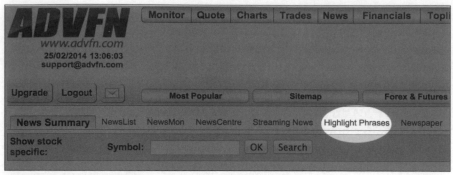

Highlight phrases on ADVFN – click 'News' to get this page

This allows you to arrange for up to 20 words or phrases to be highlighted in the colours of your choice in any news text that you read on ADVFN:

	Highlighted News Phrases	
1	challenging	Red ◆
2	difficult	Red ◆
3		Red ◆

Entering the phrases to be highlighted

With the right words and colours, you'll be able to instantly pick out the negatives and positives about any company in any report or news item.

Here's what I do – and what you should do as well:

- Put 'challenging' into the first box in **red**.

- Then 'difficult' into the second box in **red**.

And continue inputting all the other words and phrases from the following table, selecting the colour indicated as you do so:

Colour	Word/phrase
Red	challenging, difficult, down by, unpredictable, lower, poor, difficult trading, tough, below expectations, deficit
Yellow	in line with expectations, cash
Green	exceeding expectations, positive, favourable, profit up, excellent, transformational
Blue	debt, covenants, borrowings

Finally, click 'OK' at the bottom to store all the phrases.

Now look on ADVFN news at the latest company report of any share you're interested in or hold in your portfolio. Where any of those key words or phrases occur, they will be highlighted in their respective colours. The same will happen in any news item you look at. You won't see the highlighting until you click through to the articles themselves, nor anywhere else on ADVFN, but then you don't really need to.

> Problems getting the traffic lights system to work? It's usually down to your browser. I don't think it works well on Firefox, for example. But it works fine for me on Google Chrome and Internet Explorer. One other reason it might not be working is if you are trying it on a downloaded news report. It only works on news stories you read online. (Make sure you've logged in to ADVFN as well!)

Now what this tells you about companies is really rather simple:

Any company report that you see with lots of **red** is a probable sell or, at least, not a buy.

Any with lots of **yellow** is a hold.

Any with lots of **green** is a potential buy.

Obviously, the more greens the more positive, the more reds the more negative!

You may scoff at what might seem an over-simplistic technique. And, of course, my system is only the basis to start some more in-depth research.

But I don't think you can beat it for a quick judgement!

I'm not saying for a minute that you should buy every company that has loads of greens or sell every one that's covered in red, but it should give you an instant 'flavour' of the report. As you get used to the system and trading in general, you could add your own words or phrases that bring out things you're really looking for.

What about the blue highlighted words?

Well, that's all to do with working out whether a company's got too much debt or could even go bust. More on that shortly. 'Cash' is in yellow, as if it hasn't got debt it might have net cash.

So after discarding any shares with too many red negative words, the next thing is to weed out some more. This is the second stage of my quick but stern filtering process.

And the number one tool to discard a share at this point?

Net debt!

Net debt! This is what I'm now looking for. And the traffic lights system makes it dead easy to find.

Companies don't exactly like to boast about their debt, so you will often find it hidden away in their reports. But 'debt' should now be a bright blue colour throughout reports you read, and pretty simple to find.

Remember, I am not an accountant but I reckon net debt gives you a pretty good idea of the finances. Net debt is basically a company's debt minus its cash. In other words, it's probably the most accurate possible figure you can put on a company's total debts.

I believe if I rule out companies with a big net debt I can avoid a company going bust on me. So far it's worked.

Quite early on as a trader I looked at various companies that had gone bust in the past and discovered something rather interesting. Their net debt was in each case more than five times the size of their full-year profits. So I give myself a massive safety margin: **my rule of thumb is not to buy anything with net debt more than three times the full-year pre-tax profit, or what the likely pre-tax profit might be next year.**

So, at this point in the weeding out I simply go to the profit figure and then to the net debt. And if, for example, profits are £50m, I just times this by three – and won't buy if net debt is over £150m. Simple!

The only exceptions to this rule of mine are oil, mining and property companies. Oil companies often have big debts but they are rated on their oil finds. Property companies get rated more on their net asset values (the value of all their assets minus any liabilities) – i.e. houses. A different game.

> If you cannot find net debt using the blue highlighter on 'debt', keep an eye out for 'borrowings', which should also show up in blue. Also, try finding net cash (cash should come up in yellow). A good sign: it means they have cash. And that's great! If you can't find either, pick another share!

The final test of the first stage

Having made my potential shares run like Indiana Jones through a sequence of hellish trials and poison-dart fire, there remains one final set of hurdles for them to pass at this first stage. I pull the trap-door on them and say goodbye without further investigation if:

- they are a very small company, e.g. under a market cap of £20m, or have an EMS below £2,000 (too illiquid and dangerous)
- they are losing money or haven't made any yet ('jam tomorrow')
- they have a big spread (more than 5%)
- they are a small oil or energy stock (these rarely come good).

This eliminates the high-risk stocks that are left. There's nothing wrong *per se* in having the odd high-risk stock for small stakes once you're experienced. But if you're newish it's best to stay safe.

3. Dividend check

Now we're going into greater depth. The next step is to check dividend payouts.

- **Rising dividends** put a big tick in my book.
- If I see a **falling, or cut dividend**, I would probably end my research there – it's not a good sign.

If a company always increases its dividend year after year, that's a very good sign!

4. Chart check

Next is a look at the chart for the last year – that's at the bottom of the 'Quote' page on ADVFN.

Is the line higher once it reaches the right-hand side, or lower than when it started? The former is a good sign – the share is in an uptrend. If it's lower, I'd have to look into it further, but it puts it in dodgier territory.

I'd also take a look at the three-year performance chart. I'll come back to charts a bit later, but for now I want to see a share in a good-looking uptrend.

5. Company background check

The next step is to find out more about what the company does, and to look back through the last couple of years' news stories connected with it.

I like to see reports of rising profits and turnover, and a gradually improving share price. I look to see when it reports next. Is it next week or in three months? If it's next week, could there be a nasty shock on the way or will those already in the stock be ready to take profits?

To check when it might report next, scroll down and see when it reported last year; report dates are usually about the same. Also, companies tend to put out a 'notice of results' with the date a couple of weeks beforehand.

Any big share movements reported? Any institutional buys? I check all this out. ADVFN makes it rather easy, as you can click through all the news stories going back over a long time.

What I'm doing is trying to build up a picture of the company concerned, and this is what you should be doing. Keep clicking, keep reading.

Just because you see one thing you like about a company, don't buy it on an impulse.

> Don't ignore things you don't like the look of because you suddenly fancy buying a share anyway. Stay objective and keep searching.

A reader writes: Always hoover up research ...

"I'd been reading over the years about how successful Dyson had become. One day I was looking for new opportunities and saw Dyson mentioned again in an article. Without doing any further research – after all, I felt I already knew the company well enough now – I went off and bought a load of shares at 18p. They'd come down a bit so it felt like a good buying opportunity.

"A few weeks later I saw they were suspended. I never bothered to look into the reason why; I just assumed it was a restructuring or perhaps even a takeover.

"After about six months, and fed up now with seeing how well James Dyson was doing, I picked up the phone to speak to him to find out when the shares would come back. I can still hear the laughter as I learnt that Dyson was never quoted [i.e. made publicly available to trade on a stock exchange], and I'd bought a company that had nothing at all to do with hoovers. It was a small engineering company called Dyson Group, based in Sheffield.

"And I'm a very experienced trader, who's been at this for years!"

---

6. Directors' dealings

Many investors believe it's worth keeping an eye on directors buying and selling shares in their own companies.

The reason is: if a director is buying a lot of shares, it's assumed he or she has some confidence in the future of the company – and that no one should know a company better than its directors.

Conversely, if a director is dumping shares, perhaps the confidence is simply not there and one has to be careful.

Generally, directors are allowed to buy and sell shares in their own companies, but they are not allowed to trade in shares of their company in the six weeks preceding a results announcement (this is known as the *closed period*). So you will often find directors buying or selling shares on the day of results or one or two days afterwards.

Many investors believe that by following buys or sales by directors they can make money – i.e. by buying into companies when directors are buying and selling (or shorting) when directors are selling.

Interpreting directors' dealings

Of course, just because a director buys, it does not necessarily mean the shares are going to rise. You have to examine the buys and sells in tandem with doing proper research into the companies. In my opinion, following directors' dealings slavishly will *not* lead you to stock market millions.

Why do directors buy their shares?

Sometimes they buy because they think their company is doing well. Sometimes it's simply to give a vote of confidence and encourage investors to back the company (heads of credit-crunched banks did this in 2007–8 but the free-fall continued). And often it's simply because they have to do *something* with their spare cash.

Why do they sell?

It could be because they feel the company's future for the moment is not all that bright. But it could simply be because they need the money to pay school fees or buy a house.

The problem, as you can see, is that without the wider context of additional research, directors' dealings can easily be over-interpreted. And directors know that any purchase they make of their company's shares will be publicly announced, and that this could cause investors to buy in. So things are actually a bit foggy!

But it'd be just as damaging to ignore them altogether as to follow them blindly. There's a simple way of getting the most out of them.

> In my experience, the key to working out whether a director buy or sell is worth following or not is the *amount* of shares being bought or sold.

If they are buying a huge amount then I am more interested. But much more so if they are buying *a lot* of shares in relation to their current holding. The key measurement is always: how many shares they are buying/selling compared with how many they own.

For example, if a CEO of a company sells one million shares, does that mean it is time to follow suit?

Not necessarily, if the director still owns 15 million shares. He might just have needed the money to buy a better house! But if he's sold half his stake, I might get a bit worried.

It's the same with buys. **The proportion of shares bought compared to the amount owned is what you should look at carefully.**

It can sometimes be a good sign if a director buys, say, £20,000 worth of shares if they only currently hold a small amount. Not all directors are wealthy, and £20,000 might be quite a big investment for a director of a smaller company.

Summary – directors' dealings

To sum up, watching directors' dealings is something every investor should do. And sometimes seeing a deal can lead you to examine a new company that you haven't come across before.

But you should never slavishly follow a deal. There is no substitute for doing your own research into a company – and just using a director's deal as good bonus information.

Directors' dealings can be found for free on ADVFN – click the 'Toplists' tab and find 'Directors' Shareholding' in the 'Free TopLists' table.

7. Check the company website

I always check the website of any company that I'm thinking about buying.

This might seem obvious, but I bet most investors don't bother. A company's website can tell you an awful lot. It should also help you to confirm that you know exactly what the company does to make its money! By the time I've finished reading a site, I try to make sure I can say what the company does in a sentence.

And if the website is crap, one has to wonder if the company is able to compete in the 21st century.

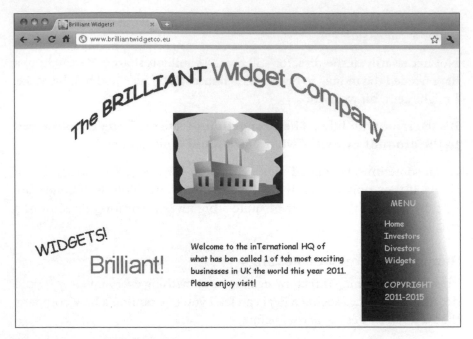

Watch out for woeful websites

If the company uses the website to offer goods to the public, how good is the presentation? Would *you* consider buying goods from its website and, if not, why not? If the site doesn't tempt you to purchase anything, it could have the same effect on others.

Google, of course, will find you a company's site in no time. It's also worth putting in the company name and the word 'reviews' or 'feedback' or 'complaints' and Googling that too.

Are customers getting their goods on time or are they slagging the company off?

All bloody good research!

If the company doesn't use its website to sell, you can still directly test its service levels in one crucial area – how does it treat its shareholders? Does it have a good news service and does it contain up-to-date news about the company? It ought to at least provide a copy of its latest financial report, which you should be able to download. You should be able to send an email to the company as a shareholder, too.

Simple test: send an email stating you are a shareholder and you want to know the date of the next AGM.

See how long it takes them to reply. The quicker the better. If they don't reply, what does that say about how they regard their shareholders?

8. P/E ratios

You'll hear a lot about P/E ratios and you may be surprised to learn that I don't take an awful lot of notice of them. Also, I just know the moment I mention them you'll close the book and go off and do something else. Have you gone? For those of you left:

What on earth is a P/E ratio and why do people go on about them?

It means price-earnings ratio and it is calculated as the share price divided by the earnings per share.

But forget about the formula, it's what it really means that's important. The P/E ratio represents the number of years it will take for the earnings of the company to cover the share price.

Interpreting P/E ratios

1. *Company A* has a share price of 10p, and earnings per share of 2p. The P/E ratio will therefore be 5 (10 ÷ 2). So, with earnings of 2p, it would take five years for those earnings to cumulatively match the share price.

2. *Company B* has a share price of 90p, and earnings per share of 3p. The P/E ratio will therefore be 30 (90 ÷ 3). It would take 30 years, with earnings of 3p, to cover the share price of 90p.

One can safely say that the investors in Company B are more optimistic than those in Company A. Company B investors are willing to pay 90p for the shares and wait 30 years (on current earnings) for the share price to be covered by the cumulative earnings. If they weren't confident, the investors would sell their shares, the share price would fall, and the P/E ratio would therefore also fall.

> I say that investors are willing to wait 30 years *on current earnings*. But the point is that the investors believe that the company's earnings will actually increase quickly and that they won't have to wait for so long.

By contrast, Company A investors are not so confident. They're only willing to give the benefit of the doubt for earnings to cover the share price in five years' time. They presumably don't think earnings will be going up any time soon.

> In general, high-growth companies (e.g. tech stocks) tend to have high P/E ratios, whereas low-growth companies (e.g. utility companies) have low P/E ratios.

If a company has a high P/E ratio, then investors have bid the share price up because they are bullish on the company and expect it to perform well.

You might therefore think that it's better to invest in a company with a high P/E ratio – it could do really well.

Sadly, it's not that simple.

The market could be overvaluing the high P/E company and it could come down to earth with a bump.

Personally, I quite like lower P/E ratios (provided all the other signs on a share are good). That's because the market isn't expecting much, so if the company can beat expectations, the share price could soar. I like my P/Es to be in the region of 12–20.

A comparative measure

The main use of P/E ratios, though, is not as an absolute measure. If a company has a P/E ratio of say 20, that isn't very meaningful in isolation. The power of P/E ratios is when you use them to compare one company's share price with another.

For example, if Company A has a share price of 400p, and Company B has a share price of 14p, nothing can be said about their relative values (as firms do not have the same number of shares as each other). Is Company B better value than Company A? We don't know. However, if we know that Company A has a P/E of 12, and Company B a P/E of 32, we *can* say that the market values Company B more highly than it does Company A.

P/Es are most useful when comparing companies within the same sector, as different sectors tend to have different P/Es. As I mentioned above, tech stocks tend to have high P/Es while utility stocks have low P/Es. Because of this, it is not very useful to compare the P/E of, say, electronics firm ARM Holdings (13,203) with that of mining company BHP Billiton (705).

If a retailing company has a P/E of 15, while the average P/E ratio of all companies in the retail sector is 20, one could say that the company is undervalued relative to the sector.

There may be a very good reason for this. But if there isn't, then the company may merit further attention as a buy.

My view

Personally, I find P/Es too abstract and only give them a passing glance.

A problem with P/Es is that publications differ on the P/E. So the *FT* might quote a different one to ADVFN. This is because some use historical earnings, some use forward earnings … blah, blah, blah. Quite honestly, the whole thing washes over me – which doesn't seem to matter, as I still make money!

Picking undervalued shares – my secret

How do you value a share?

If every share had a definite value there would be no point in trading, as every share would be around the right price. So we are looking for shares where we think the value should be higher.

This is an art, not a science.

I get emails from blokes desperate to spreadsheet it all and try and work out exact valuations. They do not exist. In the end you have to make a call. Is the company worth its valuation or is it worth more?

All the best things in life are simple, and I think the system I use to pick out undervalued shares is simplicity itself.

Here's what I do.

I am a billionaire

I use this system after researching any company that looks of interest. I pretend that I am a multi-billionaire and can buy up any company or as many companies as I want to.

But of course, as I'm a billionaire, not only do I want to acquire them on the cheap to get good value for my hard-earned cash – I also want that cash to give me a return. And the only way to do that is to buy companies that are *making profits*, enough profits to ultimately pay me back what I paid to buy them, and to make plenty of money on top of this. Why else would I be interested?

If a company satisfies these billionaire criteria, I decide that I should buy shares in them because, if I'm right, sooner or later someone big *will* buy the company or the share price will go up anyway.

So, how can I work out whether to splash out a small part of my billions on snapping up a company?

The first thing to look at is the profit the company makes; the second is the market capitalisation. In my billionaire role, the figure for how much the company might cost me to buy is the market capitalisation. So if a company's market cap is £50 million, that's how much the market currently thinks the company is worth altogether.

ADVFN provides the market cap and the profit on its 'Quote' page on the same line, so they are easy to find.

As a billionaire, I don't really care about complicated financial ratios and all that twaddle. What I want to know is: how much do you want for your company and what are the profits? In other words, how soon will I get my money back and make some more on top of that? There's no other reason for me to spend the capital amassed in my glistening dungeon of gold coins.

Putting it simply: if a company is making profits of £10 million, and its market cap is £100 million, that would interest me.

But if a company makes a £10 million profit and is capitalised at £200 million, then I'm not so interested – unless it has some kind of stupendous product that is about to dramatically raise profits. But maybe I don't want to spend £200 million to get profits of £10 million, whatever the prospects.

In other words, my rule of thumb is a maximum ratio of around 15-times market cap to profits. (Or guessing next year's profits.)

Let's go back to the company making £10 million. The most I want to see the market cap at is around £150 million. That's 15 times. Any more than that and it starts to look expensive – so why would I buy the shares?

15-times market cap is my personal rule of thumb – something I've arrived at after years of experience in the market. It's not an industry-wide standard, just my own threshold. This metric can't be used with oil or mining companies or property companies; they are a different ball game, as mentioned earlier.

Summary – selecting shares

This is a good point at which to sum up what will make me put a share on a to-buy shortlist:

- There is still growth to come.

- Dividends, profits and turnover are rising.

- There are tons of positives.

- There are no question marks.

- It is liquid.

- I understand what the company does.

- It is priced at under 15× profits to market cap (exc. property, oil, energy).

- It looks cheap.

- It is in a good market.

- Demand for its products is likely to grow.

- The chart looks positive and is in an upward trend.

- Debt is under three-times its full-year profits.

Once all my boxes are ticked, the share goes on my shortlist and then it's down to timing. And we'll come onto that shortly.

As you can see, it takes quite a bit to get a share onto the shortlist. And quite right too!

How to Plan, Manage and Close Trades (Without Going Mad)

Fail to plan, plan to ... (you know what)

Okay, so hopefully now you have some idea of where to find shares, some ideas of whether they look cheap or not.

But once you have found a share, you really like it, you've looked at the whole story and you really want to buy it ... what do you need?

A PLAN!

You really do. It's not enough just to press the trade button and buy it and hope. You need to have some idea of why you bought it, why you think it is going to go up – and then what happens. What is your timescale? Are you after a quick profit? Longer-term? How much money are you after?

And more importantly, what are you going to do if the trade goes wrong? How much are you prepared to lose?

You need a stop-loss. Maybe you even need to think about getting out quick if it starts to go down before it hits your stop – because stops aren't guaranteed, and in a crisis can be worthless. But you don't want to panic.

A plan taking all these issues into account is the answer. It needs to be jotted down and kept somewhere safe before you buy, and referred to whenever you're thinking about your next steps with a share.

Questions to ask before you press 'buy'

Putting a plan together is actually quite simple. Most people who don't bother with it are just avoiding it because they know deep down their trade is nothing more than a gamble.

The best way to put together a good trade plan is just to ask the following questions before you buy any share. Don't worry! You can keep answers brief:

• What does this company do?

• Why will the share price go higher?

• How high will I let it go before I sell all or some of my stake?

• Am I buying something that has gone down a lot? If so, why will it recover when it hasn't so far?

• How low am I prepared to see the price fall before I leave? (What will my stop-loss be?)

• Could this share be a lot lower in six months' time? What's the worst-case scenario? The major weakness? Am I really comfortable with it?

• Have I checked the net debt?

• Have I bought this because someone tipped it on a bulletin board? If so, what were the reasons for trusting the tip?

• Did I research this properly? Really?

• Am I buying because I am bored and just want to make a trade?

• Who let the dogs out? Who? Who? Who? Who?

Stop losses

A key part of any trade plan is the stop loss, just as no office building is complete without an emergency exit. We'll discuss price targets and selling in a mo, but protecting your money in the markets is so important – without it, you'll look pretty silly trying to be a trader – that I've put stop losses first.

First, what the heck is a stop loss? (It is also known as a stop order.)

Stop losses are a point at which you agree in advance with yourself or a broker or your spread bet firm or your therapist to take a loss on a share before it goes down any further.

You set them up in advance, when you make your trade, so that your account automatically sells out of a share when things get ugly and a certain price is hit (rather than being reliant on your own monitoring and changeable inclinations).

However, do bear in mind that most brokers won't allow you to place a stop on very small shares – usually anything say outside the FTSE 100 and 250. A spread bet firm might.

Stops are about preserving your capital and ensuring you don't lose more money on a share than you need to. Often shares are going down for a reason and once they start going down they can really tank.

As I said earlier in the book, one of the main reasons that people lose money in shares is their inability to sell anything at a loss. The other is selling when things go down by one or two pence. So this is where your stop loss comes in. It helps ditherers be ruthless and panickers be patient.

Let's have a look at how I used stops in this trade plan.

My trade plan for KBC (December 2013)

I bought 5,000 shares in KBC Advanced Technologies, a provider of consulting and software services to energy and other industries, in December 2013 at 100p, costing me £5,000. The share was listed on the FTSE AIM All-Share index.

KBC ticked all my boxes: from market cap to forecast profit, with everything going up, good prospects, a rising chart ... I understood it and I liked it.

But now, the plan.

I used exactly those questions I've just listed. I initially thought I wanted around 30% from it, so I pencilled in selling at around 130p, or selling at least *some* shares at that point.

Now what about if the trade failed? I like a long-term stop of 10% below the buy price, as it it gives a share space to have a few hiccups but prove itself in the long run, as well as meaning I get out fairly unscathed if it's a disaster. In this case that meant a stop of 90p. (I do also consider 5% stops, particularly early on in trades, so could have gone for that here – I'll dig into how you judge all this in the next section.)

What happened? The share didn't go down, so the stop wasn't hit. Happily, it went up to 130p after a few weeks, so I sold half my holding at 127 (I missed the 130), banking a profit of £675. I decided to hold onto the rest.

Holding onto the rest required a simple update to the plan – to raise the stop to 110, so I would still lock in some profit if it went down.

So, some profit taken and banked as per the plan, and now a new plan with a raised stop. That is the kind of plan you need to make! Simple? I know. I said it would be. So there's no reason not to create one for every trade!

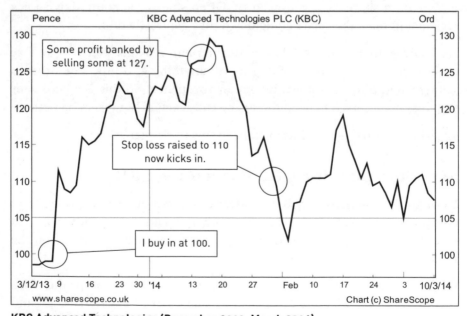

KBC Advanced Technologies (December 2013–March 2014)

Judging stop losses

The big question is: where do you set a stop? When should you be quitting a share?

Good question.

With the KBC example above I went for a default 10%. This is my standard position if I can't spot anything on the chart that shows a share has tended to drop to a certain price before and bounce back. (In trading jargon this is called 'support' – it's a point below which the market has consistently proved reluctant to let a share drop.) If there is obvious support, I'll place my stop a little bit below it because I don't want to be closed out of the trade if the share is just going to bounce back down and up again like in the past

In the KBC example, with a 10% stop loss at 90p, my maximum possible loss was £500.

So I usually start with a default 10%. Then I look at the chart to see if there are any suggestions of past wild behaviour. I look at the volatility of the share: has it swung violently before? If so, the stop might need to be further away than 10%.

As mentioned, I sometimes go with a 5% stop at the beginning of a trade because a share has yet to prove itself and I want to cut losses quickly.

One thing you really need to be aware of with stops is the potential 8am stop-out. On some shares, the price will briefly jump down first thing in the morning when the spreads become momentarily enormous because no one is trading. And that can simply knock out your stop loss.

So at 10% on some shares you can find yourself taking a needless loss, with the share almost immediately swinging back up again afterwards. We live in volatile times.

I therefore now start at 10% (away from the current price) and then tweak stops further away from there, depending on where punters have bought and sold in the past, and adding a little breathing room if it's a volatile FTSE 100er or mining share.

Let's have another couple of quick examples showing this in action:

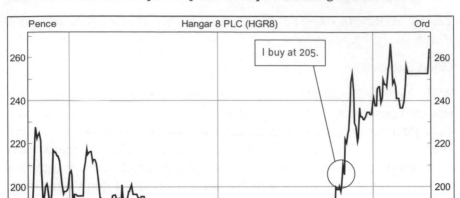

Hangar 8 (November 2012–March 2014)

I bought shares in Hangar 8 (another AIM share) at 205p in late November 2013.

So, where did I set the stop?

My initial thoughts, as ever, were 10%. And 10% away would be roughly 185.

I took another look at the chart. Where had the share been supported before?

If you look at the chart you'll see it plateaued at just under 200 for a while. So if I wanted to I could make the stop around there, about 198. That's closer to the buy price, but maybe if it does go down from this point it's going to drop a fair way since it'll be falling through support.

Hmm, what to do?

I decide: a fallback stop at 185 it is. But I'll watch this one closely. If things drop below 200 and keep dropping, I'll probably get out quick (GOQ). I don't like the idea of it crashing through support. If I'm out at the cinema or something when this happens, I still have the fallback of 185.

Another example. In early January 2014 I bought Iomart (AIM again) at 265p. Ten per cent off that is 239p. But let's look at where the share found support on the chart before. We can easily see it went to 230p before and jumped up. After that, 240 proved a support level too. We can also see that it 'likes' the 260 area.

Iomart (January 2012–January 2014)

So I went for a stop at around 240p (10% plus support) but also had a GOQ note at 257p, just below the 260 level it likes, as common sense seems to state that if it goes much below 260 it might fall quickly to 240 again – and it's better to be out at 257 and buy back at 240, right?

Now what happens if a share starts to rise nicely after you bought it? Always remember, *it is time to raise your stop*. Which brings me nicely onto …

Trailing stop losses

Some investors use what they call *trailing stop losses*. That means as the share you've bought into rises, so does your stop loss *automatically*. Not all brokers offer this, but it's pretty cool.

Example: trailing stop loss

Say you bought a share at 200p and you set a trailing stop loss of 20p.

- If the share price **falls to 180p**, your holding is sold. (This is a normal stop loss.) But, there's more …

- If the share **rises to 260p**, your stop loss will track it upwards, and then be set (automatically) at 240p.

- If the share then **rises to 300p**, your stop loss is re-set at 280p.

Effectively, your broker will sell if the share goes 20p lower than its recent high.

In other words, **your trailing stop takes a profit for you, removing emotion out of any decision**. I think this is a marvellous idea, especially for newer investors or those who can't be at a screen all day watching prices.

You can set any trailing stop loss you like as a point difference or percentage.

In the end it's down to experience – and trial and error. But better to set some targets than having no plan at all.

In the Hangar 8 example, the share rose to 250. At this point, given it has been quite volatile in the past, I would think about a 30p trailing stop. So the new stop would be hit at 220, banking a profit. But if the price keeps on going up, I stay in.

Monitoring stop losses

You have got to decide whether to set your stop loss and simply monitor it yourself or set it with your broker or spread bet firm.

Fortunately most good stock brokers – and all spread betting firms – accept stop loss orders. In other words, they will monitor the stop loss themselves – you don't have to worry about it. BUT some brokers won't do trailing stops outside the FTSE 100 and 250. Most spread bet firms will.

A stop loss warning

So stop losses are pretty great, right? What's the catch? Is there one?

There are two. One is just one of those things, the other is pretty alarming in down markets.

Firstly, your stop loss might not get you out in some circumstances. Remember your broker still has to sell the shares in the market. If you have a large holding it might not be possible to sell all of the shares at your stop loss price, simply because there aren't enough buyers at that price. Or the price might be moving down so quickly that they can't be sold in time.

Some brokers allow you to set a 'range' where you want them sold. So, say your stop loss on a share is 100. You could set 95p for the bottom of the range. If the share tumbles fast, your broker can still sell them down to 95p.

It is always worth checking what the policy of your broker is. Give them a call and ask.

> One point worth noting is that you can often change your stops when the market is shut. Usually 24 hours a day with spread bets. So if a story breaks on your share, you may want to change it before the market opens.

Secondly, **stops won't save you from overnight falls.**

This is a really important point to make. If a share tanks overnight, obviously your stop loss won't work if the shares open way down. The share has passed your stop-loss price without ever having been tradable at that price. The only possible way to save yourself from an overnight tumble is by finding a spread firm that operates a guaranteed stop. More on that in the spread betting chapter.

> So if you buy a share at 200 and set a stop at 180, and there is a profit warning before the market opens and the share opens at 100p, your stop will not work!

Now what about target prices?

Profit targets

Before opening a trade you should decide on a price level which you would be happy to sell at – this is called a profit target. I believe profit targets should be at least 20% higher than your buy price.

After all, why buy a share unless you think you can get at least 20% out of it?

But I certainly do not automatically sell once a share gets to the target price. This is a point at which I look at the share again and decide whether it is still cheap. Is there further to go? If there is, I may well set a new target and stay with the shares or even buy more.

Because I am really looking for 50%-plus profits – some big winners – as I'll discuss in more detail in my chapter on building a portfolio.

I do the same thing as when I set my stops – look to around 20% (as opposed to 10% for losses), and then tweak it to where the share has peaked before.

The art of selling

So much for profit targets. I'm still often asked: *"How do I tell when to sell for a profit?"*

And that's fair enough. It's a slightly different question. Targets are only targets, after all, and the best ones are moving ones – we want to let profits run if we can.

We've just discussed how a stop you move up under the price as a share goes up can make your decision more Spock-like. But is there anything more to the art of selling than getting stopped out on a downward slide after following along with a share like this for months?

You betcha.

There are three things that might give me an indication of whether it's time to sell or not.

1. The brick wall

If a price keeps hitting a brick wall and does so three times or so. For example, if you were crazy enough to buy Carpetright in the below example it was pretty obvious where the profit should have been taken – see how it hits 700ish three times between July and October 2013. These are alarm signals!

Time to take profits. And indeed it sank soon after the third time it hit 700.

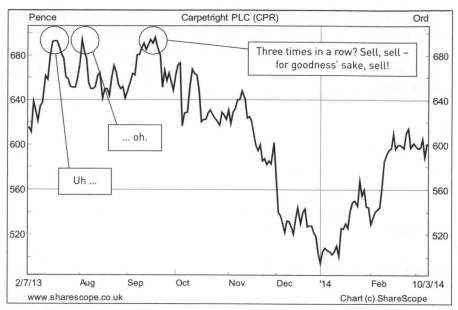

Carpetright (July 2013–March 2014)

2. The second interrogation

A way to see if you should sell after you've made a lot of profit on something is to ask yourself: *If you came across this share afresh would you buy it now?*

Stick it through the same interrogation process as the first time round. Run it through the traffic lights. Look at net debt. All that stuff.

If it fails your tests, don't hold onto it!

3. The topslice

If you are really unsure whether to sell after your share has gone up quite a bit, you'll like this one. It's called 'topslicing'.

Unfortunately, it has nothing to do with expert sandwich technique (though anything with bacon works for me). 'Topslicing' is just jargon for taking some of the profits by selling part of your stake. I do that a lot.

In fact, it is rare that I sell the whole lot in one go. If I make 30% on something, I might sell a quarter of it, or … topslice.

If it carries on up, you are still in it. If it starts to go down, well, you banked some of the profit and you can keep topslicing from there.

It's also pretty much a must if you build up a big stake in a lightly traded (illiquid) stock – stuff down the AIM or Fledgling end of the market. There's no point in waiting for that great day when your AIM shares in Tiny Speculative Company plc hit your price target, only to find that there's one buyer and he's only after £1,000-worth of shares …

For pros: Level 2

Lastly, because it's a bit of a minority sport – especially for beginners – you can also check the full supply and demand for shares using something whizzy and exciting called Level 2, and this can help in your selling decision. Don't worry about this for now. We'll cover Level 2 a little bit in Chapter 22.

Don't try to be a genius

Above all, when it comes to selling: please don't try to be a genius and only buy or sell at the perfect moment. Trying to call the top or bottom of a market is a mug's game and causes smaller profits and bigger losses from all the times people get it wrong.

What's sensible is waiting for a basic good market day before you sell (see the next chapter in a page or two!), or avoiding a day or week when everyone's suddenly got panicked over a news story that will be forgotten in a month. But none of us can always get out at the top and in at the bottom. Let's just go along for part of the ride and if we get one wrong put it down to experience.

The main thing with selling is: don't wait for it to be down 50% or more! You should never ever be in anything that's down by more than 20%.

All this stuff neatly brings me to something else to take into account when you are thinking of doing anything with your shares, and that is … the different times of the year. Seriously. It's so exciting I've given it its own little chapter.

Summary

- Before you buy a share, set yourself a stop loss (and maybe a get-out-quick price).

- Place them with your broker or spread bet firm or at least write them down!

- If you stick to a stop-loss system, your losses will generally be minimised.

> You'll see if you go to my website, **www.nakedtrader.co.uk**, that I have a list of my current positions. Every one has a stop loss and target. You need to ensure you have done this too.

Trading Times of the Year

I tend to treat shares a bit differently at different times of the year. Looked at historically, some months the market tends to be strong and some months it tends to be weak. So it's worth keeping an eye on the time of year and its likely effect on stocks.

Here's a look at the different months:

February–March

February and March tend to be middling months. After some good gains over Christmas some people take profits in February, so don't expect big advances here. I would look to have a bit of cash on the sidelines during these months.

April

It's amazing how holiday times and flowers budding put people in a good mood. Around Easter the market does really well and it's often a good time for short-term gains.

The market's typically stronger in April than any other month – on the basis of its performance in the last few decades, the probability of the market rising in April is 78%. So it may be worth thinking about buying in mid March to catch any April lift.

May–July

I'm sure you've heard the old saying:

'Sell in May and come back on St Leger's Day.'

(St Leger's day is in September.) There is a bit of truth in this, as May can be the start of some underperformance. In recent years it has been challenging September to become the weakest month of the year. 2006 saw a large fall in stocks, though 2007 wasn't too bad. Still, it's time to perhaps be wary, take some profits and keep cash in hand.

June is pretty much as weak as May – usually it's the third-weakest month. And July generally isn't that much better! So in summary, May–July ain't great. Maybe time for a holiday!

August

From the gloom of the previous few months there usually comes a great August. A lot of people are away, which for a start means there is always a lot less volume. So what happens is that shares can move much faster than normal on far fewer trades.

August is the third-best trading month of the year: good gains can often be achieved. But with the volatility you have to get the right price. I often find I can make a lot of money in August. However, beware: in part because of this volatility August 2011 proved a disaster and shares fell a lot.

One thing to look for is companies reporting in August. There aren't many, but if you find one that produces a strong statement, you often find the share price responds very well on the smaller volumes being traded. Also, it is worth looking at companies reporting in early September; August is a good time to get in early in the run up to the results.

September

Yuk! September has the worst record of any month – on average the market falls 1.4%. If you ever want to try shorting, this is the month to do it. And as things bottom out, maybe keep an eye out for bargains to squirrel away for the winter.

October–November

Well, it's not as bad as you think. A couple of famous nasty crashes have happened in October, particularly the one in 1987. Stripping out a couple of bad years, October is actually pretty decent and it's often a good time to buy. November is middling, but buying the right shares in October and November can be a good move in the lead up to the Christmas buying spree ...

December–January

December is one of the best months for share performance. January too.

Why?

Because most years, while it's cold outside, December and January markets are hot! The statistics support my argument: historically the strongest week of the year for the market is the 51st week. And the second strongest? The 52nd!

The probability of positive returns in December is a high 69%. The market's only had one significant fall in December since 1981. Both mid- and large-cap stocks perform equally well.

Why are the markets so good at the most wonderful time of the year?

I suspect it is down to something as simple as human psychology. We all feel good with the approach of Christmas, then there are New Year's hopes and dreams. But by the end of January we tend to be left with a bit of a hangover and that's why February isn't so good.

Also, as markets often fall somewhat in October and November, investors begin to come in now and buy what they perceive as bargains.

The period between Christmas and New Year often sees stocks squeezing higher on thin volumes. While I might well be tucking into mince pies, I'm usually also at my trading desk watching for opportunities to make money. Many stocks race higher during the holidays; there is frequently no one selling and institutions are shut. This often has a good effect on stocks at the smaller end of the market.

Of course, I am making it all sound too easy ... it's never going to work out every year. But the use of tight stop losses should ensure that when you meet a year without a Santa bump, your losses will be minimal.

Bad news

On the downside, one thing to watch out for is companies sneaking out bad news between Christmas and New Year. It's the same as political parties burying bad news on a day when a big story emerges elsewhere. With so many people away, the companies hope the stinker will go unnoticed. So it's worth keeping an eye on news that's related to your stocks. I get out quick if any kind of bad company news is released on one of my shares at this time.

Strategies

So where do I put my money to make the most of the benign conditions?

First (and I do this most years): I buy the FTSE 100 index in early/mid-December and I sell in early January to take advantage of the fact that the FTSE usually rises in this period.

I usually just make a simple 'long' FTSE 100 spread bet, with a stop loss in place just in case it's the one occasional year when the festive uplift doesn't happen. (I'll explain long – and short – spread bets later on.)

This worked nicely in 2013 when I bought just before Christmas at 6445 and the market had a lovely festive rally and in January went to near 6800 for a tremendous profit!

I find December is also a good time to have a look at some of the smaller, tiddler stocks in the market and sometimes have a bit of a gamble on a few stocking-filler shares. But only a little gamble, mind. Let's not be idiots.

Winning Strategies

It's time to reveal all my best strategies for making winning trades. This chapter details 20 of them – that's almost 10,000 words of winning strategies! I reckon this chapter is worth the price of the book alone and hope you'll agree.

These are all tried-and-tested strategies of mine for making money out of the stock market. Things I've picked up over the years. No one taught me these. I got them from the street, check it. Word! (Sorry.)

I also think most of them will work for a long time in the years to come. Perhaps even if you are buying this in 2030, and I'm in a home somewhere trying to find my teeth. Nurse, the screens!

It goes without saying that any shares I would trade using these strategies would also have to pass muster with the research outlined in the last few chapters. So don't think you can ignore the research or planning side of things (I saw you thinking about it!).

Okay, without further ado, let me unveil ... *Naked Trader's TOP 20 STRATEGIES!*

Oh, and I should point out that they are in no particular order of importance ...

STRATEGY 1: Buy shares just before they get into the FTSE 100

A great time to buy into a share is when it is getting close to a market cap of £4 billion. At just under this level (as I write) stocks can gain promotion from the FTSE 250 and entry into the FTSE 100.[3] Funds track the FTSE 100 and this usually gives a lift to the shares, as they will buy into it as soon as it hits the FTSE 100. Also, you may have found a good share anyway – it must have been doing something right to rise so nicely.

So I look for shares around the £3.7 to £4 billion mark that have been steadily going up. I do my usual research as well (*always do the research, please!*) but a steadily increasing share price heading towards £4bn market cap is a great sign.

Let me give you an example of a couple I am looking at now (early 2014).

I don't like insurance but Direct Line is right at the FTSE 100 entry level, with a market cap of £3.9bn. So it looks like it has a reasonable chance of entry into the FTSE 100 soon, and may be worth buying – the chart is nicely up too.

Direct Line (January 2013–March 2014)

---

3   The £4bn level can change as time goes by. If the market goes lower, the threshold could go lower.

Changes to the FTSE are made every three months. The changes are announced on the Wednesday before the first Friday in March, June, September and December.

You should be looking about a month before the changes.

One share I already own (Merlin Entertainments) is on a market cap of £3.8bn, so I am looking a bit ahead and think they could get entry in three or four months' time, which might tempt me to buy more.

It can be a good move to take profits a few days after a share gains promotion, as promoted shares can slide for a bit once funds have bought in.

You can get a list of FTSE 250 stocks at **www.londonstockexchange.com**. Look for the highest five or six market caps in the FTSE 250.

Summary

- Check for shares in an uptrend heading towards £4bn market cap.
- Look at high-ranked FTSE 250 shares on the London Stock Exchange site.
- Think about taking profits a few days after promotion.

STRATEGY 2: Get to love the phrase 'ahead of expectations'

I really love buying companies that put out a trading update stating that their current trading is 'ahead of expectations', or 'ahead of market expectations', or 'better than expected' – or that is generally extremely upbeat in a similar way. This is because you know pretty much for sure that the next results are going to be really good.

Time and time again I've seen share prices of companies issuing short but good updates in-between results go markedly higher for weeks after such a brief statement. Often they then go higher still as the good results come in, especially if good trading has continued.

I've made some lovely profits from buying into these. Here's one I bought in 2011 called Treatt. This is the paragraph from their trading update that I liked:

> "It is pleasing to announce that the **positive** news reported in the Interim Management Statement issued on 15 February 2011 has continued, and in some parts of the Group has accelerated.

Consequently, trading for the half year has significantly exceeded expectations and with order books remaining strong, full year results are now likely to be materially higher than previously anticipated."

Note that 'positive' was caught by our nifty traffic-light highlighter system and on ADVFN was a healthy green colour!

Well, okay, this statement didn't say 'ahead of expectations' – but "materially higher" is the same thing, if not even nicer.

I now knew that Treatt's 2011 results should have been, erm, well a treat.

I already had some of their shares when the statement came out, but on reading it I immediately bought more. The shares continued to motor nicely higher, as the lovely chart shows.

Of course, if I hadn't already done my research, I would definitely have looked into the share a bit more – especially its debt levels – before buying in, but having done that, "materially higher" is good enough for me!

The best place to find such statements is simply to check the share-related news reports that come out at 7am each day. You can find them by clicking 'News' on ADVFN or other such services. Keep checking through till you find one. It may well be worth the time and effort spent!

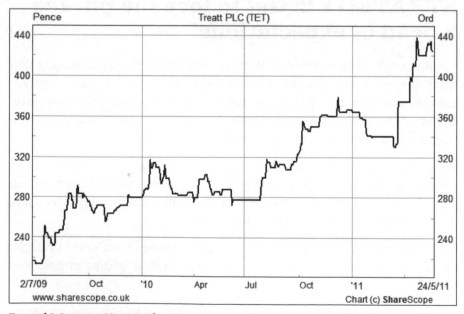

Treatt (July 2009–May 2011)

Summary

- Look for good news.

- Cherish phrases like 'ahead of' or 'better than'.

- Make the effort to find good news stories by clicking through news from 7am.

STRATEGY 3: Find out which retailers are hot

If you are looking to buy shares in a retailer, check with everyone you know.

Where are they shopping? Where are their partners shopping? Where is your partner shopping?

Visit the stores. Are they busy?

I've found a number of great trades this way over the years, including Supergroup (which trebled in value in just a few months).

Even better was Mulberry, the high-end handbag makers, after the Mrs and her mates went crazy for the bags:

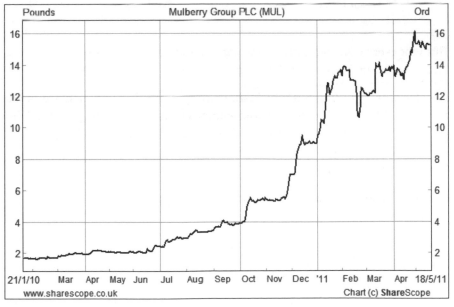

Mulberry (January 2010–May 2011)

In particular, look around your richer friends with disposable income, well, er, if you have any! Find out what they are spending their money on. And especially anything they are buying that might have high margins. Like boots and handbags!

But whoever your mates are, it's worth checking the names on most of the bags they bring back from the shops.

It's also worth finding out which shops they don't like or which are being shunned. Then you could consider shorting them, or betting on them to go down. One great short I got this way was Mothercare. I even asked women with kids at one of my seminars whether they used Mothercare. "No way!" they said.

I shorted, and Mothercare just carried on slumping.

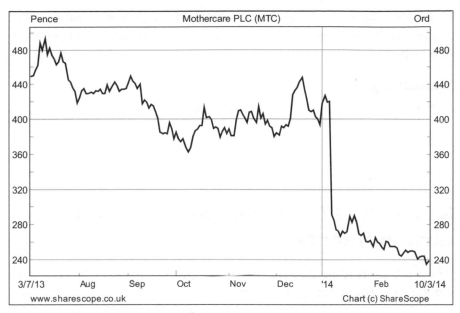

Mothercare (July 2013–March 2014)

Next was an easy one. I just asked men at the seminars to put their hands up. "Which of you have recently bought something from Next?" Almost all of them. What can I say? Check out the chart:

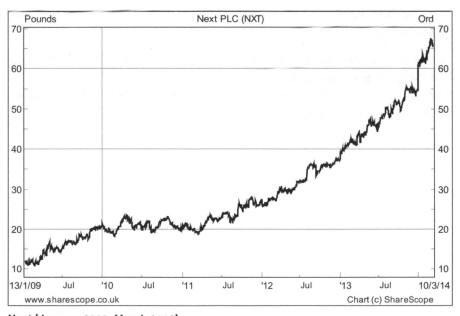

Next (January 2009–March 2014)

Remember that retailers can be in fashion for a year or two but then fall from grace. So keep an eye on your friends' changing habits and get ready to take profits!

Summary

- Which stores do your partner/friends like?

- Buy if many praise the same store.

- But don't hold onto them forever, as fashions and trends change.

STRATEGY 4: Seek game-changing developments

When you are reading through company reports (after subjecting them to the good old traffic lights) ask yourself:

Is this company doing anything new? Is it getting into a new area of business that could be a game changer and start an upward surge in the share price? Is it winning loads of new contracts that could transform its prospects?

I'm looking for companies in the doldrums that are beginning to go through a transformation. I especially like ones that at the same time state they are shutting down loss-making divisions and putting resources into profit-making areas, or indeed finding new revenue streams.

Here's an example. A statement from telecoms firm Coms in January 2014 had everything I liked to see – it was covered in green, with new contracts being won all over the place and the head cheese saying: "We anticipate 2014 will be a transformational year for Coms".

Nice one! I bought in and the following chart tells the story:

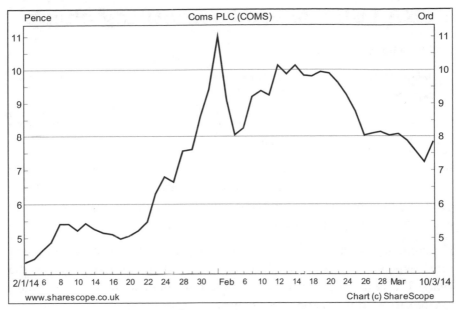

Coms (January 2014–March 2014)

How do you come across something like this? Again, it is simply a matter of clicking on company reports every day when they get published at 7am or looking at them when you get home in the evening.

Look for the word 'transformational'. Look for anything where it appears they have a new line of business or revenue stream. You could also look at a company that has bought another company. Could that purchase transform it?

One little bit of research could pay back big time like it has for me here.

Summary

- Look for companies with new profit streams or new contracts.

- Look for the word 'transformational'.

- Any company that is changing tack is worth checking out.

STRATEGY 5: Find something cheap

I know what you're thinking:

> *'Hey, Robbie, that's easy enough for you to say. How do you find cheap shares?'*

What I'm looking for is a market cap that looks very low compared to full-year profits or the likely full-year profits that are on the way.

Remember my pretend-billionaire's rule of thumb: if a company has a market cap of, say, £100m and is making £10m profits, that looks cheap. (Trading at only ten times profits to market cap.) I'd be paying £100m to get £10m a year return. Nice.

If a company is trading at over 15 times its profit, that would start to look more expensive. Again, this is just my personal rule, fine-tuned over the years. I'm really looking for something perhaps trading at eight times, where the outlook is good. *That's* cheap.

IT firm Alternative Networks came up when I was idly checking through company results in July 2010. I really liked what I saw. Its market value was £70 million. But it reported in the half-year results that profits were up a massive 30% to £4.5 million.

I doubled that for the full year, figuring a full-year profit of more than £9m. That showed the share trading at under eight times the value of its annual profits. And on top of that it reported net cash of more than £7m, which made it even more of a bargain. I had little hesitation and bought in at 154p.

When full-year results came out in December it showed a profit of £9.2m and even more cash! This time £11m! With market cap now at £90m it was still trading at under ten times its yearly profits. Plus it had all that cash. I then thought what the next full-year results could be if it kept going at the same rate: another 30% up on its profits next time would put them at around £12m. That would place the share at less than eight times its profits again, and that's not counting the cash. So I bought more!

Not long after this they were trading at 250! A very nice 70% increase thanks very much! And then I held onto them and look what happened!

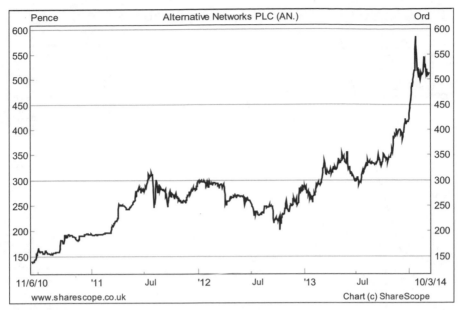

Alternative Networks (June 2010–March 2014)

Summary

- Look for companies that have a low market cap compared to their annual profits (no more than eight to ten times is good).

- Check and check again that debt is not an issue.

STRATEGY 6: Look for exciting new issues

Sometimes it is worth looking out for new entrants to the market with a product that could be big. What I'm looking for is a share that will be debuting with a great story and a great product. This tends to get people excited and that's good for a share price.

One that I spotted recently was Applied Graphene Materials, boasting a new material that everyone could use to make things thinner, especially … er, condoms! Can you imagine the huge market for that?

I bought the story so I bought the shares, and they doubled in a week!

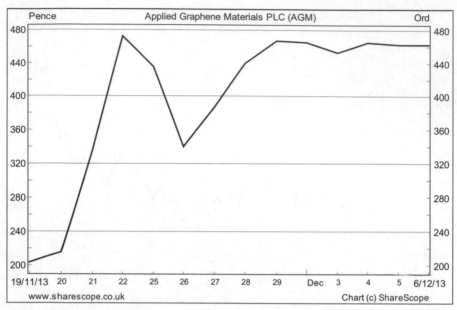

Applied Graphene Materials (November 2013–December 2013)

However, not all new issues will be winners – I can't emphasise this enough – so exit *fast* if the shares start to tank!

Trading new issues is a biggish topic in itself, so I've set aside a chapter after this one to detail all the ins and outs of finding them and trading them.

Summary

- Look out for new issues.

- Buy the ones with a great story or product.

- Beware of things not working out.

STRATEGY 7: What's the hot sector (and its close relatives)?

Sometimes you'll find that one sector of the market is hot.

How do you know it's a hot sector?

Well, it's partly down to common sense and partly down to looking for sectors where the share prices are rising.

One sector I've made money from is oil services. That is, the people who provide the equipment needed by oil companies. With oil exploration a hot but risky sector, I looked at where else might be catching some of the heat but with less risk involved. And the oil services sector jumped out.

It has continued to be a great ride, even as oil exploration has run into problems. And I suspect it will be good for a while longer. In particular, Kentz really did the business for me!

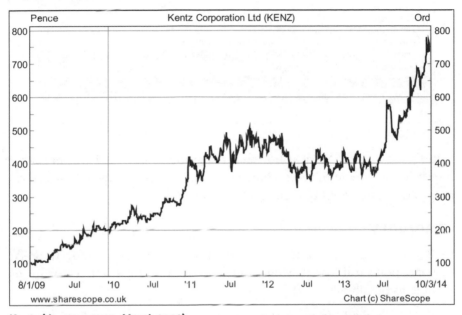

Kentz (January 2009–March 2014)

      If you find a share you like, check out others in the same sector – they might be doing well for similar reasons.

Having brought up the quote for a share, click 'Financials' on ADVFN – and near the top of the page there will be a clickable link, next to the name of the sector, named 'more like this'. Click on that to find other shares in the sector. Maybe you found a hot sector!

I don't know what the next hot sector is going to be, but I will probably find it in the course of researching shares in my usual way. When you do find it, don't be afraid to really go for it and buy well.

Summary

- If you can find a hot sector, it can stay hot for quite a long time. At some point it'll lose its shine, but it's worth riding a hot sector for as long as possible.

- Ensure you still do normal research into the particular share you are interested in.

STRATEGY 8: Recovery plays

A recovery-play strategy is all about finding a share that was once doing well, has been going down but is now starting to rise again.

The trouble here is finding the right share: one that is actually recovering and not still in the dumps and likely to get further in the dumps!

What you are looking for is some kind of statement that changes things and in late 2013 I noticed one with Pace, a set-top box developer.

It announced an excellent acquisition that would push profits higher, and as you can see from the chart the share's price soon accelerated upwards:

Pace (October 2013–March 2014)

Summary

- Have the reasons why the share will recover clear in your head.

- Don't buy if the share price is still going down and it could go bust. Check the debt.

- There must be a tangible reason for recovery.

STRATEGY 9: Get trendy for short-term gains

Sometimes I come across a share and notice something peculiar about its price performance: over a year or two it doesn't do much. It just moves sideways. But it moves sideways in a repetitive up-and-down pattern, because the market struggles to know how it should be rated.

And here I can get some shorter-term gains: I simply keep buying, selling and then shorting the same share time after time as it carries on doing the same thing.

My best example of this is with Domino's Pizza, which always seems to trade in a range.

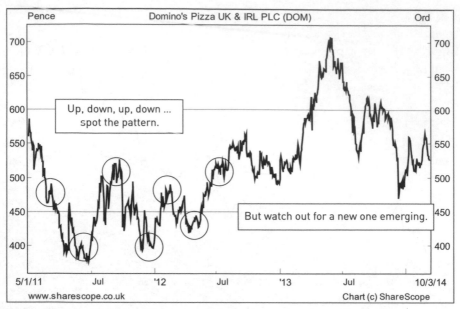

Domino's Pizza (January 2011–March 2014)

Take a look at the Domino's chart.

For nearly a year from 2011 to 2012 it was 500 to 400, 400 to 500, 500 to 400. You could easily have traded it up and down, perhaps using a spread bet for greater speed and flexibility, particularly with shorting (explained later). You'd have made decent money on this one by playing the top and bottom. How easy was that?

Of course, you have to be careful with this kind of share. They can break out of these ranges. In this case, Domino's later starts to rise fairly steadily and breaks through 500. If you held on there, rather than selling, you would enjoy the ride up to 700.

Then, would you believe it, 500ish becomes support again! The share trades down to 600, then all the way back to just below 500 – before going back up to 550, and down to 500 … and guess what I think might happen next? Back to 550. It's really quite simple.

So examine a few charts – FTSE 250 stocks are your best bet, in my experience – and find some trading range patterns and start to play them. You are looking for a share that has been going back and forth between two levels for a few weeks or months. Each time, you want to try to buy near the bottom of the range and sell near the top.

I mention FTSE 250 stocks because they are liquid and the spreads are normally tight, ideal for short-term trading. FTSE 100 stocks, though also liquid and with tight spreads, in my experience just don't work as well – they're just different beasts. And if you tried this with smaller stocks, the bid–offer spreads would be greater, which would reduce the profit.

> If you can only look in on stocks once or twice a day, it may be worth having a tighter stop loss than normal on these trades – say around 2% below the bottom of the range, in case something happens when you are not at your desk.

Summary

- Make sure it is a strong company, and of sufficient size to allow you to buy and sell easily at the price you want.

- Confirm it is in a range, then buy at or near the bottom of the range and sell or short near the top.

- Get out fast if a range is broken against your bet.

STRATEGY 10: Buy boring companies

I bet you don't want to buy boring, do you? You want excitement! I know it! You want something, ooh, that explores gold … dreammmyy! Or oil in some place dangerous!

Well, keep it quiet (and don't tell your trading mates), but what you should really be doing is looking for boring companies. In my experience, these are the ones that can make you big money.

When I look at a company's website and see a load of boring-looking cogs and widgets I get excited!

So Scapa kept getting me very excited. It makes, well … sticky tape – or what they call 'bonding materials' [I thought that was a bottle of wine and Channel 5. – Ed.] Pretty yawn-inducing!

And yet it simply sells more of the boring stuff every year. Take a look at that lovely long-term rising chart. You wouldn't have just doubled your money by buying in – you would have quintupled it and more!

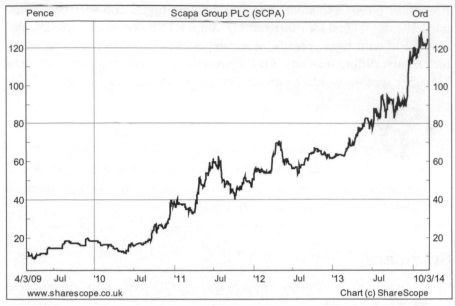

Scapa (March 2009–March 2014)

Now try telling me this company is boring! It's not a company many would buy: they want exciting oil and energy companies. But bonding materials will do me just fine.

Summary

- Think about having one of two boring companies in your portfolio – buy and hold them.

- They will keep you going during the bad times and steadily help to increase your wealth.

- They often pay good dividends too.

STRATEGY 11: Buy shares with a big growth market – or the next big thing

Try and find shares that have a massive growth market. Sounds a bit obvious, right? It's trickier than you might think – but also quite enjoyable. It's really just a question of keeping your eyes open and using your common sense to find them.

One I have made a packet on is Fusionex, a business intelligence firm.

This one seemed to me to have a big growth market. That market was to help bigger companies process massive data easily and quickly. One example would be handling all the information coming in regarding real-time traffic problems.

Fusionex was winning massive contracts, too, and looked like becoming a leader in handling what's been called Big Data. I get a bit bored of much of the tech hype out there, but massive amounts of data are here to stay – and will only get, er, massiver. Did you know that every two days we create more data than existed throughout all of human history up till 2003?

Well, now you do. I'm not sure if that's depressing or exciting, but I do know that it's the kind of thing Fusionex were making money from. More than enough for me to get involved!

So I bought in at 200 and 300 and 400ish! And quickly doubled my money:

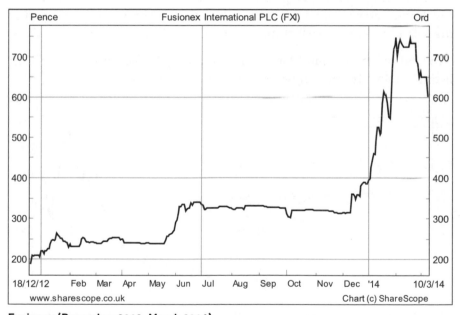

Fusionex (December 2012–March 2014)

There is nothing like finding the next big thing before it gets big. If you do, you will be rewarded handsomely. Can you imagine buying Apple early on? Or online store ASOS at 5p – a company now worth billions?

It is obviously partly guesswork. What new thing is going to be big in the next few years and can I find a company that makes it/does it etc? You need to make sure you're pretty switched on about various 'next big things' and have an informed take on whether or not they are just nonsense.

I've got lucky doing this a few times over the years. And when you do get lucky you can really make a lot.

Maybe you just have to watch more cheesy sci-fi. It's amazing how *Star Trek* foresaw a lot of today's new technology. If you had bought into *Star Trek* forecasts you'd have made a lot. After all, Captain Kirk went round holding an iPad in the 60s! And in the *Next Generation*, they pretty much had the equivalent of mobiles.

Though the most interesting Trek-tech idea, if you ask me, was the 'replicator' – a machine that you simply talk to and it made whatever you requested.

Far-fetched? Not really. The very basic start for that machine is on the way – we currently call it 3D printing. I think this technology is going to revolutionise everything. And with the costs of the machinery nearing mass-market levels, it strikes me as something about to head for the skies.

This led me to buy into American company 3D Systems (a New York listing) at $22. It's now at $65 and I'm still holding on:

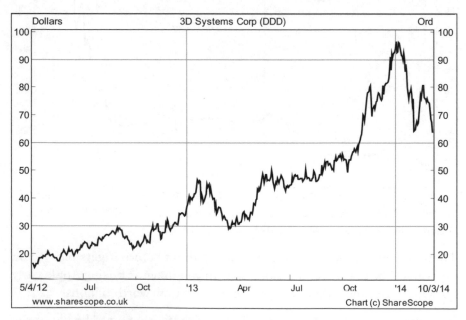

3D Systems (April 2012–March 2014)

3D printing allows actual objects to be designed and created surprisingly quickly with a computer connected to a printer-like device, using special material (often plastic, but increasingly almost anything) instead of ink and paper.

Right now, using a basic 3D printer from 3D Systems you can 'print' a kid's bracelet, a watch and so on.

Can you imagine in a few years when you can print a kid's toy instead of ordering it online or going to the shops?

I think it will overturn everything we know. We will be making the stuff at home that would now perhaps be made in China. That's my forecast. Everything will change. For the good? I don't know. Recently there was a news story that a gun had been made using a 3D printer. So there are going to be negatives. But can you imagine being able to make your own car components, toys, garden equipment?

Things are going to be different! And some retailers are going to be destroyed. I've got into the sector early on and I intend to buy more – and there are other 3D companies out there too.

So keep reading, keep your eyes open for the next big thing, and if you find it – and it proves itself – get stuck in and keep buying. You don't even have to be making big calls about the future – it can be stuff happening right here and now. Another good 'next big thing' trade, for instance, was Dialight back in 2009, then languishing at 150p.

Old bulbs were on the way out, governments were looking for longer-lasting LED bulbs for traffic lights etc, surely LED lighting was already becoming the next big thing?

And I hit it lucky, making well over £100,000 profits on Dialight as it went up and up and up. Eventually I sold most at 1300.

Dialight (January 2010–March 2014)

As said, the trick if you do find yourself being right with the next big thing, is to keep on adding shares as it goes up. You're on to a winner, and though the price won't be such a bargain, you'll still be making money.

Summary

- Imagine the future a bit – or look at developments that are already happening – and see which companies are best poised to capitalise.

- See if they keep winning contracts: a key sign.

- If you find a good one, hold on for as long as you can and don't be afraid to top up your shares – the next big thing can go up and up.

STRATEGY 12: Find strong companies in a niche market

I like finding companies that are strongly positioned in really specialised markets. There are quite a few examples around. It's especially good to find companies who specialise in areas that are growing – a bit like the massive growth market of the previous strategy, except this time we're interested in strong *niche* growth.

So when you read through a company statement and try to understand what it does, work out if they have a nice little niche market – because often, at some point in the future, they get bought out by other companies who operate in related fields. They also have the best chance of defending profit margins in tough times.

Porvair is one that I've always liked. What I'm really looking for in this strategy is the word 'specialist' and indeed Porvair describes itself as a "specialist filtration and environment technology group".

When a company really specialises in a field and does a good job while the market grows, profits can leap up. That was certainly the case here. A look at the following chart will show you what it meant for the share price! Its filtration and engineering expertise shone through.

Porvair (January 2009–March 2014)

This is the kind of share you could simply stay in for years. Indeed I bought most of the way up from 60p.

Summary

- Look for companies in unusual or specialist markets.

- Buy and hold while the market grows.

STRATEGY 13: Find bid targets

I usually manage to be in a share that is bid for about five or six times a year. Why is it so good to be in a company that agrees to be taken over? Because the shares usually increase in value by 50% or more.

And I'm sure the question you're bursting to ask me is:

Okay wise guy, how do you find a bid target?

There are four main ways, all of which can (and probably should) be combined:

1. Seeing increased buying activity in a share.

2. Buying into a company that common sense tells you would make a good bid target for others in the same area.

3. Quite simply, keeping your eye on bid gossip in the papers.

4. Would *you* buy this company if you were a company in the same area?

A good example is Fiberweb, a specialist manufacturer. Its share price had been going down to 70p, then suddenly from August 2013 I noticed the price start to rocket, with big buying coming in. So I hopped on.

I liked the company anyway. Profits had leapt to £15m. It had £25m in the bank and yet was only valued at £150m. That's just ten times profits for a decent growing company.

Sure enough, just a few weeks later a bid was announced and the price soared to over 100p.

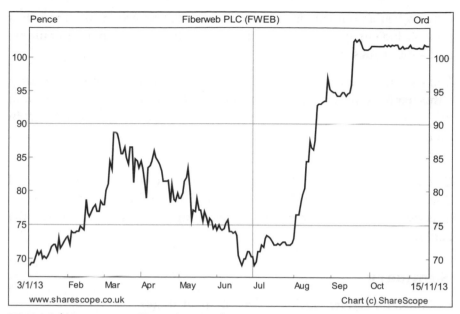

Fiberweb (January 2013–November 2013)

Something else to check when trying to identify bid targets, especially with smaller shares, is whether you are seeing quite a few small buys coming through, with a steady rise in the share price.

Although insider trading is illegal, you see time and time again lots more shares than normal in a company being traded in the run up to a bid. Because, let's face facts: those in the know gossip about it, and so the news gradually spreads.

Picking up on this activity has worked for me a few times in the past and is especially good in smaller companies. If you get to know shares on your watchlist, as time goes by and you gain experience you will develop a nose for abnormal buys or trades coming in – and it's usually worth acting fast.

Seems to me that those in the know tend to find out around six weeks before a bid is due in the smaller companies.

Of course, there are also plenty of risers in bigger companies in the run up to bids. It's worth watching for price rises and mentions in the press.

Catching a bid is often a case of picking up news and gossip from the ADVFN newswires, other websites and general bits and pieces from the newspapers.

Often when a company is mentioned in a gossipy way in the press as a possible bid target, there is still time to get on board. It's a matter of timing and a bit of guesswork.

You have to decide whether a counter bid is likely from some other party – this happens quite a lot. For example, the Boots share price was around 770 when rumours first went round about a bid. It was possible to get in then. The price rose to near a tenner and then a counter bidder came in and the price rose to 1130p.

Of course it is not all plain-sailing. If you come to the story late and a bid does not materialise, the shares can come down quite a bit. If the price is already close to where a bid might come in, you may have missed the action.

Summary

- Watch for sudden buying activity in quiet shares.

- Check daily above-average volumes in the larger companies.

- If you think shares are cheap, so might a bidder.

- Keep an eye on newspaper gossip.

STRATEGY 14: Buy shares moving up to the main market from AIM

Most companies that you will come across as an investor will be listed on the London Stock Exchange. But there are other markets that companies can join, especially AIM. These other markets are usually for very small companies; often new companies joining an exchange for the very first time. The LSE is sometimes referred to as the *main market*, to distinguish it from the other markets.

> Rather confusingly, AIM is actually owned by the LSE, but it is in all respects a separate market.

A fairly common progression for a new company is to first join AIM and then once it has grown to a certain size to leave AIM and list on the main market.

One of my favourite strategies is to look for AIM shares that have just moved onto the main market or are about to move to the main market.

You get about ten companies a year who decide to move onto the main market.

Why is it a good move and why do the prices tend to rise?

It shows the company is serious about its growth prospects and wants to be a big player.

Also, fund managers can now start to invest in shares they wouldn't have wanted to get involved with before, which can help give the price a boost.

Companies with a value of £600m or so will get in the FTSE 250 – and inclusion in that index will see tracker funds buy in. Or even in some cases the FTSE 100.

So whenever you see an announcement that an AIM share is planning to move to the main market, it's pretty much a buy signal.

Of course, again you need to make sure you do the normal research and don't just buy anything. But if you like a company, it's invariably worth getting stuck in when you hear they are going on up from AIM.

How do you find out? A company normally announces it is going to make the leap when it announces results, so it is worth flicking through results every day.

Kentz, an engineering and construction company I was holding in a spread bet (see strategy 7), announced it was going to join the main market. It said it would probably do so in 2011. I'd already bought Kentz at 200 and had other reasons for it going up. When it finally made its move, it got an automatic entry onto the FTSE 250, which helped the price gain even more!

As I write (early 2014), one share that is shortly to move to the main market from AIM is Quindell, an outsourcing company, which announced this back in August 2013. Again, once the move is made it will get access to the FTSE 250 and fund managers will buy in.

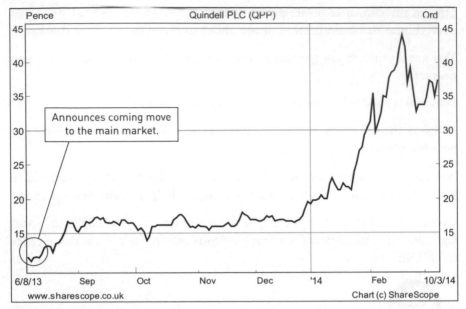

Quindell (August 2013–March 2014)

Summary

- It's a great signal when a company goes to a main listing from AIM. Very well worth noting and thinking about buying.

- You have to keep your eyes open for these announcements. Check daily results.

STRATEGY 15: A company's division booms

Sometimes a company that has varied interests suddenly sees one of its divisions begin to do very well. And that is a great time to buy in.

A read-through of a company's report can bring this to light. What you're looking for is a company that is already doing okay with its revenue streams, so you have the income coming in. It then takes just one division to begin to outperform and you get a share price uplift.

Avon Rubber is a good example of this. Its main business was in the dairy industry. It's a good business but not exactly an exciting growth area. After all, there are only so many cows!

What caught my eye was its defence division, where it supplied equipment such as masks. The statements revealed it was finding lots of new markets for its masks, including in the US and in the Middle East. Unfortunately, troubles in the world seemed to be multiplying, and there was not much doubt for me that orders were likely to continue to come in. On top of that, the results showed profits were heading up fast and debt coming down.

Avon Rubber (May 2010–March 2014)

As the chart reveals, the price went from a quid to close to three quid. And then doubled again.

Summary

- Look for companies where one division is picking up steam.

- With income coming in from other safe but dull divisions, that should help underpin the share price.

STRATEGY 16: Oil exploration – but be sparing and careful

Oil exploration companies, especially small ones, are loved by investors, but sadly these days they rarely provide much profit. There was a small boom in these companies a few years ago but now you really have to get the right one.

You have to realise they are high risk and not put too much in. Researching them is a little harder than it is exploring other companies, and I find it difficult to get my head around production rates etc.

In summary there are four things to look for:

- Has it already found oil?

- Has it got enough cash to keep going?

- What is the management like?

- Is the area it is operating in likely to produce more?

I had success with Coastal Energy, which I bought at 430. Someone bid to take it over at a tenner per share. This one had plenty of cash, management with a good track record, it was already producing lots of oil and the area it was in kept on giving.

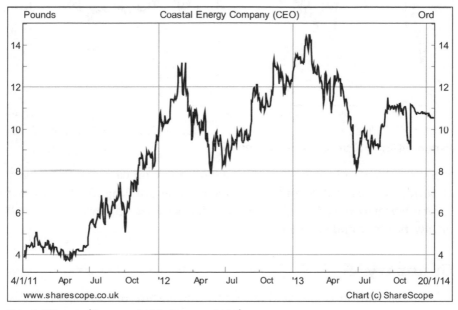

Coastal Energy (January 2011–January 2014)

If you are looking at smaller oilers you must beware that any investment in smaller oil companies is fraught with risk and should be a distinctly small part of any portfolio – almost for fun, if you like. The problem is that a dry well could see 50% marked off a price overnight. Management is key here.

Parkmead, like Coastal Energy, was another buy on the strength of management. The main man it had got on board was Tom Cross, a seasoned oil man who had helped take Dana Petroleum from a penny share to the dizzying heights of 1800! Obviously it seemed worth taking a punt given his experience. He even said he was trying to do another Dana!

For a small stake it has gone well, but if you get it wrong or they struggle to find anything get out quick!

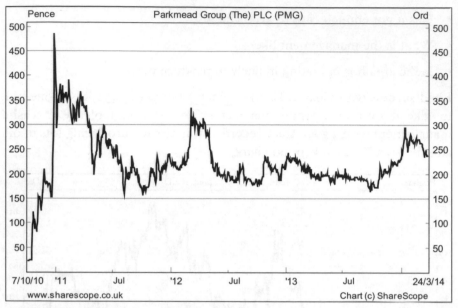

Parkmead Group (October 2010–March 2014)

What you have to be careful with is any oiler low on cash (they will need to fundraise), as well as any that has kept disappointing. And you must remember: it is next to impossible to value an oil company, so they will always be scary and volatile!

Summary

- Oil exploration is an exciting sector, but beware of having too many oilers.

- Look for ones that have already found oil or have good cash reserves.

- Check the management team and the drill areas.

- Watch out for serial disappointers.

- Go easy on them.

> **A reader writes: A sad reminder**
>
> "I still have a sad oil co. in my account – Rockhopper. I keep it there so that every time I look at my portfolio I can see I should never listen to tipsters. I will give myself a break one day and sell it!"

STRATEGY 17: Buying on overreaction to news

It doesn't happen that often but occasionally a share will slump suddenly on a news story that might affect its products. There is a big knee-jerk reaction and the share in question gets hit, but using common sense you can estimate whether the reaction is overdone and the share will go back up.

One morning in 2013 (you might remember) the horse-meat scandal broke in the UK, when it was discovered a lot of ready-made beef meals were actually ready-made horse meals.

I saw that a provider of these ready meals – Greencore – had plunged on the news and thought this could be an amazing time to buy ... yummy!

When a company has fallen a lot you need to do some quick thinking.

How much has it fallen in percentage terms? Now look at how much you think it *should* have fallen after the news and how likely it is to bounce back. You need to get a good look at the actual damage done. Sometimes the market is way off.

Greencore had fallen to the low 80s, nearly 30% lower than its recent high. But I saw this in its statement to the market:

> "Beef Bolognese Sauce represented c. £0.3 million of Greencore's £1.16bn turnover in its last financial year. The annualised revenue of all products withdrawn represents less than £1 million."

The company also seemed to be saying it was unlikely it supplied much else horse-flavoured stuff. It was just a horsey sauce. So, in essence, withdrawal of the sauce meant little to the company's overall performance.

A 30% fall? Way too much for a company whose withdrawn products *didn't even account for 0.1% of its turnover.* So I bought tons and tons of Greencore in the 80s, both on spread bets and in my ISA too. I figured that at the very worse a quid would be a fair price, but there was actually no reason why the price shouldn't at some point head back up to its old high.

Well, the price gradually lifted up and guess what … it went all the way to 300.

I took some profits a bit earlier than this, after it bounced up from the 80s, but was along for a very enjoyable ride.

On the initial bets in the low 80s, I placed stops at a hyper-cautious 75p – if the worst came to the worst, I knew I would then only lose small amounts if the price kept falling. And I could start again later.

The amount of work I did to make giant profits here? Well, very little really. In fact, it was all just a bit of common sense. No complex technical analysis etc. needed. Bad news can make you good money. Just give yourself a few rules and boundaries. Make sure you understand the company and are *sure it has been oversold*. I don't want you going out and buying up every company going through a disaster.

But the good news these days is that bad news companies almost always bounce back to some extent.

If you buy a bad news share that you think has long-term potential and it keeps falling, set a tight stop, get out and try again when it's lower. You must make sure you are not trying to catch a falling knife that simply continues to fall.

If you get in near the bottom and it goes up, raise your stop under the price. Keep buying as it heads up. Keep raising the stop.

Right, I am starving – I fancy a steak … nice and rare …

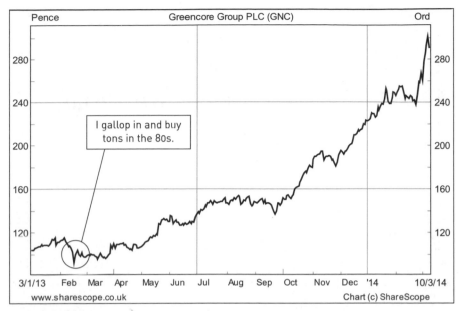

Greencore (January 2013–March 2014)

STRATEGY 18: Buy health and safety

Yep, I can't stand it either. These days you can't move for new health-and-safety rules.

When researching companies, though, I always like ones in this area – firms that have a health-and-safety product that could become the next paranoid must-have, or which might really start flying if some legislation tightens regulations up somewhere.

One I only recently found was Seeing Machines. This was truly safetylicious! The company had technology that could work out whether a driver of, say, a digger in a mine was too tired to continue safely. Or a car driver. Or a pilot. Or ... well, you can imagine the different uses.

And I could definitely imagine these sort of things maybe becoming compulsory in the future. Say, for lorry drivers?

To me this looked a nice one, especially as the company was quite small.

So I went in and bought a load at 5p. It is already going well and up to 8p. I've no idea yet whether this one is going to work out, but I'm buckled in for the long term, with a stop loss safety hat on just in case.

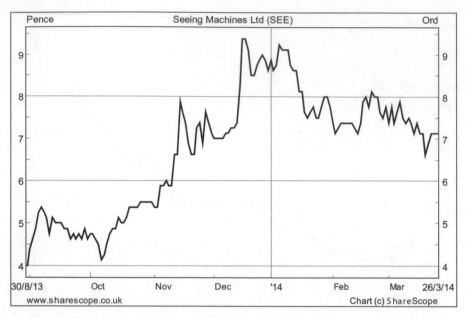

Seeing Machines (January 2014–March 2014)

Summary

- Look for companies providing health-and-safety products.

- Think hard about why such a company's products could boom.

STRATEGY 19: Profits and dividend rises over three years

This really is quite a simple strategy.

If a company has managed to raise its profits and dividends every year for three years in a row, you have got to get interested.

A company that fulfilled these criteria and more was Hilton Food Group, a meatpacking firm. This has been a terrific share for me.

The following chart tells the story:

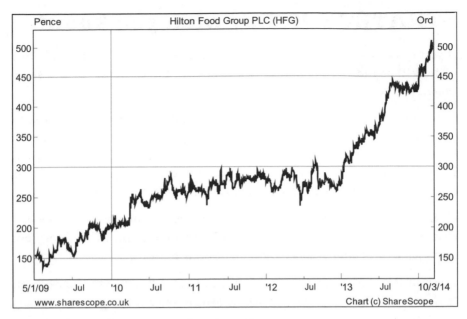

Hilton Food Group (January 2009–March 2014)

Its dividends rose by a penny every year from 2008 to 2014 and so did profits and revenue. While profit rises weren't dramatic, it still meant a nice slow rise in capital.

Dividend rises show a company is confident – they're giving away their cash after all – and coupled with a capital rise thanks to increased profits, it means they're almost certainly doing well. Hilton also paid out nearly 5% per year – that's pretty good!

I'll keep holding this one until a question mark creeps in. Say it suddenly says one of its divisions isn't performing as well as it has been. Or there is a problem somewhere. Or, indeed, if profits begin to fall for any reason. That's when I will take my gains and sell.

So it's always a good idea when checking out a company to see how well it's done over three years. Look back over the results and see if it has maintained a consistent uplift. There cannot be a better sign!

Summary

- Has the company shown consistent profit gains?
- Has the dividend risen every year?
- Keep holding unless question marks appear.

STRATEGY 20: Buy what you know!

If you work in a particular industry, you ought to have a pretty good idea of how that industry is doing. You probably have friends in the same business too.

For example, maybe you are in the house-building industry. If you keep your ear to the ground you should be able to gain good information about how your industry is doing. Make sure you chat to people in your industry. Do things look good or are there worries? If there are problems in your business there might be comparable problems in similar listed businesses.

Or if your business is going well, take a look at some comparable businesses that might be listed on the market and research them. Maybe they are doing as well as your business and for similar reasons.

I was in the media business for a long time so I was pretty clued-up on that area and that helped me make decisions as to whether to buy media companies.

Of course I haven't had a conventional job for many years, but I always ask people: What do you do and how is that business going? Sometimes it gives me ideas for new sectors to research.

As mentioned elsewhere, I do continue as an independent distributor for Telecom Plus, which under Utility Warehouse provides energy and telephony. So I meet a number of people in that industry and have an idea of how it is doing. It enables me to keep my ear to the ground on margins on phones and energy, for example.

And I've bought what I know – indeed a lot of what I know – and own a significant amount of Telecom Plus stock. And I expect to keep hold of it for a long time to come. I've made around £700,000 on this one.

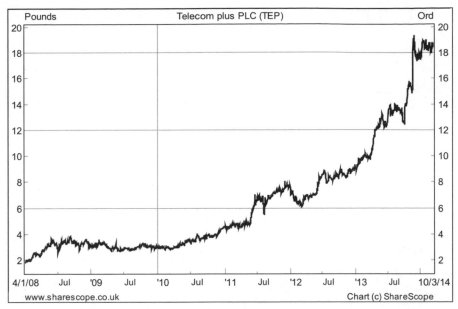

Telecom Plus (January 2008–March 2014)

So think about your job and the industry you are in (or once were in, if you've quit the rat race). Then look at the stock market listings. Is there anything listed that is comparable? Talk to your mates and get their feedback.

Summary

- Think about your sector and the expert info you have on it.

- Talk to peers and get their views.

- But *do not deal* if you have any specific price-moving information the general market does not also have access to. That's illegal, you dodgy bastard.

New Issues

New issues or IPOs were the subject of strategy 6 in the last chapter. They're interesting beasts in a number of ways so I think they deserve a little extra chapter of their own.

They are well worth talking about! Over the years I have made a fortune out of backing some amazing ones which doubled, trebled and more.

And what is an IPO?

It's basic jargon for companies coming onto the market for the first time. IPO is the abbreviation for: *Initial Public Offering*. Unfortunately, the *public* part of that is a bit debatable, as it's not always easy to get your hands on them.

If the market is going well, there can be lots of companies debuting on the stock exchange like this. But if it's tanking, there will be fewer.

I look at all new issues coming onto the market, as I find that there can be gems amongst them that prove eventual long-term winners. Over the years I've had some massive successes with these. Some have gone up 400–500%! Many doubled.

In the last book I was sniffy about looking at AIM market launches and preferred main market ones, but that was because of the tax rules at the time – they couldn't go into ISAs so I would have to pay tax ... so now I am not so sniffy. Perhaps just cautious when it comes to AIM new issues.

First, though: how do you keep track of what's coming onto the market and what's just been launched?

There are various ways.

- One is simply to check news stories on ADVFN or something like Investegate or many of the other newswires each morning (which you should be doing anyway). Usually along with results at 7am you will see the odd 'Intention to list' news story. Those are the ones to click on.

- Papers like *The Times* tend to keep track of them.

- Investment mags like *Investors Chronicle* and *Shares* highlight them.

- If you put 'IPO' into the search engine of your fave finance site, they'll come up.

After finding them, I usually research them by just Googling the company and tracking down whatever I can find out about them: recent profit figures, what they do etc. Sometimes there is quite a bit of information in the intention to list statement.

Then I wait till they announce what the likely market value will be.

I especially like IPOs valued at £600m or more as they'll get automatic entry into the FTSE 250, where trackers will buy. Anything over £4bn will see it get into the FTSE 100. But smaller ones, as said, are also pretty interesting.

Buying into new issues

Very occasionally companies offer shares to anyone who wants them. This happened recently with Royal Mail.

You'll probably see these come up on your broker's site and you can put in a bid for some shares at the issue price. If the issue is popular, like Royal Mail, then you might not get all the shares you ask for.

Usually you have to buy a new issue once it is actually listed on the market.

So, you've found a new issue and you want a piece of the action. Getting in on the first day just takes a bit of determination. The thing is, your broker or spread firm probably won't have heard of it yet so there's no chance you'll be able to deal online.

First things first, you'll need the stock code of the company. You ought to be able to find it from around 7am on the ADVFN news service. Trawl through and it ought to say:

"Blah blah ... company lists today ... the code is XXX."

If you want to buy the shares in the market you may want to buy in pretty early. So call your broker and say:

"I want to buy this company. It's a new issue today."

He'll faff around a bit but then he should come back and ask you how many shares you want and you should be able to deal.

If you want to trade via a spread betting firm it might be more difficult; it's a question of which firm you use. Some might give you a price and some might not be able to straightaway. Not much you can do if they won't give you a price, it's up to them really. Sometimes they've said to me they could give me a price but needed half an hour to set it up.

Sometimes I wait and sometimes I dive in on the first day. It's a difficult call and something that takes a bit of experience and some luck too. Because sometimes buying on the first day is a mistake and you could wait for a better price.

If it starts trading on the market way higher than the issue price, you may want to consider holding off as the price could come back a bit in the days after the IPO. But the main market new issues tend to do so well that, even if you buy in and it comes back a bit, it may go up over time.

Main market new issues are not as frequent as AIM, which is why they are so precious. But there is usually, on average, one a month. A company has to satisfy many criteria to get a main listing – AIM is far easier – such that it means a company is serious and wants to get somewhere. One of the many reasons I like the main market launches.

Evaluating new issues

I don't simply buy every new issue – obviously not every one is going to be a winner. The problem in the end, really, is working out which new issues are worth buying and which might be stinkers. It's not easy. With new issues you are very much buying a story as well as a company – always remember that.

Firstly, I always have a read through the statement issued. How much money are they raising and how much is the market cap going to be?

Then, in addition to the standard company research we discussed earlier, I ask myself:

- How likely is it that whatever the company makes or produces will be in more and more demand?

- Has the company got something tech-wise that others don't or have they got a nice edge over others?

Things to avoid? That's easy. Anything floating on AIM with 'oil' or 'gas' in its title. I'm just not interested. I have no idea whether they will find oil or gas and in my experience it rarely happens. After mug punters buy in at the start, such shares usually drift. If I wanted to gamble I'd go to Kempton Park.

Also, I tend to avoid a company where there might be a lot of competition in its market or growth looks slow or simply, well, it doesn't look very exciting. Recently I looked at RM2 before it floated on AIM. It's in the pallet market. Pallets are big business and the company had some kind of improved pallets that lasted longer than others.

But I just couldn't get excited about pallets. I know that boring businesses can be good, but when it's an IPO you're looking for a bit of a buzz to be there to lift things quickly. A decent recurring revenue and the ability to to rent or sell quite a few products is a good start, but with IPOs I'm not sure it's enough.

RM2 was in such a competitive market, another company could come out with an even better pallet – and in any case how long would it take for this solid business to be reflected in the share price? A long time, I suspected. Could I see the share price doubling anytime soon? Not really. So I stayed out.

Another example was when Betfair floated. I liked the Betfair business and used it myself. I really thought I might buy in.

But I was very cautious about confirmation bias, as discussed earlier in the book. Since I liked and used the business, I was in danger of building a one-sided investment case. What were the negatives? I had to be brutally honest about the company. One thing in particular bugged me. I thought: hang on, it's been going for a long time, where are all the new customers going to come from?

Then on the day it floated I saw the market cap was £1.5 billion. I Googled its profits. It had only made £18m last year and was forecast to make £40m that year.

What?!

Would I pay £1.5bn for a company that was going to make £40m?

No way.

So I completely turned around and shorted it at 1500. I closed my short at 1000 – too soon, as it happened, as it continued down to 600!

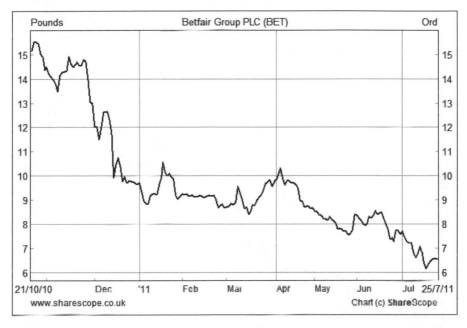

Betfair (October 2010–July 2011)

When it all goes well

So there were two losers to avoid. How about some winners? My most recent IPO buy rather amazingly doubled in just a week!

This was Applied Graphene Materials, the manufacturers we met in the previous chapter. One of graphene's biggest potential uses, you may remember, was in making thinner condoms. I thought that could perhaps harden the share price even more. Which is exactly what happened. I picked up the shares at around 200 and soon they were 450 – at that point it seemed crazy not to take the profits.

So, I had a bit of luck with it, but as the technology excited me, it was likely to excite the market too. Suddenly, I am feeling excited … where is the Mrs?

Fusionex, the Big Data play from the previous chapter, was another good IPO trade as well. Fellow Big Data firm Wandisco likewise. This floated in 2012 at around 200 (the same as Fusionex). Again, I liked the Big Data angle – it was definitely exciting. Wandisco seemed in a good place and I thought others would see the same too.

So I bought in at 200 and 400 – and the shares raced up past 1000! At which point I sold most of them. After all, the rise was too good and profit has to be banked some time.

Wandisco (June 2012–October 2013)

Turning to some that were floated on the main market: of course, Royal Mail was a no-brainer! Offered to everyone, I got my grand's worth and it nearly doubled...!

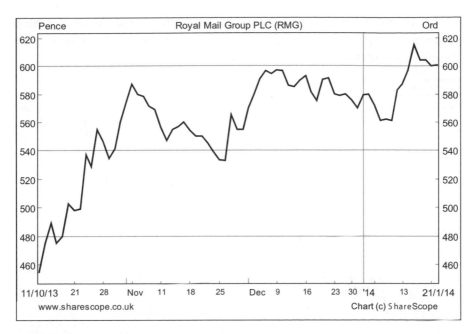

Royal Mail (October 2013–January 2014)

Merlin Entertainments was also quite good. I mentioned it earlier because I reckon it'll be promoted to the FTSE 100 soon. But it was also once an attractive main market IPO trade. It's only gone up a bit as I write, but it is a business I can understand as it runs all those vile theme parks that us poor parents get dragged along too. Full of people eating overpriced crap. But that is good news for us canny investors!

They operate horrible parks like Legoland (hell), Chessington (really vile), Sea Life (boring) and the London Eye – which is actually brilliant.

In 2013 they reported some good results, with revenues up over 11% and a plan to build more tedious parks all over the world so that more parents can spend a fortune entertaining their spoiled children.

The more overpriced crap they stuff in their gobs, the more money us investors will make, I thought. Bring it on, load me up with high-margin pizza and pasta!

Of course, I knew the shares could be a rollercoaster ride. [I'm certainly feeling nauseous! – Ed.]

The forecast for the firm's profits was about £270m, so a market cap of £3.5bn seemed reasonable. I bought at the issue price of 315. These were offered to anyone who wanted some, as long as you didn't want too many.

With this one I wasn't expecting a massive ride up quickly, but a nice company with prospects over time, and still a bit more excitement to drive things than pallets.

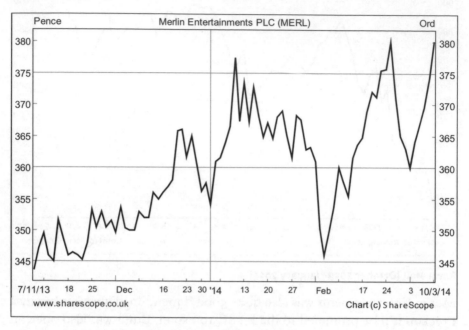

Merlin Entertainments (November 2013–March 2014)

Last example: Conviviality Retail. I understood this one too. Conviviality sells cheap alcohol and owns a couple of very well-known booze chains, Bargain Booze and Wine Rack.

It had lovely growing profits, was debt-free – and people are always going to buy booze. Plus Conviviality seemed to have enough pulling power to draw people away from the supermarkets, with a growing market as (sadly) more and more pubs close and people drink at home.

I bought in at 130 and it went to 180 over the next six months.

Darling, pass me another glass of Merlot … thanks!

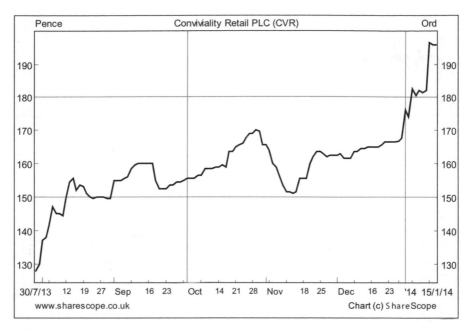

Conviviality Retail (July 2013–January 2014)

Handle with care

How do you handle new issues once bought?

Pretty much the same as any other share. Always use a stop loss. And maybe be just a bit harsher on any share that starts to go down. I really don't like any IPO that goes down 10% – I think any one like that is well worth quitting *fast*, before it can drop any further.

Here's a good example. Look at the chart of 24/7 Gaming. Without a stop you'd have lost nearly the lot. But following a strict 10% rule, if you bought at 50p, you'd have been gone at 45p.

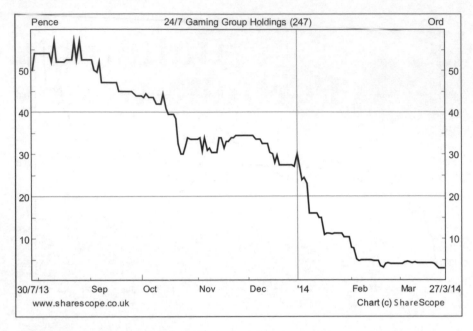

24/7 Gaming (July 2013–March 2014)

Mind you, at 50p there was no reason to buy. Why? Because it was making a heavy loss already. In a very competitive market.

But the point is: if you had bought in, you should have got out – fast!

Summary

- You are buying a story as well as a company.
- You need to use common sense to judge whether to buy the story.
- If you get it wrong, get out quick!

Building a Portfolio Gently

Building a portfolio gently is, in my opinion, absolutely crucial to making money out of the markets in a way that won't sooner or later implode. It is harder to do than you might think.

After all, we are TRADERS right?

And everyone out there in the market is DESPERATE for you to trade MORE.

When in fact to make money you should trade *less*.

Yep, I really do think that the less you trade the more you will make.

It's worked for me. I don't trade every single day. I have even let a week go by where I have seen no good reason to trade – *and therefore haven't traded*.

Over-trading

Why does everyone want you to trade, trade and trade some more? Because they all make money out of you when you trade and they don't when you don't.

Over-trading is also about EXCITEMENT! We want some ACTION!

People simply press the buy and sell button too often – they feel like they should be making a trade every day – or most days. And this is quite common with new traders. They get the bug and want to chase every stock that moves.

This is okay if you're a really hot day trader, but sadly there are hardly any of them around. I've had it said to me time and time again (especially from people I've met who work for spread betting firms):

"Our losing accounts are those which make too many trades."

In fact, spread betting sites are pretty much designed to make you over-trade.

The desire to over-trade probably stems from our emotions (one of the less helpful *Dad's Army* parts of us). We want to make money quickly and we think if we keep trading, the money will come pouring in. Wrong! It's more likely to go pouring out. Plus ...

The more trades you have running, the more time you have to spend monitoring them, the more stress you'll feel and the poorer your decisions will be.

And on commissions alone you'll waste a small fortune.

So don't go bananas and have a whole raft of open trades everywhere. Stick to a sensible number that you can keep control of.

The gambling mindset

For a couple of years in the 1990s, I was a professional gambler on the horses. I even owned a couple, so I had access to a bit of inside info on form and the like. But even with that info, I didn't make a lot of money – just about enough to get by. Never anything big.

It's next to impossible to make a living on the horses. However, the stock market is different because if you stay disciplined and calm you can definitely make big money.

It's not about who crosses the line first, but about picking businesses whose performance will keep getting better – and there can be plenty of winners in that race.

But you have to invest and not gamble to become a stock market winner who makes real regular money.

What's the difference between a stock market gambler who loses and a stock market investor who wins?

Quite simple: a market gambler is itching to trade and press that exciting deal button almost for the sake of it. And gamblers make up 90% of spread betting accounts that lose.

- **Gambling** is putting money on shares that you know nothing about. Buying something for a punt – and with no trading plan in place.

- **Investing** is buying into a company you've done your research on and trying to get your timing right.

I get so many emails starting:

  'I am going to have a punt on … '

Don't have 'punts'. Invest. Make money. If you have punts you will lose, maybe not right now but eventually. Punts are just lazy gambling.

So there – have I made myself clear?

Tea-and-toast trading

Successful traders, then, are those who don't overdo it or gamble – they're the ones who aren't afraid of not doing anything!

They're the ones who are quite happy to put their feet up and have some tea and toast when no trades are necessary. I really recommend it. Instead of trading, just drink tea and eat toast.

You will often find that this downtime will save you a lot of money. Especially given that bread and teabags are still very cheap. If you don't like tea and toast, go out and take the dog for a walk. Or take up a new hobby.

Because sometimes markets are volatile – up 100 points one day and down 150 the next. When markets get volatile I sit back and tea-and-toast it. Or sometimes, if it gets really nasty, I hide behind the sofa. Had plenty of experience doing this during *Dr Who* when it was really good in the 70s. It's also a good place to hide if the wife's come home and I forgot to tidy up.

Every time the entire market has got very volatile, I rely on history – as long as I know I am holding good, strong companies, I can be sure they will in time bounce back.

Just remember: every time you exit or enter a trade it costs money (spread *plus* commission *plus* stamp duty).

So when you first enter a trade, your initial aim should be to hold it for a bit.

Not that you bought it on a tip and, 'Oh it'll find oil next week and be double the price'.

Big returns

Remember when we looked at an example portfolio earlier on when discussing cutting losses and running winners? That had lots of tiny losses but several strong wins. Within the second lot of trades there are a rare number that will make you tons of money over time. They're rare but they are out there, and I want to share a couple of examples to prove that it's possible – and that the secret of crazy returns (well over 200 or 300%) really is trading less rather than more.

It's all about building a portfolio gently!

Now, I am not a fan of Vimto – it's a horrible purple abomination – but boy do a lot of people love it! A while back I saw the shares of Nichols – the drinks manufacturer behind Vimto and several other brands – starting to rise. So I had a look at it.

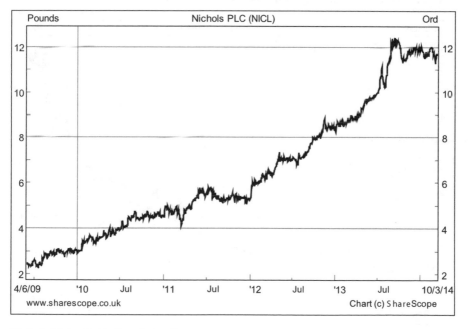

Nichols (June 2009–March 2014)

After running Nichols through all my various tests and the research methods I told you about earlier, I found I liked the look of it a lot. So I bought some shares at 220p. It kept going up. I let it run. Its statements remained strong and every time it released results its profits had fizzed up (see what I did there?).

Rather than cashing in when it had doubled, or going off to find the next attractive maker of disgustingly sweet fizzy stuff, I just bought more shares in it every six months or so – at 350p, 450p, 550p – building up a nice stake.

There was always a reason to buy and rarely a reason to sell. And that's remained true up to the time of writing. It's trading at 1170p (up 400% on when I first saw it) and I am still holding it.

Who deserves the credit here?

Well, okay, I did some good research and happened to pick a good share, and I then built up a good holding in it. But everything after that was a combination of Doing Nothing + Time.

It's amazing how good that combination can be.

It's a similar story with Telecom Plus. This is easily my best trade of all time, netting me nearly £700,000 profit – so far!

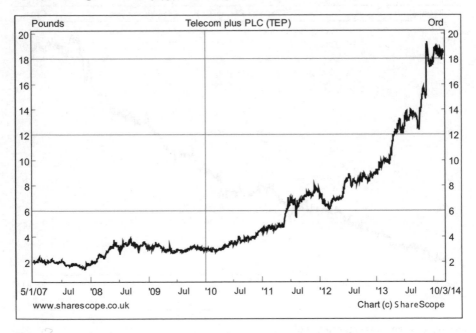

Telecom Plus (January 2007–March 2014)

I bought loads at 82p and 120p, adding more in the 300s and 500s – and even recently at 1475!

So I am sitting on a massive profit. And still holding! I've done nothing much but watch it rise over the years. Profits are still rising. I'm in till there is a big question mark!

I suppose what I am saying is that once you get a good one, stick with it. That's how I've made a lot of my profits.

Gentle trading really is the way to build a nice portfolio, especially if you are a beginner.

Start slowly. There is no rush. Wait until you find the right share, buy it and hold it if it's good, then move onto the next.

Terrible Trading Mistakes

This chapter is about mistakes, cock-ups, blunders, gaffes, screw-ups, clangers ... you get the idea. It includes the top mistakes made by traders and investors, my biggest idiocies, and more.

If you've been losing money on the markets, I reckon you should find it all pretty enjoyable (or possibly painful!). But seriously, it's amazing what you can learn from making mistakes. I know I've learned a lot. And it really is true how many of us make exactly the same ones.

The secret is to learn from mistakes. Some do, some don't. But a few in this chapter are probably the biggest ones you can make – so you could save thousands by not making them.

As long as you aren't losing a fortune, mistakes are rarely disasters. The lessons can be invaluable, and going forward you should be less accident-prone. There are no right and wrong answers to the markets but the following boobies can be easily avoided. Doing so will save you/make you money over time.

Mistake 1: Buying crap with no thought

I'm starting with what is probably the biggest trading sin: buying the next big thing that *isn't*.

Greedy traders always want to make a million fast and they think by buying a company with the next cure for cancer or similar outlandish claims they are going to make their millions.

They read about it on all the bulletin boards, make the mistake of believing what people are saying, buy in and then lose – before continuing to hold it for ages … still believing.

One of the shares like this that always comes up is Sareum. Apparently it might have a cure for cancer. So they say. In 2013 a number of punters bought in at 2p. A lot of them lost around 75% of their money.

Don't believe crazy claims made by people you don't know!

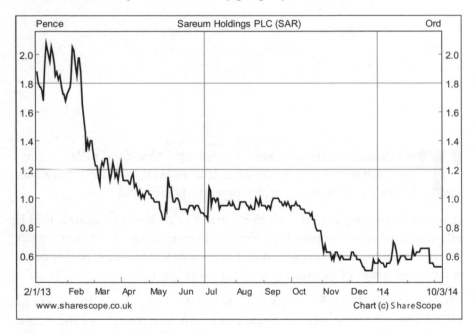

Sareum (January 2013–March 2014)

Mistake 2: falling for a pump and dump

New investors often fall for the pump-and-dump merchants that can be found on many different sites.

Pump and dump means to buy tiny illiquid shares, then pump them on the BBs, promising the price will go to the sky. Mug punters then buy in. As soon as they've bought and the price goes up, the pumpers dump, selling their shares at the higher price and leaving those they conned holding the baby.

Gowin New Energy on 13 January 2014 was a good example of this. The pumpers hit the BBs and started pumping up the stock with comments like "Money to be made on this one again." As you can see from the trades for the day, one of these pumpers had bought 14,518 shares at 6.8 and later dumped them at 7. Another bought 10,000 at 6.85 and dumped at 7.5. One bought 15,000 at 7.39 and dumped minutes later at 7.55.

The pumpers aren't interested in big money. They just want to turn over a few quid every day. Watch out for pump-and-dump heavy forums, usually very busy with dozens pumping tiny shares to make a few quid from mug punters. Don't let them take your money!

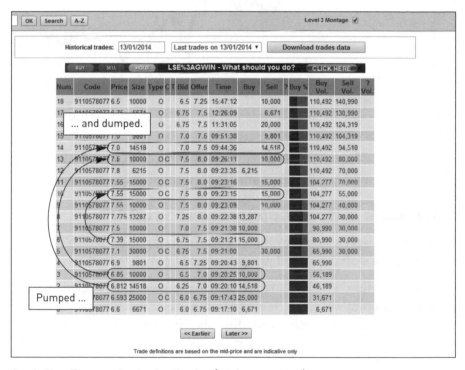

Gowin New Energy – trades for the day (13 January 2014)

Mistake 3: not using stop losses

Stop losses have already been discussed quite a bit in this book. Remember, a stop will get you out and keep you from having a portfolio full of big losers. Of course, stops sometimes get you out at the wrong time – but you can always buy back.

For example, say you traded Centamin without a stop …

Centamin (January 2011–March 2014)

You could easily have bought and held on and hoped when in fact a well-placed stop would have ensured any losses were pretty minimal.

Mistake 4: setting stop losses too tight

So you want to set a stop loss. But be careful on the stop level! It is silly to set too tight a stop as you will just get stopped out all the time!

If you're trading a volatile stock, setting a too-tight stop can be a particularly pointless move. It's understandable; you want to be out of something fast with a small loss. But the problem with doing this on volatile shares is that you are pretty much asking for each of your trades to be closed out too early.

So think carefully about where to place your stop.

Many traders get closed out as the market opens with wide spreads – don't be one of them. Set sensible stops a reasonable distance away. Use levels below resistance and support to make sure those stops do not get hit.

The one time this really got me was in a share called Spirent. I bought at 107 and stupidly placed a stop at 102. This was *really* stupid. I was asking to get stopped out on a wider spread at 8am – and of course I did!

I should have set it at 95p.

Remember, it's a good thing to go through and check all your stops every night and ensure they are in the right places!

Mistake 5: not investing or trading ... just gambling

It's amazing how many people go gung-ho into the markets and just gamble!

I received an email from a 19-year-old who is obviously very intelligent and could end up being a good investor. But I despair when I read paragraphs like this (I've X'd out the company names):

"I have read a lot of contradictory info on XX and XX across many of the message boards you will undoubtedly be familiar with. Being 5% to 10% down on both, reading this info begins to place doubt in my mind. I do, however, believe these are both potential ten-bagger shares. Could I have your views?"

I took a look at the two shares he mentions. Oh boy. They both turned out to be tiny, illiquid penny shares that should not be touched with a barge pole the length of a pier.

For heaven's sake, one of them had a spread of 13% – you lose 13% just by buying it! Both were high risk, loss-making companies that could just as easily go bust as go up.

What my emailer – and so many other new investors who buy into these shares – don't realise is that they are not investing or even trading ... just gambling.

The words *ten bagger* is what really gets them going. Believe me, ten-times increases are highly unlikely to happen. Trouble is, it all seems so exciting to buy a share at 4p hoping it will become 40p. True, it does happen occasionally. But for every one that makes it, ten go bust.

You will simply lose money over time by buying rubbish and that's all there is to it.

People who make this mistake are invariably egged on by penny share pushers on the bulletin boards. Such pushers are only trying to get them buying something they haven't researched and know nothing about in the hope of getting a big, quick return themselves.

Mistake 6: buying companies with big debt

I covered this a little earlier in the book, but buying companies with big debt really is one of the biggest mistakes you can make.

The one thing no trader wants is to wake up one morning and get a lurching feeling in their stomach as they read:

"Shares suspended at request of company."

What's going on? Well, you hope it's good news. Maybe the company's about to be taken over and the share price is going to soar. But you kind of know something bad is probably up. And that possibly the share you're in ... could be going bust.

Eeek!

How could you have made such a terrible mistake? It's a great share, it's been going up, directors were buying, it wasn't even really very risky! How are you going to tell your spouse you lost ten grand just like that?

Where did it all go wrong?

Did you check the debt?

If it went bust, it will, almost every time, be down to unsustainably large amounts of debt – and the banks have pulled the plug.

Remember my rule for debt (not including oil and mining): get the figure for the full-year pre-tax profit from the company's own last full-year report (not ADVFN financials). And don't buy a company if the net debt is more than three times that.

If you cannot find debt, look for net cash instead. Use my traffic lights system!

A punter favourite that went bust in 2009 was Aero Inventory – I remember going through this one at a seminar. Profits were rising, as was everything else, but I immediately refused to touch it.

Why? Profit was £40m – but net debt? Nearly £500m! I thought anyone would be crazy to buy it. It went bust soon afterwards.

Same with poor old Woolworths. A tremendous debt. I do miss it, though – you could find all kinds of great crap in there.

Example – Homebuy ... definitely not a buy

Homebuy's results looked great in June 2006. Profits up 343% to £12m! The chairman said they were making 'excellent progress'. All the way through the report everything looked fantastic.

Why didn't I buy the shares after the great report?

When I read the Homebuy statement, at first glance I was very tempted. The company had everything in it I like: a growing business, booming profits and turnover and an encouraging outlook. The shares looked like they had plenty of room for growth and I thought about buying some. But then, as usual, I used my traffic lights system to check the company's debt.

And my system picked out this sentence:

"Net bank indebtedness has increased from £28m to £78m."

Full-year profit for Homebuy? £12m. *With a debt of £78m.* That's six and a half times profit. Way over my limit.

Once I established that, I had a look through the report using traffic lights again to find out what the banking facilities were (banking facilities are highlighted in blue by my traffic lights).

I was shocked. The banking facilities were just £75m. In other words:

They were already at the limit of what the banks were currently prepared to lend them!

At this point there was no way I was going to buy the shares. Although the company report was bullish in the extreme, the debt was way too high.

In the days following, the shares were tipped as a buy by many magazines, newspapers and tip sheets. And then, just a few days later, on 17 July, there was a further statement. Homebuy's chairman bought 25,000 shares at 231p, nearly £60,000 worth, and the deputy chairman bought 100,000 shares costing him a massive £231,000!

This provided the impetus for many other private investors to buy shares.

Amazingly, just a few days after these directors had bought shares, investors in Homebuy were greeted with this statement on the newswires:

> "Trading in the shares of Homebuy has been suspended at the company's request pending the outcome of discussions concerning further funding arrangements for the business."

Homebuy went bust and shareholders never got anything back. *They lost all their money.* Judging from the bulletin boards, there were an awful lot of people who lost everything.

If they'd looked at the debt, they would never have bought.

Mistake 7: buying tipped shares

When you're new to buying shares, a huge temptation is to buy shares you have seen tipped in the papers or a magazine or a tip sheet.

Be wary!

Firstly, if the tip is a very small company the market makers will see you coming a mile off, and the shares will be marked up before the market opens. If you buy, you will probably be buying at an inflated price. Market makers could well add 5% or more to the price of the share. And once they've got you in their clutches, what's the next thing they want you to do? Panic you into selling them – and that often works.

Using these wily tactics, the market makers will have sold you shares at a high price, and then buy them back off you at a much lower one. The only people who win ... yes, you've guessed it, those dastardly market makers.

And with any tipped share, whatever its size, you'll see bogus uplift. This is where the bulletin boards (or just searching Google News) come in handy. If a share is rising, check carefully it hasn't been tipped and you're not buying into a false rise.

Okay, so maybe you like the sound of the tipped share, but do your own research first before buying in. And if you still like it, maybe wait a week or two till the shares settle after the tip.

The worst tips to buy are the ones in the weekend press. So many people read these but so too do the market makers. The *Mail on Sunday* can move shares a lot higher on Mondays from its 'Midas' column and so too can weekend commentators in the *FT*.

Mistake 8: selling on ex-dividend day

You must know your ex-dividend dates!

Shares normally drop on ex-dividend date by the amount of the dividend. So a 20p dividend share will drop by 20p. What often happens on ex-day is you see a lot of small investors selling because they think the share they're in is going down fast!

But it's not really going down, because as the shareholder you are getting the equivalent of the drop in cash as a dividend. It's amazing the number of private investors who sell because they think their share is going down for a different reason. It may even be worth buying some more stock on the cheap when this silly blip happens.

So always, always check your ex-dates. If a share you own has dipped in price, it may just be because it's the ex-date.

A good place to check is: **www.digitallook.com/company_diary**. Shares nearly always go ex on a Wednesday. You can also find ex-dates in full-year and interim reports.

Mistake 9: ignoring profit warnings/negatives

Profit warnings

It's crazy to buy into a company that has just produced a profit warning. And it's crazy to hold onto one of your shares that has just issued one.

It's more than likely it'll issue another one, and just because its share price has gone down doesn't mean it won't be going down some more!

Why take the risk? A profit warning means the company is in some kind of trouble or having problems. Why get, or remain, involved on the off chance of a quick bounce back?

A company issuing its first profit warning could even make a good shorting candidate.

Negatives

If you see the odd negative word creeping into a company's statements, don't hang in there, get out! Get the hell out! What's the point of being in a company with negatives coming out when you could be in a company with loads of positives?

If you skipped the chapter on confirmation bias earlier, the time to read it is now.

Mistake 10: over-trading/smugness/greed

Sometimes traders have a good run and make some money.

Which is great. Except that after three or four winning trades they start to get a bit too smug and consider themselves masters of the universe. They feel they know everything and will never lose again.

And so, fuelled by an irresistible urge to carry on the good work, they go nuts and start to trade too much. The discipline goes (after all, they are always right now) and soon the wins become losses.

I get told time and time again by spread betting firms, for example, of people who quickly make big money and then in just a few weeks not only lose the lot but begin to go heavily into the margin and start owing the firm money!

"It's pure greed," said one. "They think they are king of the world when they start winning and blow it."

I guess it's the same as someone who wins a lot at the horses. He bets too much and ends up giving all the winnings back to the bookmaker.

Or someone who goes to a casino. A casino *loves* winners. Because they know the winners come back to win more. Then they lose and try and win back the money they've just lost. And so lose even more.

So, if you've had some nice profits, don't be tempted to change your tactics. Stick to what you were doing and use your normal stakes.

And stop being so smug!

Mistake 11: buying boys-toys/one-product companies

If you're a woman reading this book, you'll know what I mean. Boys love toys! That is: gadgets, technology, computer games, iPod imitators, in fact anything at all which has an *i* in front of it, things that go whirr … kzzpt, ping! – you know what I'm talking about.

And because boys love those toys, when boys look for shares they get drawn to companies that make the toys. There is a rationale behind it in their minds. The company that makes the gadget is going to go up in value 20 times because everyone is going to buy the toy they are developing!

This was the reason why so many of this type of investor lost money in the year 2000. They'd all bought into tech companies. And look what happened! Most of them went belly up. Or, at least, they lost huge percentages of their original values.

But lessons haven't been learned and investors still buy into tech companies with one or two products that may end up being a toy that's used in every household. Unfortunately, nine times out of ten a new technology struggles, time moves on and it becomes obsolete. I'm afraid there are dozens of these types of companies – and I can promise that boys will continue to buy them in the hope of that elusive big share win. Not everyone can be Apple.

Mistake 12: catching a falling knife

Don't try to catch a falling knife – it's an old stock market cliché, but it is so true. Don't be tempted to buy a share that keeps falling. This is the stock market. It is not like going to the sales and picking up a bargain.

One of the few traders I personally know loved buying fallers – he'd never buy anything I bought, because "it's gone up".

I wasn't so different when starting out. I thought I was pretty smart when I first began trading and I thought trying to buy into shares that had just plunged down a lot was a great idea.

Why?

Well, it's obvious! Surely because they've suddenly dropped a lot they must be a bargain, and they're going to go up! Buying shares that have come down a lot appeals to us traders – we start to think about how much money we'll make if the shares go back to their levels of just the previous day.

I remember the first falling knife I tried to catch: a textiles company called Hartstone. This was in the days before you could get prices on the internet. I used to watch the biggest percentage fallers page on Sky Text. I saw Hartstone shares had fallen from 450p to 280p on a profit warning. And they were starting to go back up …

Easy money? You bet.

Excitedly, I bought some shares at 280p. And what a flipping genius I turned out to be. Within two weeks the shares were at 320p and I had dreams of them going back towards 450p. Needless to say, I'd done zero research. Suddenly my dreams were shattered, another profit warning was announced and the shares slumped again – to 175p. I ended up getting out at 120p and with a lesson part-learned.

Only part-learned because I still tried to catch a falling knife another three or four times after that.

It doesn't only apply to me; buying shares that are falling is irresistible. Every single day of the trading year, you can look at ADVFN's list of the top percentage fallers. You will find a share that's down by 20% – and inevitably you can watch as punters pile in to catch that knife.

Of course, during the noughties downturn there were any number of examples. The stop loss will always get you out. Use one!

Mistake 13: buying lots of penny shares

Beware of buying shares with a market cap of less than £15 million.

It might sound tempting to buy a company with, say, a market cap of £4 million. That's because you want to delude yourself that the company could really find its feet and suddenly quadruple its market cap, and you'll be in the money.

The fact is it is highly unlikely, and it's much more probable that you are buying a stinker. On top of that, they are usually very illiquid.

Some of the smallest AIM shares are the worst. They can fall very rapidly and often it can be hard to sell them if everyone else is trying to sell at the same time.

Shares in companies valued at less than £15m also have quite wide spreads, which make them even harder to make money on.

So unless you really think you have spotted a super company at the start of its life, steer clear.

I have met so many people that have bought them and had their fingers burned. The one that comes to mind most is called Provexis.

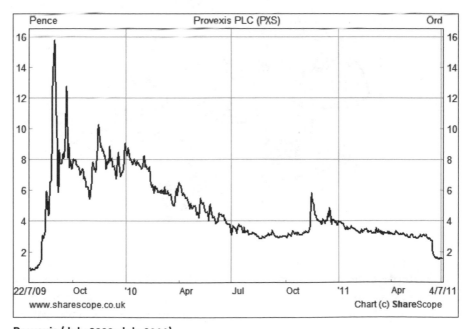

Provexis (July 2009–July 2011)

I remember during one seminar everyone telling me they had bought in to Provexis at around 15p. Apparently it had developed a new sweetener that was going to be bought by Coke or something. One chap excitedly told me in the bar afterwards that he'd bought millions of these shares and that it would turn him into a multimillionaire. It went to 3p.

I just really, really hope he got out in time.

Mistake 14: averaging down

Averaging down usually means. "I'm buying more of the crap share that I originally bought at a much higher price. It's fallen quite a bit, but if I get some at a lower price maybe I'll end up breaking even when the shares bounce back … "

For example: you bought shares in Terrible Prospects plc at 500p, it is now 400p and you buy the same number of TP plc again at 400p. Your effective buying price is now 450p. This means that at any price over 450p you're making money, whereas previously your break-even was 500p. Good news, no?

No. This is a terrible strategy, as your share is going down for a reason and if it goes down some more you will make even bigger losses. (And you've now almost doubled your position size so your losses are going to be twice the size they would have been.)

Of course what you should have done is cut your losses on Terrible Prospects plc at 440p, got the hell out and moved on. This does not mean averaging down will never work, but more likely than not it won't.

It's far better to *average up*. That is, buy more of a share you've already bought and which is rising healthily.

So take my hint: don't average down in the hope you may break even!

A reader writes: When you hold on with your cold dead fingers ...

"I bought Tanfield at 366p and sold at 35p. The price dropped sharply over a two-week period, but I ignored all news and held on and on. Lesson: pay greater attention, respond to market news, drastic price movements and do something when a stop loss is hit. I learnt to let a share go, but not the cheapest way."

Mistake 15: trying to trade indices/day trading

Don't get involved with trading indices too early on in your investing life. Indices are things like the FTSE 100, the Dow, etc.

Index-trading is very difficult. Indices move very fast and a winning position can turn into a big losing one in just an hour or two.

Say you decide the FTSE is going to go down or up and bet on that happening with a spread bet. The index can move fast and unless you can keep a very close eye on it, you can get in trouble. It is quite compelling. You see the FTSE 100 has fallen 70 points in the day and it's lunchtime. 'Well,' you muse to yourself, 'it can't fall much further. It'll probably go up from here!' So you take out a daily up bet. But it goes down some more and you get closed out at a loss.

Take it from me – this type of trading is hard.

Avoid it if you are new to the markets; this also applies to betting on indices like the Dow and the NASDAQ.

> Index trading is like blind knife-throwing – not for beginners.

Mistake 16: hanging onto losers/snatching profits

I covered this a lot near the beginning of the book but it remains the biggest problem for newer traders. That is, hanging on to losing shares hoping they will go back up.

You have to learn to ditch the losers early. And the best way is by setting that stop loss discussed earlier. Quickly dump anything that is beginning to lose you a lot of money. If you have anything in your portfolio down by over 10% take a good look at it, and unless you really have a reason why it might come back up it's usually best to bail.

Snatching at profits is the other big no-no. You need to be looking to make 20%-plus on your trades even if it takes a while. If you are certain you have a good one, give it space to breathe and rise, and don't snatch at a very small profit – because if you do you will never make money overall!

Don't just take a profit because a share you bought has gone up 2p.

> You'll find this cutting losers/running winners theme running throughout this book. I am hammering it home to you ... but it's on purpose.

This is one of the most important things to remember!

Do I have to carry on nagging you?

Mistake 17: buying against the trend or trying to spot a turn

This can end in disaster. You think, 'This company's share price has gone up quite a bit. It must be time for it to go down. I'll go short.' But it keeps going up, you keep your short open and you end up a sore loser. This can happen time and time again. Better to let the trend of your share dictate what you do than trying to guess when the trend has changed.

Try to follow trends and not go against them. Smart arses generally end up as just arses.

Remember: your few quid will be flattened by the rush of much bigger money. Trends stay in place longer than you think and they often go against all reason and logic.

> ### —— A reader writes: Trouble with uptrends ... ——
>
> "I have trouble buying shares that have risen a lot. I refused to buy Optimal Payments at 120 even though I thought it stacked up and loved the business model. It is currently 425. I still think I should buy it and I still haven't!"

Mistake 18: buying small drugs companies

Many people get very excited about smaller drugs companies. They reckon all they need is for one such company to discover a miracle cure or the next Viagra. Then, having invested in their shares, they will wake up millionaires.

I just don't buy these companies. In all my trading years I have seen so many more failures than successes.

The biggest punter favourite that got hit really hard in 2011 was Renovo:

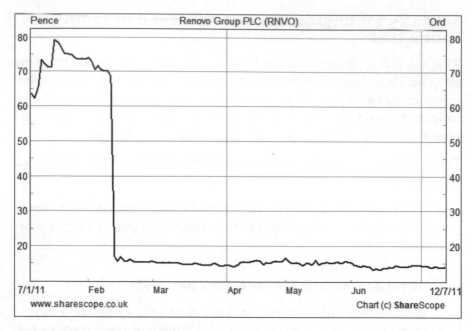

Renovo (January 2011–July 2011)

Traders bought steadily into this one, up to nearly a pound. One morning they woke to the news that Renovo's flagship scar treatment hadn't met its goals in a major trial.

The shares sunk 70% the next day.

Cue plenty of wailing and gnashing of teeth. However, those investing should have realised what a major gamble this actually was. It's the same with lots of other smaller drugs companies. The share prices tend to get too high because of excited investors hoping for the big one. And then they collapse.

Mistake 19: buying just small oil and mining shares

A common one this. ££££ signs are in the trader's eyes. His big idea is to buy small oil and mining stocks – followed by some more small oil and mining stocks. *I bet they find loads of gold in them thar hills, and plenty of black gold beneath them!*

Of course, what usually happens is that the companies keep raising money, they keep finding nothing and the share price keeps going down ...

A recent popular trade like this was Avocet Mining. It mined and it mined and everyone bought in and everyone lost.

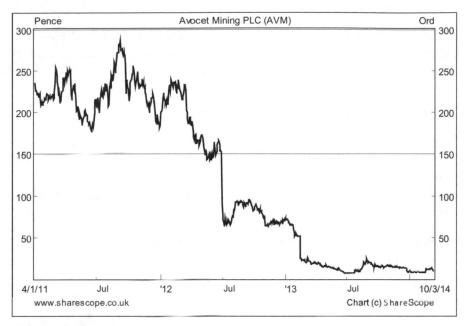

Avocet Mining (January 2011–March 2014)

It's amazing the amount of new traders who go into the market and solely buy small oil and mining exploration stocks like this and very little else. This really is crazy. Portfolios must be balanced.

I have met so many traders who lost fortunes backing a whole host of small oilers. Or actually, even worse, backing just one! Some really do put massive amounts into just one small oiler in the hope of making it big. But it is just too much of a risk.

A reader writes: My petroleum lament ...

"I went crazy and bought just Desire Petroleum. And lots of it. Too much. Unfortunately I bought at 150 and now it sits at 40. What a lesson to learn. Wish I had bought other shares too, now. Having all my money in one has turned a single loss into a portfolio-wide disaster."

At least if you back a few, one might do well, but even then concentrating in one area – and an exceptionally volatile one at that – is still putting it all on one horse.

If your oil and mining shares are merely a sensibly controlled part of a balanced portfolio, and a couple go bust on you, it won't be too bad. If they're all you have, you're in for a world of hurt.

Mistake 20: not running profits

Running profits is one of the hardest things to do in trading. But it's amazing how much money you can make from keeping hold of a really good winner. We've discussed the 20–30% you should be aiming at. How do you know when to hold your nerve in reverses, or whether to hold on past this?

It's important you work it out. For example, I bought Petrofac in the mid-300s and held onto it while it kept on rising!

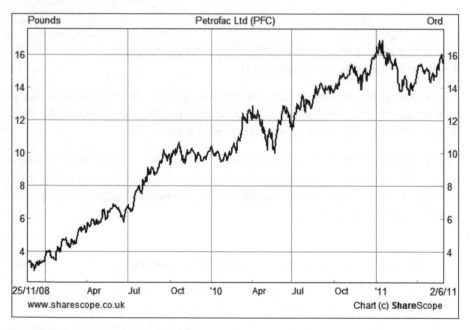

Petrofac (November 2008–June 2011)

If I had taken the profit along the way I might have come out and never gone back in. This can happen so easily and has happened to me.

The best course of action if you're unsure whether to take a profit or not is this: pretend you never saw the share before. Would you buy it from new?

Yes? Hold onto it then. This has helped me hold onto Petrofac even when it has gone down by 70 points on a bad market day.

If you have a winner, try not to let the market push you out of it, as long as no question marks appear.

Mistake 21: buying a system

Over the years I have never come across even one person who has bought a trading system that on its own has made them serious money.

Always ask the person selling you the system why they have not yet retired to a beach somewhere with it.

The worst systems, I believe, are the ones that claim to be able to make you loads of money trading Forex/currencies. Nearly everyone loses trading Forex so it isn't possible. Don't fall for it.

Systems appeal to our laziness – something else is going to do the work for us, yippee! You lazy git. Do some work!

A reader writes: Systematic crapness ...

"I spent £3,000 buying the XXXXXX system. I was told it would be guaranteed profits. I was asked if I wanted to renew it after a year – I said I would love to, the only trouble was that I had lost £24,000 on it so far."

And now, my big mistakes ...

... and the lessons learned!

Don't imagine I always get everything right. I certainly don't! I'm not like those dodgy tipsters who claim every little thing they do is magic. But over the years I've managed to put a stop to most of my original bad habits.

Coffee Republic

My worst trade ever was Coffee Republic. First off, I bought the shares without doing any proper research. I bought them because there was a branch near where I lived and I liked their coffee. What kind of reason was that?

I bought loads at 28p. The share price started falling from the moment I bought it. I bought some more – averaging down. Coffee's got a great mark-up, I argued to myself. The company will do better. I got emotionally involved with my local branch. I started buying more coffee in the hope it might drive up the share price ...

I started interfering:

> *"Why don't you put the muffins up there where people can see them?"*

After all, if everyone bought a muffin with their coffee the share price would start to rise.

I bought more at 8p. Then it became a terrible spiral. I was drinking so much coffee I was having sleepless nights for more than one reason. The company issued one bad report after another and eventually I sold at 3p, losing £7,000.

What a relief once I sold. And sod Coffee Republic.

I go to Starbucks now.

What were the mistakes I'd made? Want the list? Okay, I had:

1. got emotionally involved

2. hadn't set a stop loss

3. averaged down

4. threw good money after bad

5. ignored all the warnings.

Take heed and don't do as I did.

Senior

A slightly different mistake I made was selling a share too early, prompted by fear of losing profits.

I bought shares in engineering and manufacturing firm Senior at 25p. They did really well and doubled up to 50p. Hmm, I thought, yes that'll do – I think I'm going to take profits.

But I didn't do what I usually do and try and re-evaluate it. I never asked myself: if I was coming to this share for the first time, would I buy in at this point? I just lazily sold it. Guess what happened next?

It kept going up ... and up ... to more than 150p.

Why didn't I buy in again as it did so?

I let emotion get in the way. I decided the share was rubbish, really, and hoped it would go down. What stupid trading from me.

And I thought I was the master of holding onto winners. No, sir.

> ### A reader writes: Got greedy, got hit!
>
> "When Avanti Screenmedia went bust I lost £2k. I could have got out with a 50% profit earlier but I was greedy! The biggest lesson of this for me is to make sure I understand what companies do so that I can make not only sensible investment entries but also sensible exits."

Shares don't go up in a straight line and if you have a good one which falls slightly one day, if it still looks cheap, keep holding!

Want another mistake?

(Of course you do, you're lapping this up, I know. 'Robbie – what a plonker! Call yourself a shares expert, you pillock?')

Hardy Oil

Hardy Oil does not bring back happy memories. I simply bought too much of what was a risky oil stock. So when it plummeted overnight on some bad news, I lost more than a grand!

I'd bought in the late 400s and only got out at 350. 'Harmless punts' are not victimless crimes!

 # When Markets Go Down

AKA when the excrement hits the air-circulation device ...

Obviously, shares don't just go up. They can go down, too, and sometimes savagely – often when you least expect it.

You probably hear all the time about bull and bear markets:

- **Bull markets** are basically when shares go up most days, but with the odd sudden correction when shares fall for a short period (say a month).

- **Bear markets** are when shares are generally going down most days, with the odd sudden upward thrust.

If we look at the FTSE 100 chart from 1994 to now, it is rather interesting:

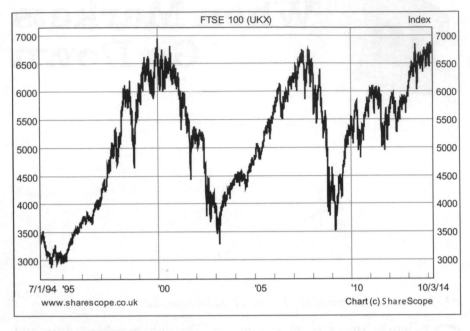

20 years of the FTSE 100

Over a long period of time, look what happened. Ultimately ... not much! In 2014 the FTSE is much the same as it was in 1999. And in 2008.

But it wasn't exactly plain-sailing all that time. We had a bear market from 2000–2003, a bull from 2003–2008, a violent bear from 2008–2009, then a bull through to 2014.

The bottom ended up being around 3500 each time and the top around 6900. Kind of makes me think we are in a holding pattern – perhaps awaiting a new industrial revolution. It may revolve around 3D printing, but I think a new form of transport will change things too. Anyway, time will tell!

If you managed to buy and hold stuff in the bull markets and ditch stuff before the bear markets you should have made your fortune. Unfortunately, no one has timing that good. So we need to know what to do when a bear market strikes.

Fighting bears, bank runs and ... robots

There is nothing worse than seeing your profits made over time suddenly start to disappear. There have been all kinds of events to make the market scared. The worst of recent times, of course, was the fall of Lehman Brothers and the banking crisis. Thousands queued outside Northern Rock branches in the first run on a British bank since the 19th century, and centuries-old titans such as RBS and Bank of Scotland (HBOS since the Halifax merger) had their value decimated.

Indeed we were pretty close to a major financial crash here, and then all bets, as they say, would have been off.

And then there's been turmoil across the Middle East. Bailouts across Europe. Debt swamping weaker countries and scaring even the stronger ones. The US had its credit rating cut in mid-2011.

And to make matters worse?

At the same time, a very real problem – and it's a recent one – is that *Terminator*, and the rise of the machines, has actually started coming true in the markets.

Yes, Arnie is back. The robots really are taking over. Only, rather than being sophisticated humanoid murder machines, these robots are programmed by banks (and other financial companies) to buy and sell stocks as part of computerised trading strategies.

It turns out this can be rather more dangerous for the average citizen; it means a *lot* more volatility in the markets than there would otherwise be.

In May 2010, for example, there was what's been called the 'Flash Crash'. The Dow Jones crashed nearly 1,000 points in just a few minutes, leading to widespread panic. Remarkably, by the end of the day, it had bounced back up again. How? Why?

A large mutual fund had sold off a lot of futures contracts, which caused an initial decline. However, the robo-systems of 'high frequency traders' – those looking for quick hits – then started selling them furiously too. After an incredible bout of buying and selling, their machines decided to slow down or pull out of trading altogether. Liquidity in major shares dried up almost instantly. This caused all the other robots (of banks, hedge funds, ordinary funds, perhaps central banks – all sorts of institutions) to start selling stocks.

Prices rapidly went further down. Lots of stop losses in the market were hit, resulting in countless other automated sells. Some shares even briefly went to zero!

The authorities are trying to stop this happening again by introducing circuit breakers to halt trading. In the UK, any stock down by more than 10% on the day gets halted and goes into auction for five minutes.

Now, in the grand scheme of things, this kind of thing doesn't matter much to me – I'm a medium to longer-term trader. However, if you are new to the markets then you can easily lose a lot of money by being forced out by these events. And all because of Arnie's cousins.

So what do you do if things start to turn ugly?

There are various approaches you can take to all this volatility. One is to conclude: 'The stock market is a [naughty word. – Ed.] and I'm selling up and not coming back. I'm off into premium bonds and lottery tickets.'

Alternatively:

- 'I'll sell most of my stuff as I'm scared I'll lose the lot, and then buy back when things look better.'

- 'I'll try and short loads of stuff while keeping my long-termers open.'

- 'I'll hide behind the sofa till it's safe to come out.'

- 'It doesn't matter, my shares will be higher in six months so I'm off out for a game of golf.'

- 'If everyone is scared, I'm going to buy in at the height of the panic.'

None of these is the correct answer, because there ain't a correct answer.

All I can tell you is what I do. And that is broadly *follow* the market as it changes rather than second-guess where it might turn. So, for instance, as markets turn down, I might start to gradually sell things and go short. As they lift up again, it's time to start buying. And I'll only go against the grain now and then if I think bargains are available and people have sold off unnecessarily, or if I think a rise looks unsustainable.

When to buy and when to sell (when all is going to hell)

My strategies when markets are falling

When markets are falling:

1. I tend to cut spread bets back a lot.

2. I go right through the ISA portfolio and skim a few profits off the top and dump anything that I have any question marks over. However, I usually hold onto my longer-term winners.

3. After that I make sure that there is some cash sitting in the ISA and plenty of legroom in the spread bet accounts.

4. I short the FTSE 100 and use an ETF to make money in my ISA from the market falling (more on that in a sec).

5. I keep an eye open for when to get stuck in somewhere near the bottom, if I can.

Industrial-strength portfolio protection

When things are bad market-wide, the FTSE 100 index as a whole (obviously) goes down. Perversely this gives you an opportunity to protect your portfolio rather than having to sell everything off: you can hold onto your stocks and short the index. And short it with a *vengeance*.

I use something which sounds rather scary but is actually quite easy once you get your head round it. It is the snappily named:

ETFX FTSE 100 super-short strategy (2×) FD

See, told you it was snappy (you can imagine what a barrel of giggles the person who came up with this name must be).

Now, I know what you're thinking. 'Screw this, it sounds complicated, I'll skip it.' See, I also hate finance books when they seem to get complicated. Try and bear with me for a sec. Off for a cup of tea? Coming back to this bit after *Match of the Day*? You bottler!

This really can make you money tax-free in your ISA if the FTSE 100 tanks. It's an ETF, which means *exchange-traded fund*, seemingly a scary dull-sounding thing that will never be worth understanding – but which couldn't be simpler. ETFs are just funds that are purchasable in the same way that shares are – by being listed and traded on exchanges. Easy bloody peasy!

And this *ETFX FTSE 100 super ...* monster is ISA eligible. Its code is SUK2.

So you can tap SUK2 into your monitor and it should come up. If you want to use it, just tap SUK2 into your broker's dealing screen and you should be able to easily buy it in your ISA, just as you would with any share.

But what is it and how does it protect portfolios?

Here's the brilliant thing: it goes up twice as much as the FTSE 100 goes down! (Kind of, there is a time element to be wary of which is too complex for my pea brain.)

So if the FTSE fell, say, 10% and went from 6000 to 5400, this little beauty could make you nearly 20%, as if the FTSE had actually risen to 7200!

Which is why it is called a 2× super short! (In reality, because of some slippage, it doesn't quite do 2× after a while, but it's close.)

You can buy and sell it just like you would a share. You don't have to worry about market makers or market manipulation or anything like that. It simply goes up as the FTSE goes down.

Fairly obviously, if the FTSE goes *up*, it goes down! And twice as much. **So use with caution.**

If you are a medium-term investor and think the market may go down for a bit but then spring back up, this super short is a great portfolio protector.

How about an example showing how I used it last, eh? Good idea!

Example – super short time

It's early 2014. The FTSE is at 6700. My portfolio has done very nicely. But the FTSE has tried a number of times to get through 6700 and I reckon, given it is near the top, and the US is tapering back its bond-buying, it looks unlikely to go much further.

I think my shares are likely to go down a little but I think the market reaction to the downside won't last long.

So I don't want the hassle and cost of selling some of my strong companies. I would rather keep them but try to make some short-term money from the downside to counteract the likely small falls in the portfolio.

So I short the FTSE in a spread bet at 6700. More on that in a minute.

And what about the ISA portfolio?

Here's where SUK2 comes in! I buy 20 grand of SUK2.

The FTSE falls and my stocks fall a bit – not too badly, though. The FTSE drops to 6000. Then tensions ease in the markets and it starts to go up. I sell the SUK2 at the 6000 level, banking around £20,000 profit. The market has gone down 10% so the SUK2 has paid out near 20%. This nicely covers some of the losses made in the ISA on the shares.

The shares then start to go back up with the FTSE. I never had to sell them, so no cost to me. Eventually they recover. The SUK2 has done its job.

> *What about if I was wrong and the shares carried on going up and I had the SUK2?*
>
> Well, okay, that's fine! Let's say the FTSE carried on going up. I would have lost a few quid on the SUK2, but my shares would have probably gone up. I could have sold the SUK2 for a small loss, no damage done, especially as shares would be going up anyway.
>
> If the FTSE had continued to go down I could have carried on holding – and perhaps increased – the SUK2.

Now tell me: what have we really been doing using the SUK2?

HEDGING! Yes, we have indeed been acting like a hedge fund, and making money on the downs as well as the ups! Clever old us!

Look, I hope I managed to explain it. If you are still unsure, stick SUK2 on your monitor and see how it moves against the FTSE.

The other strategy is easier to explain and that is simply shorting the FTSE in a spread bet account. Just log into your spread account, and sell the FTSE at whatever pounds per point you think you can afford or would help hedge your portfolio.

> In spread betting you don't need to own something in order to sell. There is no magical shorting button – 'sell' basically just means 'short' if you don't have a position open in a particular share.

Shorting the FTSE at 6700 – closing the bet as it turns at 6000 – makes 700 points profit. At, say, £20 a point, that's a lovely gain of £14,000.

We could also be clever and as it goes down use a trailing stop loss to seal in profits (see Chapter 19, on spread betting, for more!).

The FTSE trades 24 hours a day with spread bets and the price can change a lot overnight, so if you're using a stop loss be prepared to get stopped out overnight …

Other things to think about when the market is sinking

- In general it is FTSE 100 stocks that get hit suddenly and quickly rather than the smaller stocks.

- In particular, commodity stocks tend to get hit a lot as investors bale out.

- Do a stress-check: can you afford to lose, say, 40% of what you have in the market if it crashes badly? Have you overdone it using leverage with spread bets or CFDs? It's a good time for a rethink and some checks and balances to ensure you are not in for more than you should be.

- It's also a good time to think about whether you need a few more 'defensive' shares in your portfolio. For instance, shares in supermarkets and utilities often go up in downturns, as people may abandon luxuries but they'll always need food and water.

Consider what sort of downturn you are in

Above all, you need to think carefully about why the market is tanking. Is it just a short-term overreaction thanks to a load of sell-happy robots? Or is it more serious?

The fallout from the Lehman Brothers collapse and the credit crunch was the most serious crisis of recent times. There was a squeak of a chance the whole financial system was in trouble and so it really did seem sensible to keep a lot of cash on the sidelines to be on the safe side. Even if, when we were out of the woods, markets rallied.

In general, massively calamitous events don't happen very often. But perhaps one day we'll all get caught out.

Black swan events – a time to buy?

A 'black swan' event is not when your wife suggests renting a Natalie Portman film. It's simply a neat, slightly buzz-wordy phrase for a highly significant event that comes right out of the blue.

There are usually one or two a year. For example, it could be the terrible earthquake that hit Japan in 2011. Or some kind of awful unexpected terrorist attack.

And this might surprise you: whilst a black swan event can often be a terrible time to be a human being, it's usually a great buying opportunity for shares. Sad but true. Often just a day or two after the event itself, you can pick up some very good bargains. I know it's not nice to think about, but it probably shouldn't be ignored.

Of course, if something apocalyptic happens – like a nuclear bomb being detonated in London – then all bets are off. But during nearly every unexpected bad event, the markets initially knee-jerk downwards, helped by crazy robots. Then when we've had time to think about things, everyone realises, 'Hey, it's not as bad as we thought it was,' and the market duly heads back up.

> I keep one spread betting account open with nothing in it except for the funds to buy cheap stock if there is a black swan event.

Look at any event. The 2011 earthquake in Japan. The uprisings in Egypt and Libya the same year.

At each such event, the market gets scared and sells off, thinking the end of the world is nigh. Then a few days later it says, 'Oh, actually, it's not all that bad, things will work out.'

So don't be scared.

If you are a real scaredy cat then is trading really for you? I have a friend who thinks the world is going to end up like some brutal war-torn sci-fi movie. She has about 300 cans of Tesco's value baked beans stashed away. Oh, and just for variety, 100 cans of Tesco's value sausages and beans.

Personally I would rather kill myself staggering about in an alien-ruled nuclear winter than end up in a basement with cans of old beans.

Which leads me to two rough rules for trading:

- Buy when everyone is selling.
- Sell when everyone is buying.

In other words, buy when everyone else is crapping themselves that they will lose all their money. Sell when they are all feeling smug and that they've made a lot of money.

In either case, they are almost certainly wrong – fear or greed, not sensible investing, has got the upper hand with them – and you can make money from being a cool, calm, collected Mr Spock who is right.

> These rules refer to the market as a whole diving or soaring – not to individual shares. And they don't mean you can disregard research and buy any old thing. They're just good times to get in or out of worthwhile shares.

Simple? Well, it does work. But it's easy to write and harder to do. We are like pack animals and want to do whatever everyone else does.

That's why you don't walk down the street with no clothes on.

Okay, if you do, congrats, you must be very pleased with what's down there.

Downturn strategies summary

- Consider cash and cutting positions but don't panic.
- Cut stakes in volatile stocks.
- Use shorting tools like SUK2 and spread betting.
- Consider buying after a black swan event.

Do you know what the biggest clues are that a bear market might be about to get underway? Here they are ...

Incoming bear market signs

- Sunday newspaper headlines say things like: 'Markets soar as investors pile in', 'Our experts predict the FTSE will hit all-time highs'.

- You take a cab and the cabbie says: "Got some shares? Mine are doing really well."

- You visit the doctor or dentist and you see share prices instead of medical notes on his computer screen.

- A friend says: "I've got this really hot share tip, this company's got this amazing new product, everyone'll want it and you'll be in right at the bottom!"

- The bulletin boards are full of subject lines like "Fill ya boots with _____".

- Coffee shops are jammed with people paying £5 for a coffee.

- And the possible tipping point: Starbucks starts doing tastings and free coffee afternoons ...

> A bear market is a 6 to 18 month period when the kids get no pocket money, the wife gets no shopping and the husband gets no sex.

PART V
The Next Level

"The great rule is not to talk about money with people who have much more or much less than you."

– Katharine Whitehorn

Spread Betting

Introduction

Ooooh, spread betting ... I don't mention this in public much. If I do mention it at a gathering I usually get a pitying look and am instantly classified as a gambler itching to stick his last quid in one of the fruit machines at William Hill.

Or else people immediately look bored and go onto someone else more interesting.

However, as a trader or investor, you should definitely be interested in spread betting.

I can happily tell you that some of the profits from my spread betting accounts this year helped me buy a property and do it up! I withdrew profits of more than £350,000 from spread betting recently – and I still have more than half a million in spread bet accounts as I write.

I have used it more and more and I've surprised myself by how much money I have made: and those profits are all tax-free, too! My belief is that all investors and traders should use spread betting alongside their ISA to trade totally free from the clutches of the bowler-hatted Revenue men.

There have been the odd noises that they want to tax spread betting. Given most people lose at it, that seems pretty unlikely, though of course it's always possible – particularly if they can work out a way of zapping those who make profits on it regularly. So obviously tax rules may have changed by the time you read this. But I hope not!

> There is a very small grey area already in regards to tax: that is, if all you do is spread bet and nothing else and have no other income it is vaguely possible they could argue you are doing it as a profession rather than simply gambling. Unlikely, I think, but you never know. Anyway, it's best to think of spread betting as an extra rather than a mainline, so hopefully this wouldn't affect you anyway.

I meet people at seminars who are simply scared of spread betting. Others struggle to get their heads round it at all. Some say: "Oh, it sounds like gambling."

Okay, there's no way round it: it *is* gambling. You never own any shares – you're simply betting on a price to go up or down, and you win or lose depending on what the market actually does. Your spread betting portfolio is literally just a list of bets. But this also means that spread betting is another way of tax-free trading. And it comes with its own advantages (and disadvantages) that make it well worth exploring, even if just as an adjunct to your ISA trading.

Also, it *is* worth being scared of – but only in the sense that you need to respect it and use it with care.

But difficult to get your head round? Not after this chapter, I hope!

In a nutshell

Okay, so explain what this strange-sounding activity actually is in a nutshell, please!

It's really simple. With spread betting, instead of buying or selling shares in the market, you are betting on the shares to go up or down with (what's essentially) a bookmaker. Which is why it's called spread *betting*!

The *spread* part simply comes from the fact that, as every trade is commission-free, firms make their money from the spread between the buy and sell price (that and the monumental losses that quite a lot of people build up through twatting around with leverage).

So, you're having a *bet* something is going to go up or down rather than making an investment in a company by buying its shares. You do not buy or sell any real shares at all in the process.

Spread betting is like visiting a bookie at the races, rather than buying an actual share in a race horse.

But why bother with it at all – why not just buy or sell shares in a normal account? What's the big deal about having a spread betting account?

Well, there are some amazing attractions.

Attractions of spread betting

Attraction 1: it's tax-free

Spread betting is tax-free because it's considered to be gambling. Governments reckon you are more likely to lose and don't fancy you being able to offset spread betting losses against tax! As I said above there are a few noises about taxing it but I think for the foreseeable future it should remain tax-free. There's also no stamp duty.

Attraction 2: you can trade on credit – but be cautious!

Being able to trade on credit is quite amazing when you think about it. It's a bit like having a spread betting credit card.

For many trades, spread betting firms give you what's called *margin* (or *leverage*). What this means in practice is many firms will let you trade on credit!

There is no sign up at the spread firms like in shops in dodgy areas to the effect of: 'Don't ask for credit or you'll get a punch in the mouth.' Indeed, the motto is more like:

'Please ask for credit and we will give you as much as we can.'

Why are they so keen to give us credit? Well, spread firms make a profit out of every trade (winners and losers: the spread nets them something each time). Therefore it is in their interest for you to bet as much and as often as possible.

And boy, they give you a lot of credit. Give them £10,000 and in many cases you will be able to trade up to £100,000 of shares! In other words, you only have to put down 10% of the money to trade.

So you could buy ten grand's worth of a stock for just a grand. You're thinking: "Ah, now I can see why it's so popular … "

However, this must come with a warning. You shouldn't use all the credit available – the mantra *only bet with money you can afford to lose* must be followed if you are to avoid life-shattering disaster.

Attraction 3: bet on things to go down (short)

If you think the market is going to crash or you want some insurance against that happening, you can go *short*. (More on shorting a bit later.)

Attraction 4: play the indices or commodities

With spread betting you can make money on whether the FTSE goes up or down, and ditto for the Dow. Or gold. Or oil, the Yen, sugar – loads of other things.

Attraction 5: You can get guaranteed stop losses

If you have a stop loss with a normal broker and shares tank before the opening, your stop will not save you. But with a spread bet account you can get a guaranteed stop – and that *will* save you. You will be stopped out at the price you ask for, even if the share collapses before market opening.

So what are the downsides to spread betting, then?

Downsides of spread betting

Downside 1: wider spreads than brokers

Well, it's fair enough – the spread firms aren't a charity and part of the way they make money from you is by charging you a wider spread than brokers when you open your bet and when you take a profit or loss on it. So it costs. In other words, if the spread in the share market is 500 to sell and 501 to buy, expect the spread betting prices to be 498 to sell and 503 to buy. That's why they make a profit every time you bet!

Downside 2: longer-term trades get pricey

The longer you keep open a spread bet, the more it costs you. Every three months or so you have to close your bet and re-open it, which means you pay the spread again. And the further out you set the expiry date for your bet, the bigger the spread. More on that in a mo.

Downside 3: spread betting could make you over-trade

Spread bet sites are designed to be addictive. After all, the spread bet firms make more money the more you trade. It's very exciting to see the amount of money you are making or losing going up and down. And everything is made out to be sweet and simple. But this can make you trade too much, so beware!

Downside 4: losses are unlimited

If you don't set a guaranteed stop loss when opening your bet (which costs you even more on the spread) your losses aren't limited to your stake.

We'll discuss all of this shortly. But first I want to show you how easy it is to spread bet (either shares or indices). The best way to describe spread betting is to dive right in and look at some examples.

Example – a spread bet, long, and held to bet expiry

BSkyB shares are going up and you want some of the action. The shares are currently priced at 500 501 (500 to sell, 501 to buy) in the stock market.

However, you only want a relatively short-term exposure (say three months), so you decide to take out a spread bet.

You log onto your spread betting firm's site (or give them a call on the phone) and find the BSkyB spread betting price is 500–505 (i.e. 500 to sell, and 505 to buy).

Now it's very simple:

- If you think the shares are going *down*, you want to short them. Sell at 500p.

- If you think the shares are going *up*, you want to go long. Then Buy at 505p.

In this case, you think BSkyB shares are going up, so you buy at 505.

The next decision is how many pounds a point you want to stake. If you're very optimistic you'll bet a high amount, but if you're more cautious (and risk-averse) you'll bet a low amount. In this case, let's say you bet £10 a point.

The following table shows what your profit will be, depending on the BSkyB share price at the expiry of your bet:

BSkyB price	Profit (£)
480	-250
485	-200
490	-150
495	-100
500	-50
505	0
510	+50
515	+100
520	+150
525	+200
530	+250
535	+300

For example, at bet expiry if the BSkyB share price is 530, you will make £250. (This is a cash profit that will be deposited in your spread betting account.) But if the BSkyB share price is 485 at bet expiry, you will lose £200.

The formula to work out your profit is simply:

```
stake amount × (final price - price bought at)
```

So, if the final price is 515, the calculation is:

```
£10 × (515 - 505) = £100 profit
```

If, instead of betting £10 per point, you had bet only £1 per point, then the profit numbers in the above table would be divided by 10. Or, if you had bet £100 per point, then the profit numbers in the above table would be multiplied by 10.

It's usually easiest just to think in terms of numbers of points made or lost. For example, if the BSkyB share price is 520 at bet expiry, then you've made 15 points (520 minus 505). Then simply multiply the points you have made by your original pounds per point.

Example – a spread bet, short, and held to bet expiry

In the previous example we looked at the case when you were *bullish* (optimistic) on BSkyB and so went *long* (i.e. you bought a spread bet).

In this example, we'll look at the case where you are *bearish* (pessimistic) on BSkyB and so will *short* it (i.e. you will sell a spread bet).

Don't get confused here: you don't have to own in order to sell. It's just the way they phrase a bet on something to go down.

To quickly recap prevailing prices:

- the **share price quote** is: 500–501

- the **spread betting quote** is: 500–505.

In the first example, you bought the spread bet at 505. This time you will sell at 500. Again, you will bet £10 per point.

The next table shows what your profit will be, depending on the BSkyB share price at the expiry of your bet.

As you can see, the profit profile of the trade is essentially the reverse of that in the first example. If the share price falls to 490 at bet expiry, then you make a profit of £100. But if the share is at 535 at bet expiry, you will lose £350.

BSkyB price	Profit (£)
480	+200
485	+150
490	+100
495	+50
500	0
505	-50
510	-100
515	-150
520	-200
525	-250
530	-300
535	-350

The general formula for calculating profits for *short* trades is:

```
stake amount × (price sold at - final price)
```

So, if the final price is 495, the calculation is:

```
£10 × (500 - 495) = £100 profit
```

As before, just think in terms of points made or lost. And then multiply that by the pounds per point to get the cash profit.

Example – a spread bet, long, and closed before bet expiry

Quarterly spread bets have a date at which they expire. At expiry the bet is settled at the prevailing price in the underlying market (i.e. the price of the underlying shares). In the first example above, if the underlying market (BSkyB shares trading in the stock market) was priced at 520 at bet expiry, the spread bet is settled at 520. Expiry of a spread bet can be considered like the end of a horse race – when the result is known, and the winnings paid out.

However, unlike a horse race, spread bets can be *closed out before expiry*.

Think about that for a moment – that's quite a useful option!

Imagine placing a bet on a horse race and after two bends your horse is out in front. Wouldn't it be good if you could stop the race right there and collect your winnings immediately? But you can't. You have to hold on until the end of the race and possibly see your horse overtaken by others.

But this isn't a problem with spread betting. You can effectively 'stop the race' whenever you like. This is what is meant by closing out before expiry.

This can happen because the spread betting firms are quoting prices all the time – even after the 'race' has started.

Let's look at the first example again.

You bought the spread bet at 505 for £10 per point. After a few days the spread bet price is 515–520. The price has moved up and you want to close your bet immediately and bank your profit, instead of waiting until expiry of the bet.

No problem. You close your bet by making an opposite bet. In other words:

1. If you *bought* the bet originally (i.e. had a *long* position), you would close it by *selling* the bet.

2. If you *sold* the bet originally (i.e. had a *short* position), you would close it by *buying* the bet.

In this case, you are long, and so you would close the bet by selling the bet (at the same pounds per point: £10). To recap, the spread bet price is 515–520, and so the selling price is 515.

The following table summarises the prices and action taken to open and then close out a bet before expiry:

Market action	Value
Original spread bet price	500–505
Spread bet bought at	505
Stake (pounds per point)	£10
Spread bet price a few days later	515–520
Spread bet sold at (effectively closing the bet)	515
Points made	10 (515 - 505)
Profit	£100 (£10 × 10)

So, we can see that this facility is very powerful indeed. It allows the spread bettor to close bets when they're winning.

You can't do that at Goodwood!

Expiry dates

Most expiry dates for spread bets are set at three-monthly intervals – March, June, September and December. The expiry date itself is usually the third Tuesday of the month for shares, and the third Friday for indices.

Recently spread bet firms have tended to allow expiry well into the future – at IG, for example, you've been able to go nine months ahead.

I usually go for the furthest quarter possible. Otherwise you can go for a rolling daily. Here the spread is tight but you pay a small charge every day for keeping the bet open.

A rule of thumb is that a rolling bet usually works out as costing more after two to three weeks. But in the end there isn't that much in it so I wouldn't worry too much.

But one other thing to note: although you have chosen an expiry date you can *extend* that date if you want to. That's called …

Rolling over

… rolling over. Normally, when your bet expires you will *have* to take your profit or loss – not a bad discipline. But you can keep a trade open by what's called a *rollover*.

A rollover means you close out the current trade, and open a new position in a spread bet with a further-out expiry date. Effectively, you roll over the position. You take your profit or loss and a whole new trade is set up. Unfortunately, you have to pay for this via a new spread, but most firms will give you a decent discount on that.

Some people argue that you should just let all bets expire on their expiry date, clear your slate and start again. Some merit to that, I think, as it forces you to re-assess your current strategy.

Phew – that was a lot to get through. Still with me? Look, if you're not, don't worry, put your feet up and read it again. It will sink in, I promise. Took me a while to get my head round it too.

Dangers of over-exposure

When you're spread betting, you get exposure to shares without putting up all the money you'd have to if trading in a normal share account. That's good and bad news.

For example, I could buy £10 a point of BSkyB – giving me, in effect, exposure to £5,000 of shares without having to put up the five grand. Most spread firms will allow you to trade that with only 10% upfront – so you'd only need to have £500 in your account.

This is called 'margin', 'leverage', 'gearing' and 'being an idiot'.

What happens if the shares sink 200 points and you suddenly owe £2,000?

Can you afford to pay?

And what happens if you open a lot of trades and they all go wrong, leaving you with a whopping great bill?

Always check your spread account. Think about a few worst-case scenarios and check carefully that you are not overdoing it. You must work out what your exposure is and whether you can afford that exposure.

Here is my handy cut-out-and-keep guide to spread bet exposure. Make sure you don't put on a bigger bet than you realise.

Cut-out-and-keep exposure check!

Spread bet size	Equivalent size in share market
£5 per point	500 shares
£10 per point	1,000 shares
£20 per point	2,000 shares
£50 per point	5,000 shares

Your bet	Share price (p)	Exposure
£10 per point	500	£5,000 (10 × 500)
£10 per point	1000	£10,000 (10 × 1000)
£20 per point	100	£2,000 (20 × 100)

> **NT Note!** Exposure is where you have to be careful and make sure you are not playing with money you can't afford to lose. Always remember: you don't *have* to use margin! You are perfectly free to spread bet just using cash you've deposited in your account.

> DON'T GET HIM STARTED
> ON HOW HIS TOTAL EXPOSURE
> PARAMETERS WORK···

(Cartoon from *The Naked Trader's Guide to Spread Betting*.)

Spreads and costs

There is no point in moaning about being charged extra spread whenever you do a deal with a spread betting firm. Remember, you do not have to pay commission when spread betting *and* you don't pay the dreaded stamp duty *and* you don't have to pay capital gains tax on any winnings.

How do the costs compare between normal trading and spread betting?

It's quite hard to work that one out. Different spread firms charge different spreads at different times. It also depends on how you like to trade.

Let's take the BSkyB example again and work out a rough cost comparison between normal share dealing and spread trading.

In this example we will say the shares were 500–501 in the stock market and 500–505 in the spread market when the shares were bought.

Then we'll say the shares go up to 549–550 in the normal market and 548–553 in the spread market.

Normal share trade

- Buy 1,000 shares at 501p. Value = £5,010

- Buying costs: broker commission = £12.50; stamp duty = £25.05

- Sell 1,000 shares at 549p. Value = £5,490

- Selling costs: broker commission = £12.50

- Gross profit = £480. Costs = £50.05

- Net profit = £429.95

Spread trade

- Buy £10 a point at 505p. Sell at 548p. No costs.

- Profit = £430

The comparison trades are summarised in the following table:

	Shares	Spread bet
Position opened	Buy 1,000 shares at 501	Buy at 505 for £10 per point
Broker commission	£12.50	£0
Stamp duty	£25.05	£0
Position closed	Sell 1,000 shares at 549	Sell at 548 for £10 per point
Broker commission	£12.50	£0
Trade profit calculation	1,000 × (549 - 501) = £480	(548 - 505) × £10 = £430
Costs	£50.05	£0
Net profit	£429.95	£430

So, not much in it there – and I reckon generally there is no difference. The above calculation assumes a quarterly bet that you close out before expiry, though. If you use a rolling daily remember you get charged a little every night to keep it open.

It is probably cheaper to use spread betting if you are a larger trader, not particularly holding for the longish term, and you easily make more than £11,000 profit a year (the CGT allowance for 2014/15).

Say you'd already used up your capital gains tax allowance: top-rate taxpayers would have to pay 28% tax on our example profit of £430; a massive £120! In this case, it would be much better to spread bet than buy in the normal market. An ISA should be your first port of call for tax-free profits, though.

I could come up with loads of different examples and each one would throw up a different cost comparison.

For example, Vodafone – one of the most actively traded shares on the market – would probably be cheaper to spread bet as the spread will always be very tight. But a company with a 3–4% spread might be better off being traded elsewhere.

> The rule of thumb is: the tighter the spread given by the spread firm, the more cost-effective spread betting is.

Also, remember, if you are rolling over you are increasing your costs again.

Stop losses

I've nattered on about stop losses throughout the book. One of the greatest benefits of spread betting is that their stop losses tend to get you out faster than a broker can.

But there are a few points you should understand.

Let's say you've bought a BSkyB spread bet at 505p. You decide your stop loss should be about 50 points, so you set a stop at 455p. If the share goes below that, you'd rather take the loss now than rack up any more.

There are *two* different types of spread-bet stop loss:

1. Ordinary stop loss

The spread firm will try to get you out at the stop price, but if the share is moving fast you may end up being closed out at, say, 445p rather than 455p.

2. Guaranteed stop loss

A guaranteed stop loss means what it says – you will be closed out at 455p. But a guaranteed stop loss will cost you a bit of extra spread, so your 505p buying price may be adjusted to something like 507p, costing you the equivalent of £20 on your £10 per point buy.

> I would say it's generally worth paying the extra spread and getting the guarantee if you are a very new trader. Once you are confident then perhaps it isn't worth paying the extra spread every time. I generally don't use guaranteed stops myself.

Take this example. You've bought BSkyB at 505p but a week later the company issues an early morning statement. The market doesn't like it and the shares open at 355p.

Under an ordinary stop loss you will be closed out at 355p – a full 100 points lower than your stop loss. That would cost you £1,000 more (at £10 per point) than if you'd used the guaranteed stop loss of 455p. Because the firm guaranteed you 455p, that's the price you'd get even though the shares opened at 355p.

Here's another view on guaranteed stop losses from one of my readers who is a profitable trader using spread bets:

"I think of the charge for the guaranteed stop losses as an insurance premium, debited via the greater quoted spread. It's an insurance policy with an agreed excess. You have to consider whether routinely paying the premium and occasionally falling foul of the excess whenever the stop loss is triggered – either by the real dive which you wanted protection against, or by the all-too-frequent momentary spikes in share price movement – is justifiable in relation to your own circumstances.

"It probably makes sense, especially in somebody's first year, and particularly where s/he is unable to constantly monitor the market. But the user needs to be aware that it is an expensive form of protection – thanks mainly to those unexpected and unwanted excess charges which kick in unnecessarily whenever a transient spike occurs or is engineered. They kick in far more often than the real situation of a share price collapse. What's more, the spread bet companies know that when the annoyed punter has been kicked out of a bet by one of these many false alarms, s/he will quite likely reopen the bet – paying the added spread again each time."

One word of warning on stop losses in spread betting – as with those in your broker trading, set them at a decent point away from your trade. That's because, during the first few minutes of trading, spreads can be stupidly wide and you could get caught and stopped out on one rogue early trade.

I've had horror stories from several readers who got stopped out early in the morning by some rogue trade. And if your spread firm is especially nasty they might even close you out on purpose!

You must handle and control your stop losses in the best way you can and learn by experience. It could well be that the best plan is to use guaranteed stop losses on all your trades. At least then you know, and can control, your maximum possible loss.

Margin calls

A margin call is a call you don't want to get! I'm glad to say I haven't had one since 1999! (When obviously I partied like it was ... 1999.)

A margin call means one or more of your positions are losing heavily and the spread firm wants to see the colour of your money. Don't worry, they are very discreet, so if you don't want your other half to know you've been losing they won't find out. (But keeping trading secret is never the *best* of ideas for long-term happiness.)

They will normally ask you for the money needed to cover some of the losses you are racking up. The best solution is to use a debit card and hand the money over right away.

Is it a wake-up call?

If you get a margin call, you may also want to consider whether it is a wake-up call. Have your positions got away from you and should you close out, take the loss and go flat for a few days? Are you definitely playing with money you can afford to lose?

Be honest with yourself. Don't pretend the losses aren't too bad and you're 'gonna get them back'.

> When you get the margin call, treat it as a wake-up call!

If you owe a spread firm money, it is backed by the law – so they can send the boys round. Cough up!

The case of Nick Levene, who famously lost £50 million-plus spread betting, shows how big debts can mount up – quickly. Google him for a hair-raising article or two.

Spread firms have actually put some structures in place to try and stop this happening, and will call and email you very fast if you go over your limit. Even so, the above scenario could still happen.

Here are my thoughts on margin/leverage.

Say you have £15,000 you can afford to lose and you want to spread bet. Put £5,000 into the spread account. This could give you access to £50,000 of shares. But only use a little of that leverage. In this situation, ensure you only give yourself access to £20,000 of shares. Once you have too much exposure, close out some positions or bank profits.

Spread betting strategies

My main uses of spread betting are (in no particular order):

- shorting FTSE 100 and FTSE 250 companies in a bear market
- buying companies when I'm out of cash in my ISA to be free of capital gains tax
- buying or selling the FTSE 100 index at certain times
- buying shares on a shorter-term basis.

I treat most trades as short-term (anything between a week and six months). But if they are going really well, I'll stick with them; I have held the odd spread bet for over a year.

> The major lesson I've learned with spread betting is: keep an open mind and change strategies as the market changes.

Playing the indices via spread betting

One of the advantages of spread betting is that it does give you the chance to bet on the indices – e.g. the entire FTSE 100 taken as a whole – although this is not something I do a lot of.

To spread bet the indices is similar to buying or selling a normal share. You're just betting on a number (in this case the index value) going up and down.

So, if the FTSE is, say, 6500, you can take out a quarterly or daily spread bet. You can buy at the offered price or sell at it. You can bet on it to go up or down. Or you can bet on the Dow, Nikkei or any other index.

As I've already said, I don't buy or sell the indices much, as to me it's just gambling. One use I do have for it is to have a short on the FTSE if the market has had a very good run and looks toppy.

For example, if you had a FTSE short open during 2008–2009 you could have made a lot of money!

Opening an account

In the days of yore, there were only two companies that took spread bets – IG and City Index – but now there are tons of spread bet companies with various offerings.

Many traders have two or three accounts and use different firms depending on a particular trade.

Some firms specialise in tiny bets, others have minimum stakes. Some have smaller spreads than others.

Most spread bet companies want you to win. That's because every time you put on a trade they should make money. They should simply put on whatever trade you make themselves in the market and they pocket the extra spread charged.

A winning client is more likely to carry on spread betting, and so make them a profit, whereas a client is more likely to call it a day after racking up losses.

But some companies take what can be described as an adversarial stance towards you. You put on trades and they don't take out a similar trade in the market to ride the trade with you and just make money on the extra spread. In effect, they want you to lose!

It's up to you to pick one or two firms – get to know them and see if you like the way you get treated. If you don't like them, there will always be plenty of others!

The companies that I use and why

I have visited all the companies I use to check they are not out to get me! In each case there definitely wasn't a shady looking bloke in a peaked cap trying to bet against clients or stop them from winning.

So here are the four spread bet firms I use all the time:

IG

www.ig.com/nakedtrader

IG is excellent. It offers a huge range of bets including sectors and covers most small caps. It even tells you how many of its clients are long or short of a share (do the opposite of their clients to win!). Great platform, super execution.

Spreadex

www.spreadex.com/nakedtrader

If there's a small company IG won't let you bet on, Spreadex will! It is happy for you to bet on pretty much everything, including the *very* small companies. Customer service is excellent. It even sometimes sees what I have in my account and emails me reports on those companies. That is truly good service!

Capital Spreads

www.capitalspreads.com/ntrader

A Capital Spreads account is a nice account for new starters because it makes a stop loss compulsory. One is set up for you the moment you place a trade, though you can of course change it. This firm is probably the most competitive for spreads for FTSE 250 and FTSE 100 shares.

Spreadco

www.spreadco.com/nakedtrader

Spreadco is one of the best for trading indices like the FTSE as it offers a spread of just 0.8 on the FTSE, when most others are wider at 1 or 2 points. If you trade the FTSE a few times, it will save you a fair few quid. Execution is very fast here.

So that's spread betting. It's a really useful tool – as long you don't go crazy! If you want even more spread betting strategies and do's and dont's, I think you'll really enjoy my spread betting book. It's called, well, *The Naked Trader's Guide to Spread Betting*.

It's packed with tons of trading examples, the biggest mistakes spread bettors make, investigative visits to the two top spread bet firms, and plenty of spread betting ideas and strategies.

You can probably find it in the bookshop near where you found this one, or else it's easy to order on the internet. You can grab it from my site (**www.nakedtrader.co.uk**) or wherever you like.

Naked Trader's 10 golden rules for spread betting

1. Make sure you know what you're doing!

2. Use it for shorter-term trading.

3. Beware of trading volatile indices.

4. Don't open too many positions.

5. Keep stakes to a level you can afford.

6. Be strict with your stop losses.

7. Remember to trade the opposite way when closing.

8. A margin call could be a wake-up call.

9. Consider a guaranteed stop loss on every trade.

10. Don't tell the wife how much you're losing.[4]

---

4   That's a joke. If you're having to hide losses, STOP BETTING NOW. Gambling is even more dangerous in spread betting. Houses have been lost.

CFDs and Other Stuff

CFDs

CFDs or *contracts for difference* are becoming increasingly popular. Though I don't use them that much myself. Why? Simple: unlike spread betting they are subject to that nasty capital gains tax.

I would actually advise new investors to avoid CFDs. They are way too easy to trade using credit and that could lead you to over-trade.

But once you are experienced there is no reason why you should not add them to your trading arsenal.

Like I said, I don't tend to use them that much – but I *do* use CFDs in my SIPP. And I have found that quite profitable.

If CFDs interest you, make sure you read up as much as you can about them and only go ahead when you're sure you know everything. Make sure you understand completely what you are doing!

What are CFDs?

Instead of buying a share, with CFDs you are buying a contract for difference (hence CFD). In effect, like a spread bet, you are buying a contract with a bookmaker or broker, rather than buying the share directly.

So, if a share is 500 to sell and 501 to buy, you should be able to buy or sell a CFD at that price. The difference is:

- You can *sell* at 500, without having to own the share (i.e. you can short easily). So you can make money on it if it falls.

- You don't have to pay any stamp duty. But you *do* have to pay an interest charge each day instead; expect roughly 70p a day on a £5,000 long.

Because of the interest charge, CFDs should be treated as a shortish-term tool: say one day to three months.

You will find there are two types of CFDs:

1. *Straightforward* (no difference really to shares); expect to pay about £10 a deal.

2. *Direct market access* (DMA); expect to pay nearer £20 or a percentage.

With DMA CFDs you can put your order directly on the order book and therefore become, in effect, a market maker and try to buy at the sell price.

As this is generally a book for beginners, I'm going to leave it there. If you want to know how to place DMA orders, I can show you live at a seminar. Explaining it here would take too long.

I do believe CFDs are going to get more and more popular. The main thing, if you open a CFD account, is to *take it slowly*. Start with one or two small trades until you are certain you know what you are doing.

Remember: CFDs are not suitable for long-term investment. If you are thinking of buying a share with a one or two-year view, just buy it in the normal market as it will end up cheaper. **Six months max for CFDs, okay? (Personally, I'd keep it at three.)**

Another problem like spread betting could be addiction. Beware.

Covered warrants

I gave a talk at a conference a while back and a speaker was on after me dealing with covered warrants. After he'd spoken for ten minutes, my wife nudged me and whispered:

"Look at that row over there, they're all fast asleep."

And indeed they were. In fact, some of them were dribbling a bit. Well, I guess it had been a long day.

Covered warrants sound extremely boring, and they're also quite difficult to explain. Which is quite handy for me as this book is for beginners and they are a complex derivative, so I'm not going to cover them here.

If you want to learn about them, check out the book *Andrew McHattie on Covered Warrants* by (you guessed it) Andrew McHattie. He is the expert on this subject and the book will tell you everything you need to know.

Warrants *are* useful and I do use them occasionally if I need to do any shorting for my pension fund. However, for the moment ... forget about them.

If you are a real beginner, I would suggest you leave covered warrants alone until you've had at least two years' experience in the markets.

Investment trusts

Investment trusts (ITs) are often overlooked by investors, but I've bought a few of these and made some decent profits.

Investment trusts are funds that buy shares in other companies. You invest in them just like normal shares – there's a buying and a selling price for each. Usually the investment trust has a theme, so it will buy shares of a particular kind and, in some cases, buy shares in other investment trusts.

In essence you are buying a fund. And you buy or sell them just like a share.

One investment trust I made nice money on was the Diverse Income Trust – I realised it held a lot of the shares I did.

I've also done well out of the Templeton Emerging Markets Investment Trust. That gave me exposure to emerging markets (surprise, surprise!). In a similar way, if you fancy getting exposure to the Japanese market you could buy a Japanese investment trust. Or, if you fancy growth in India, there are some that invest in Indian companies.

And so on.

One of my recent favourites has been the Montanaro European Smaller Companies Trust – this one buys shares in small companies across Europe and has done very well. It would be difficult for you to buy smaller European companies directly; buying the Montanaro IT, they are bought for you. Easy.

There are many types of ITs specialising in smaller companies, pharmaceuticals, German markets, etc. The list is endless. ITs give you exposure to a sector you like the look of with a bit less risk than just buying one share in that sector.

Are they worth buying?

Well, why not? Personally, I don't buy that many or that often, and I treat buying them like any other share, though they do require a different research focus. Investment trusts rise and fall in line with their *net asset value* (NAV). This is a rough calculation of the aggregate value of the fund's holdings at a point in time. These get published monthly, weekly and even daily.

Certainly, having one or two ITs in a portfolio could be a solid move. But if you choose a risky one it will definitely be worth imposing a fairly tight stop loss.

Investment trust summary

- Research them as carefully as ordinary shares.
- Check the net asset value.
- Find out the top holdings and research them.
- Work out how risky/volatile the trust is.
- Make sure you want exposure to its particular market.

Other funds

Elsewhere, ETFs are increasingly popular, but I don't really use ETFs beyond the SUK2 example we looked at earlier. I have nothing against them but I've never felt the need to use them very much.

ETF trading is ultimately a different game to share trading and I prefer judging individual companies. And, generally, I don't use other types of funds (e.g. unit trusts) because I'm basically running my own fund for myself and very happy doing things that way.

Shorting

One of the major uses of spread betting is shorting, where you are doing the opposite of buying a share. You make money if the stock goes *down*.

I would urge new investors to tread carefully before getting into shorting, but it's something that must be considered because it means you can make money during a period when the market is otherwise pretty pants. And while I do urge caution, it is something you should learn about quite quickly.

There are various ways of shorting: CFDs, covered warrants and spread betting. But the easiest method is to spread bet. That is the method I use.

I tend to only take out short positions in quite large companies. The reason is mainly the spread. The spread firms usually quote much wider spreads in smaller companies, and for shorting purposes I find the spread is simply too much. So in general I'd only short the top 350 companies.

During crisis years I have held more shorts than longs (buys) because it made sense. I believe at some point in the future I will do the same again.

Hedging

Many investors use shorting as what's called a *hedge*. That's not something that separates you from the nosy neighbours; it's a way of protecting a long position.

For example, you may hold 5,000 shares in a company, but are worried for a short-term period (perhaps the company is about to announce results). You could sell the shares, and buy them back after the cloud has passed, but that could be very expensive (what with broker's commission and stamp duty). You also may not want to sell if some shares produce a capital gain that is taxable at an inconvenient time.

An alternative is to hold the shares, but take out a down spread bet in the company to an equivalent value of your holding. If bad things do happen, and the share price falls, the amount you lose on your share holding will be approximately offset by the gains in your spread bet.

This is only a short-term strategy! It is not a magic formula for avoiding a loss forever. And if the market doesn't fall but goes up, then the profits on the shares will be off-set by the spread bet position. So use wisely.

Finding shorts

So how do you find shares that are going to go down and make you money?

Well, during the bear market of 2007–2009 it would have been easy: short pretty much anything and it would have made you some money! Ditto for early August 2011. And ditto for tech stocks in 2000 and 2001.

If you are in a bull market (shares on the whole are going up) there is not much point in shorting as you're going against the crowd.

But outside of a bear market, if you want a short, you have to do the exact opposite of finding buys. You need to look for shares that are overvalued, on a downtrend; or, if the market is in a downturn, a share that should sink with it.

Beware. It's not enough to just find what you think are over-valued companies and short them. Remember what economist, investor and general 20th-century egghead John Maynard Keynes wisely observed:

"Markets can remain irrational longer than you can remain solvent."

You need signs that a share really is going down. **A trigger is required before you open a short trade.** Otherwise, mistakes will be common and expensive.

I am personally not much cop at trading indices, but I can see the point of setting up a FTSE short if you're generally holding loads of share buys. If something happens, like a terrorist attack, and the FTSE 100 goes into free fall and your shares with it, at least you'll make some money.

However, I would advise you to hold off from shorting indices until you are confident in your trading. It's the kind of thing that could kill you in the markets.

Here are the kinds of things I look for in shares I'd like to be short on. You can use these to draw up a watch list while you wait for a potential trigger (also listed below).

Signs of unhealthy shares

Profit warning

Profit warnings tend to come in threes. If a share issues a profit warning, there could be worse to come. For example, furniture store Courts began issuing profit warnings long before it went bust in 2003 – you could have shorted and made a killing.

High P/E

If a company has a very high P/E or it's making, say, £5 million but has a market cap of £280 million, it may be all the promise (and more) shown by the company is already in the price and it could fall heavily on any negative news. However, it is extremely difficult to get the timing right on high P/E shares hitting trouble: some can carry on defiantly for a long time. Don't rely just on this.

Watch for negatives

Check the latest reports on the share you're interested in shorting. If you see the words 'challenging', 'difficulties' or 'problems', then it could be in trouble.

Big debt

Check the net debt of the company – if it sits at much more than six times pre-tax profit, that could be a big burden. I made a fortune backing Yell to go down and it went bust eventually!

General downtrend

A share that just keeps going down, maybe breaking through 52-week lows. It often means there is something amiss.

Some shorting triggers

Broken down through support

Remember earlier in the book I talked about support levels for shares? You don't remember? You skipped that bit? Bad reader! Go back and read it again.

If a share has been coming back down to a price a number of times and then falls through it, a lot of people sell up, pushing the price down even more, so it could be time to short. You can find shares going down through support by going to ADVFN's premium breakout lists but selecting breakout *downs* instead of ups. You should then get a nice list of shares that are breaking down and could be worth considering as a short.

Bad news breaks

If you've found a fragile company, and bad news breaks in its sector – or, even better, they're caught up in the story itself – that's a very good time to initiate a short.

My ideal short

My ideal short is on a share that is:

1. breaking down through support

2. in a sector that is not in favour

3. has issued a not-so-positive statement recently

4. is unlikely to be a bid target in the short-term.

--- **Short example 1: Yell** ---

One example of a short I made some good money on is Yell.

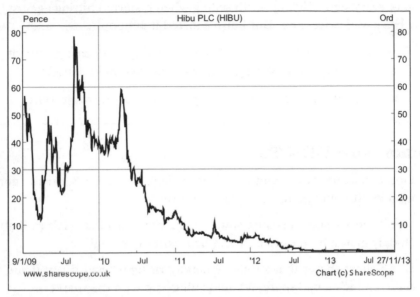

Yell (Hibu) (AKA Aaaaaaaaargh!) (January 2009–November 2013)

This one simply had a massive debt: something like £4 billion compared to profits of just £200 million! So I shorted at 50p or so – and it kept on falling ... all the way to under 10p. Then it changed its name to Hibu and promptly went bust.

Hibu? Honestly it deserved to go bust just for the awful name change.

Short example 2: Carpetright

Another good example is Carpetright. I mentioned earlier that it gave every sign of being worth selling when it started hitting against a brick wall price-wise. But I also shorted it at 700p!

This was an easy one. Continual profit warnings, forecast profits of £9m yet a market cap of £450m (how does *that* make sense?).

Plus every time the price knocked up against 700, down it went.

Some short DON'TS

- Don't go against the trend and short a share because it's already gone up a lot. It could go up an awful lot more!

- Don't short a share because some big market guru has. He's probably already in at a better price … and he might be wrong!

- Don't short shares in a strong, generally rising market. Even if you're right, and it's a bad share, it could still go up with the market.

- Don't hold on to your shorts for too long [Robbie, please, have some self-respect! – Ed.] – consider them as much shorter-term trades than normal. If you see them starting to rise after you have obtained a good profit, it might be time to take your profits.

- If you're a bloke over 40: just don't wear short shorts in public. Well, someone had to tell you.

Remember: indices like the FTSE and Dow can move very fast – be very careful when shorting them that you don't get blown away by a big move.

Market Timing: Level 2 and DMA

It's all very well having a nice share you want to buy. But what if there are loads of sellers about in the background and you're buying just at the point it is about to sink? Level 2 tells you how many sellers and buyers there are.

But just what exactly is Level 2 and is it worth having?

Two very good questions which I will try and answer for you now.

But just before I do, I have to say that it's next to impossible for me to go over Level 2 properly here. It would take 1,000 pages to do it and even then I'm not sure I could. I just about manage it, but only live at my seminars. I can give you a little summary. No need to get frightened, it just takes a little time.

If you are just starting out I wouldn't worry about it until you find your feet. But if you're starting out you *could* get into this now – the reason being it will help you to understand more about how shares move and why.

You will find it an eye-opener and will quickly understand much more about how and why shares go up and down.

There's no way I could trade without it. When it comes to timing a trade, I always use Level 2 for a final decision. Personally? I'd look at it now. I think even if you're very new to the markets it's worth considering finding out about Level 2. But expect it to take *ages* before it's of help to you.

So what is it exactly?

Level 2 used to only be available to professional traders in the City, but thanks to new technologies and price cuts by the stock exchange, it's now available cheaply to anyone who wants it. In short, it provides far more information about a share, including not only full details of the current bid and offer price but also prices that exist at other levels and the offers of individual market makers.

Without Level 2 you simply see the current best sell and buy price. But you have no idea what other bids and offers there might be in the market.

Let's say you are interested in buying or selling Avon Rubber. Without Level 2, here is what you would see:

Name	Symbol	Market	Type			ISIN		Description	
Avon Rubber	LSE:AVON	London	Ordinary Share			GB0000667013		ORD #1	

	Change	Change %	Cur	Bid	Offer	High	Low	Open	Volume	Time
▪	+0.00	+0.00%	610.00	604.50	613.50	-	-	-	1,580	12:19:11

Industrial Sector		Turnover (m)	Profit (m)	EPS - Basic	PE Ratio	Market Cap (m)	RN	NRN
Aerospace & Defence		124.9	13.2	32.7	18.7	189.24		

Simple (Level 1) price quote for Avon Rubber

You can see the sell (bid) price of Avon Rubber is 604.5p and the buy (offer) price is 613.5p. These are the *best* prices, meaning:

- 604.5p is the *highest* selling price in the market
- 613.5p is the *lowest* buying price.

This is all very well. *But those aren't the only selling and buying prices in the market at that time.*

Now here's a Level 2 quote for Avon Rubber. You can see it is completely different. You can now see the other orders in the market:

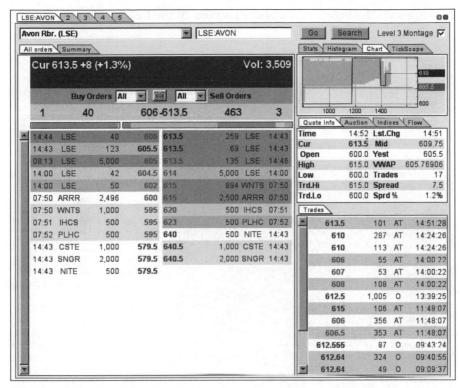

Level 2 price quote for Avon Rubber

What's the use of it?

Well, you can see the market makers begin to move their prices *before* it makes a difference to the Level 1 price. And what that means is, you can get in and buy or sell *before* the crowd knows there is going to be a price change. I find I can often get in ahead of a big price jump.

On this Level 2 screen you can see the market makers such as WNTS and all the others. On Level 2 you can see them start to move their prices up or down. This means you can buy or sell *before* most people know the price is about to change. Which is rather handy!

When you see a lot of market makers moving up it is a good sign.

Moving onto the bigger stocks, here's a view of the Level 2 for Sainsbury's:

LSE:SBRY 2 3 4 5

Sainsbury(J) (LSE) | LSE:SBRY | Go Search | Level 3 Montage ☑

All orders / Summary | Stats Histogram Chart TickScope

Cur 309 -1.4 (-0.5%) **Vol: 3,192,400**

Buy Orders All | All | Sell Orders

| 2 | 1,111 | 308.8-309 | 10,156 | 13 |

Time	Exch	Size	Bid		Offer	Size	Exch	Time
12:00	LSE	845	308.8	309		1,036	TQ	12:02
12:04	LSE	266	308.8	309		1,018	LSE	12:03
11:59	LSE	1,024	308.7	309		962	LSE	12:03
11:59	LSE	1,876	308.7	309		751	LSE	12:03
11:59	LSE	196	308.7	309		1,000	CHIX	12:03
11:59	LSE	845	308.7	309		33	CHIX	12:04
11:59	LSE	770	308.7	309		1,233	CHIX	12:04
11:59	LSE	1,690	308.7	309		222	CHIX	12:04
11:59	LSE	279	308.7	309		470	CHIX	12:04
11:59	LSE	397	308.7	309		222	TQ	12:04
11:59	TQ	969	308.7	309		1,551	LSE	12:04
11:59	TQ	196	308.7	309		813	LSE	12:04
12:00	CHIX	597	308.7	309		845	LSE	12:04
12:00	LSE	5,670	308.7	309.1		1,036	TQ	12:02
12:00	CHIX	2,724	308.7	309.1		1,002	LSE	12:03
12:00	TQ	1,328	308.7	309.1		331	LSE	12:03
12:00	LSE	4,798	308.7	309.1		956	LSE	12:03
12:04	TQ	3,000	308.7	309.1		845	LSE	12:03
12:04	TQ	355	308.7	309.1		509	LSE	12:03
11:55	LSE	1,908	308.6	309.1		1,690	LSE	12:03

Chart: 312 / 310.4 / 309.1 / 308 — 0900 1000 1100 1200 1300 1400 1500

Quote Info / Auction / Indices / Flow

Time	12:04	Lst.Chg	12:03
Cur	309.0	Mid	308.9
Open	313.9	Yest	310.4
High	314.0	VWAP	311.1601
Low	307.6	Trades	2359
Trd.Hi	314.0	Spread	0.2
Trd.Lo	307.6	Sprd %	0.0%

Trades

Price	Size		Time
308.9	226		12:04:03
308.9	446		12:04:03
308.9	606		12:04:03
309	135		12:03:59
309	51		12:03:59
309	3,348		12:03:59
309	89		12:03:59
309	947		12:03:59
309	253		12:03:59
309	18	AT	12:03:59
309	796	AT	12:03:59
309.1	53		12:03:49
309.1568	1,650	NT	12:01:34

Level 2 price quote for Sainsbury's

With bigger stocks, you still have market makers, but there can also be all and sundry putting in buy and sell orders. You can also see buy and sell orders from all the exchanges: LSE (London Stock Exchange), TQ (Turquoise) and CHIX (Chi-X).

The prices and amounts of shares you can see are all real buy and sell orders. The price of the share moves when someone has bought or sold the amount you see on the screen.

What may confuse you is that it says 'buy orders' on the left and 'sell orders' on the right. This is from the point of view of the people putting on the orders. For you, you are therefore 'buying' the right-hand side prices and 'selling' the left-hand side ones.

A quick way to remember this. You always have to:

• *buy* at the **higher** price, and

• *sell* at the **lower** price.

In other words, you always buy or sell at the more disadvantageous price!

You may look at this Level 2 screen and think: "Bloody hell, I'm never going to understand it."

But once you're used to it, it's much easier than you might think. What you're looking at here is not only where the market makers are, but with larger stocks you can see *all* the buy orders and *all* the sell orders. By seeing how big the buy orders and sell orders are, you can judge where support might be on a share price. And this information really is valuable.

The other valuable thing about it is that it teaches you how and why share prices are moving – you can see everything going on in the background that affects a price.

Level 2 will stop you from taking profits on a share too early and buying a share at the wrong time.

The best way to understand Level 2, though, is really to get it and play with it on your favourite stocks. And as I said, expect it to be a long process but one worth persevering with.

How do you get Level 2?

Level 2 is available (at the time of writing) at anything from free to £600 p/a. If you trade an awful lot, some brokers and spread bet firms will give it to you for nothing – a rule of thumb is roughly 30 trades or more per quarter to qualify. However, this can be dangerous. You don't want to over-trade just to get it free.

ADVFN promise to offer it to *Naked Trader* readers at way cheaper than their normal price for the first year. Click on my website for news on that or email me at **robbiethetrader@aol.com** with 'Level 2 offer' in the subject line.

If you don't trade that much, don't worry – it's a lot cheaper than it was, and costs keep coming down all the time.

I personally use the ADVFN Level 2 because I like the layout. Also, at the time of writing, it is the only Level 2 that includes all the trades made through all available markets and not just the London Stock Exchange, so you get to see everything out there.

I really wish I could do an in-depth book entirely on Level 2, but it's too difficult to get across the complexities in an easy, non-terrifying way. It's just one of those things that really is much easier to explain in the flesh. At my seminars I go through everything I do with Level 2 right there and then, using live shares, and I think this works really well. If you really want to get on top of Level 2 quickly, it may be worth coming along to one of those. Check my website to see if I have one coming up and come and do it live with me. It is actually quite fascinating.

Direct market access (DMA)

More and more brokers and spread betting firms will allow you direct market access.

What's it all about, Alfie?

It means you (yes, *you!*) can be a market maker, and you can put your own buy and sell orders directly into the market.

Let's say a share price quote is currently 500–502 (500 to sell and 502 to buy).

Now, normally if you wanted to buy the shares you would have to pay 502 – that is the buying price.

But DMA allows you to input an order direct onto the order book, which means you could input an order to buy at 500.25. You would then become the best (i.e. highest) selling price, and the share would officially then be quoted as: 500.25–502. If someone then wanted to sell some shares, your price would be the best and they would sell to you at 500.25.

Brilliant for you, because you are effectively buying them at the sell price.

Alternatively, if you wanted to short the shares you could put in a sell order at 501.75 and effectively sell at near the buy price.

Most direct market access is done via CFDs. All the orders, including yours, will show up on your Level 2 screen.

As I said, you can get DMA at many places now.

As with Level 2, in the end DMA can only be properly explained live and again if you come to a seminar I would be happy to show you. I place orders live on the book at the seminars so you can see exactly how it works.

One of the best things about it is trying to buy shares with big spreads at the sell price. Nice if you can get it and I do sometimes.

Charts and How I Use Them

I am definitely *not* a chartist! I don't visit charts as my first port of call. They come at the end for me, as a further aid.

Don't mistake me. I strongly believe charts *are* very important to look at because they tell you at a glance a lot of important info about the history of a share price; where it's been, what it's been doing, which TV shows it likes, and who it's been knocking around with.

But ...

> I believe it's simply crazy to buy and sell shares on the basis of looking at a chart and nothing else.

There *are* some people who do this. They call themselves 'chartists' and I reckon most of them can hardly afford to get their round in. This isn't going to make me popular with chartists, but who cares if I'm not popular with everyone. Evict me and see if I'm bovvered.

Chartists say things like:

> *"The MACD divergence touched off by the Fibonacci Bollinger band at 202.4 shows an increasing likelihood of a golden cross over the 40-day moving average on the triangle double-bottom formation ... "*

Which is almost certainly just a load of cobblers. (Well it definitely is in this case, as I made it up, obviously. But the terms are real.)

I gave a talk one day and the guy on before me, who was talking about charts, moaned like hell to me that he was having a rough time on the markets, saying he was fed up with being a chartist. He mentioned none of this in his speech.

You'll often see bulletin board punters talking chart theory because they think it makes them look good. Bit odd considering it's done under pseudonyms and no one knows who they really are, but people are funny aren't they?

Market commentators and tipsters tend to split into two camps:

1. Chartists (also known as technical analysts): they reckon they don't have to know anything about a company beyond its share price; they don't care what the company does, what sector it's in, whether it makes profits or not, or when the next dividend is due.

2. Fundamentalists: they feel you should be looking at the accounts, profits, etc.

What am I – a chartist or a fundamentalist?

Well, very much more a fundamentalist than a chartist – but one doesn't have to be, er, a fundamentalist about it: I always want to look at the whole story of a share, and that includes looking at charts. I like them for breakouts and for setting targets and stops.

But you've got to be careful about charts. They can easily be abused, and if you rely too much on interpreting them you can start to fall victim to wishful thinking or end up, like some heavy chartists, in a land of pure make-believe and extremely vulnerable to losses. But there are some basic ways of using them that will prove very useful. And this is what this chapter is about.

Although I don't call myself a chartist I probably use them more than I realise. Chart and TA guru Zak Mir in his very nice review of the last edition of this book commented:

> "Thumbing through the pages of *The Naked Trader*, it quickly became clear to me that our cheeky friend has a relatively low opinion of technical analysis. I am usually amused by this stance, especially when such people are often quite sensitive to the charting position of stocks. Robbie Burns appears equally susceptible to this

particular quirk. On the one hand, he is fairly critical of the dark arts of which I am so fond, but on the other appears very conscious of market timing. He also seems to pay a great deal of attention to, what I would regard as, the technical health of stocks he researches for the first time. For example, his methods include assessing volume, using a rising price as a buy signal, historical price movements, proximity to 52-week highs and so on."

Fair comment from Zak!

Charts and price ranges

You will very quickly come across charting jargon when you begin visiting bulletin boards – there are a lot of amateur chartists out there. I see no need, especially for new investors, to get bogged down in all the terminology.

I think it's far too easy to get tripped up by chartism – and many investors come a cropper when they rely on it. They read a few books about charting and then feel they're invincible! **Of course, what inevitably happens is the chart turns on them and bites them on the bum.**

So let's keep it simple. The main purpose I use charts for is checking out a share's *price range* in the recent past.

Here are the major ways in which charts might prove helpful for your trading.

Playing the range

As we discussed in the strategies chapter, charts are useful for flagging up shares that are trading in a tight range. A share price might move back and forth in the range 200–220 over a few months, and you could try to play that trend: buy at 200p and sell at 220p. Take a look at the Domino's Pizza example in that chapter.

Breakouts – my favourite

A breakout is when a share price is moving out of a previously established price range. As looked at earlier, a breakout is an excellent indication of a potentially juicy share. And without a check of a chart, and seeing its price range in the past, you would never be able to spot them.

Let's have a look at the chart of Monitise. Go on, you know you want to.

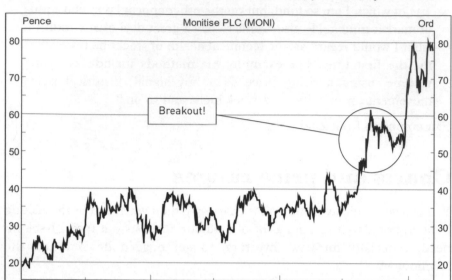

A 52-week upward breakout – Monitise (January 2011–March 2014)

The related ADVFN toplist gives you all the shares currently breaking out of previously established price ranges, and enables you to search for 52-week, 12-week and 4-week breakouts. My preference is for 52-week breakouts. A 52-week upward breakout often means a share is about to rise steadily higher.

Resistance and support

As well as breakouts, you need to know about resistance and support.

- *Support* is jargon for the level a share's price doesn't tend to go below.

- *Resistance* is the level the shares can't seem to rise above. (Resistance is futile, after all.)

How can this help us?

Well, it helps with setting the trigger level in a stop loss order. With Monitise, you can see resistance is around 40p many times over a couple of years. That's a selling signal.

And it could help you to decide when to buy. If it fell back to 30p, this was support a number of times, and 30p going back to 40p is around a 30% gain.

It's quite handy, really. This is probably what technical analysts would call back-of-a-fag-packet technical analysis. And they will hate me for it. But keeping it simple like this has worked wonders for me. This is how I look at a chart of any company I am interested in.

Think: where is support and where is resistance? Then you can more easily plan a buy or sell strategy.

Trend-spotting with longer-term charts

I often look at charts over some longer period. I find this works better – any trend you find is then generally more reliable.

I like to hop on a share whose price chart continues to go up like this:

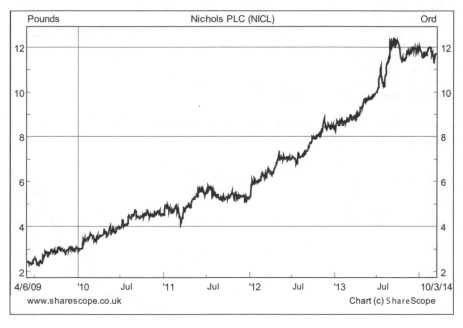

Nichols (June 2009–March 2014)

I don't like to buy charts like this:

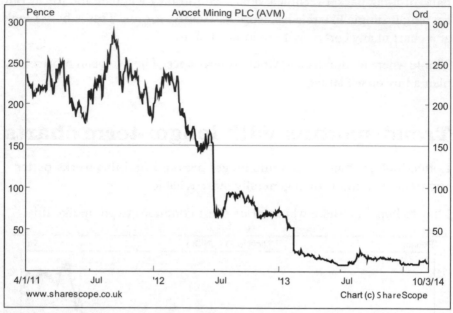

Avocet Mining (January 2011–March 2014)

I am just looking for a chart that is simply gradually going higher – say, a beautiful one like this:

Optimal Pay (January 2013–March 2014)

As you can see, this one just gradually keeps going profitwards in a nice rising uptrend.

I do *not* like charts like these, which show a falling price and very little meaningful support:

Kazakhmys (January 2012–March 2014)

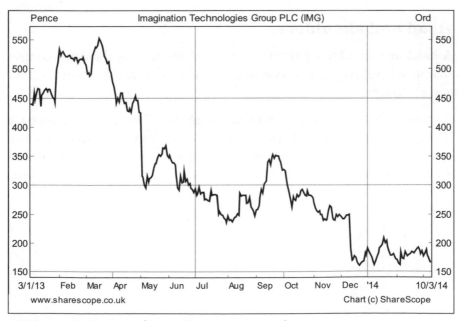

Imagination Technologies (January 2013–March 2014)

Basically, they're disaster zones!

As I've said elsewhere in this book, a lot of traders prefer things the other way round: nothing looks more like a buy to them than a share with a chart that has just kept on plunging downwards (and vice versa for shorts).

I'm afraid you must always remember that in such matters shares are no different to human beings: falling a great height is not a guarantee of being able get back up again and go higher. In fact, after a loud splat, usually quite the opposite is true.

> ### A reader writes: Gravity doesn't work both ways
>
> "I 'invested' in Marconi because the price had dropped from £12 to £4 – surely, therefore, it was good value … I lost several thousand pounds on that bit of common sense."

Chart patterns

So now you have hopefully learned about support, resistance and breakouts. What about chart *patterns*? I'm not really so keen on these but let's have a quick look at them. The most famous chart pattern (let's call it Sir Chart Pattern) is called *head and shoulders*.

Head and shoulders

A head and shoulders pattern (and we're not talking dandruff-control shampoo here) is so called because that is kind of what it looks like: a head and shoulders!

It's formed because the share hit a new high then fell off, tried to get back up again but couldn't and tried again. It really shows the share has run out of momentum for the time being and it might be time to take profits. So if you're ever going to consider looking at chart patterns, this is the one!

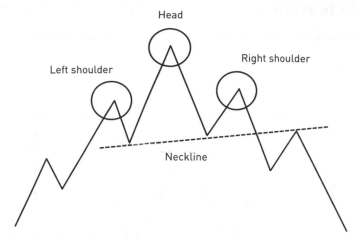

Head and shoulders

Double top

Another popular pattern where a share is expected to move lower is called a *double top* – as you can see it, well, looks like two tops:

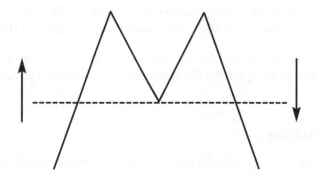

Double top

When the share has tried to break up though a certain point twice it gets tired, needs a rest and a cup of tea and therefore goes down. So chartists argue (and boy do they argue!) it should be sold once the second peak is reached … thus forming the double top.

Double bottom

And now the naughtiest sounding pattern – the *double bottom*.

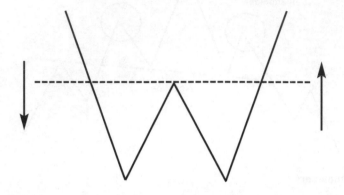

Double bottom

This is where the stock is expected to go *up*! It has gone down to the same price twice and bounced off that price. That, say chartists, is a bullish signal and the share should now rise a lot as it has found support.

Oh, talking of tea, another chart pattern supposedly bullish is the 'cup and handle' – i.e. the chart looks like, you guessed it … a cup and handle!

The share's gone up a lot, gradually fallen away, risen back up to form the cup shape, goes down a bit (to form the handle) and then is expected to rise sharply.

Round bottom

Then we have the err … (cough) round bottom. Lots of people like round bottoms (so I'm told). This is when a share falls away slowly, then bottoms out slowly before gently rising to form, err, the bottom.

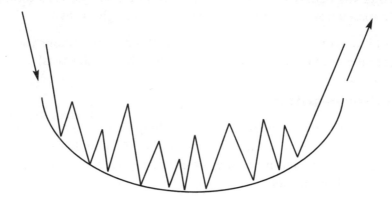

Round bottom

This is a bullish chart and the share should rise.

Triple top

And there's also the triple top. This is not good news. A share hits the same-ish price three times. After it has hit the price for the third time it is expected to drop away sharply.

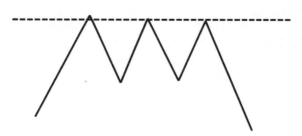

Triple top

Whether you believe in all this is up to you. The chart patterns sometimes work, sometimes don't, but they are worth a thought or two.

I would look on all these as things to just think about before you buy or sell; as an extra rather than using them solely. Sorry, chartists!

Further reading

An excellent guide for beginners, and to help you get more advanced in charts, is *The Investor's Guide to Charting* by Alistair Blair. This covers charting in depth, and if the subject interests you, the book covers most angles. And bottoms too.

Buybacks, AGMs and Perks

Share buybacks

Sometimes you'll see a company announce that it is going to buy back some of its shares. Companies can seek authorisation from their shareholders to do this. Generally, companies seek to buy back their shares because they feel the market is undervaluing their shares and the price is too low. By starting a buyback programme, the value of the shares is usually underpinned and might gradually see a rise in value.

But **I'm not a great fan of buybacks**. If the market is undervaluing the company then there is probably a good reason. So don't rely on buybacks to improve the value of the share you are holding by that much.

I would even consider selling the shares concerned, because buybacks, in my experience, don't tend to lead to fireworks for the share price.

However, for those wanting a steady income from a steady share, I suppose a buyback programme would give you confidence that the share will have some support.

Shareholders' meetings/AGMs/presentations

If you're a shareholder of any company, you're entitled to go to the annual general meeting (AGM). These are usually pretty dull affairs, but if you've got a long-term holding in the company it may be worth considering.

Sometimes companies even invite shareholders to the company premises to have a peek. These are called investor/analyst open days. If you've got the time and energy, why not have a look and visit the company? I've visited a couple and enjoyed the experience. Although, one of the ones I visited went bust two years later!

Another way of finding out more about the company directly is by going to presentations – **www.proactiveinvestors.co.uk** is good for this. What they do is get two to three company bosses together of an evening to tell you why their shares are worth buying. You also get the chance to put questions directly to the bosses of the companies involved.

I've been to one or two of these presentations and thought they were well worth the time and effort. The website tells you which companies are presenting, so I usually research them before I go. It's quite fascinating to meet the people behind a company and it can be very useful. These presentations are free.

Often the companies involved are smaller oil and mining outfits, which can be quite hard to research. To be able to talk to the management is a definite bonus.

A friend of mine who regularly goes to these meetings has an interesting way of deciding whether to buy the companies. She analyses the shoes of the chief exec. Apparently this works rather well. A nice pair of shiny brogues? Tick! A horrible old tatty pair? Black mark!

Well, look, it works for her! Personally I go for bald CEOs. Bald, good; hair, bad! Don't ask me why.

Share perks

You'll often see articles in newspapers and magazines written by lazy hacks regarding share perks. When I say 'lazy', this is because articles on perks are one of the easiest features for them to write – they can re-write an old perks feature in about ten minutes!

Perks are special privileges you can get if you own a certain number of a company's shares. For example, hotel chains might give you a 10% discount on their room rates.

You should buy shares to sell them at a profit: all perks do is make you hang onto a share longer than you should. But of course there is no reason not to enjoy a perk if you happen to have a share.

Merlin Entertainments gives you discounts off theme parks, for example.

And my holding in Telecom Plus gives me an amazing perk: 10% off my whole year's energy and telephone bills. Now *that* is worth it!

But never buy for the perks alone.

 # Your Pension

SIPPs (*self-invested personal pensions*) mean you can take control of your own pension fund rather than letting the professionals look after it. I think they're brilliant. The question is:

Should you take the plunge and run the fund yourself?

The answer is: could you do any worse than the fund managers?

I watched the pension fund I had with the company I worked for, BSkyB, go up for a few years and then sink like a stone between 1999 and 2001, at which point I'd had enough. So when I left full-time work I immediately transferred all the money from two frozen company pensions into my SIPP and began trading.

I'm glad I did as I soon built it from £40,000 to £165,000. Much of that rise was detailed in my *Sunday Times* column 'DIY Pension'. Now it sits at around £400,000. I reckon if I had left the pension money with the company scheme it would probably be floating around the £60,000 mark.

So I run my own pension fund, buying and selling shares. Of course, I'm confident when it comes to dealing in shares, but other people need to think carefully about whether to run their own fund.

For this section, I'm going to assume you feel reasonably confident about investing. Or you are going to be confident. So I'm going to discuss how to set up a SIPP and what to do with the money once you get hold of it. If you are a total beginner I would do some trading first in your ISA etc. and ensure you feel comfortable trading before handling your pension.

One rule of thumb is: only go for a SIPP once you have about £25,000 or more to put in your pension – it's not worth it otherwise, taking costs into account. Also if you still have a final salary scheme, it might be worth keeping hold of that instead.

Setting up a SIPP

Setting up a SIPP used to be a pain in the bum. It used to take absolutely ages and it was a paperwork nightmare. Ah, but things have changed for this edition of the book! I've talked to loads of people who have set up SIPPs who tell me the transfer has become quite easy and smooth.

There are still lots of forms to complete. But some of it can now be done online. Assuming you mainly want to trade shares, you need two things:

1. an execution-only stock broker

2. a pension trustee.

The trustee basically looks after the money and keeps it secure for you – usually for a yearly fee of around £150. You then trade the shares as normal and hopefully watch your fund rise.

It's probably best to choose the broker first – maybe the one you use for normal dealings – as they should have a list of trustees they recommend and work with. Trustees are much of a muchness, so just choose the cheapest.

There have been big changes in tax rules since the last edition. Then you could put in as much you wanted. Not so now. After the financial crisis they have clamped down on it and now the max you can put in each year is the same amount as your salary (up to a limit of £40,000) and the lifetime max is £1.25m.

Currently you then get 20% added by the government, and can claim back a further 20% higher rate tax relief if you're in that tax bracket. For instance, if you're a 40% taxpayer and put in £10,000, the government essentially adds another £4,000. (This could obviously have changed by the time you read this, so you need to check.)

You just send the money to the trustee, it's put into your stockbroking account and away you go. Buy and sell shares using the money as you wish – and that includes AIM shares.

It's slightly easier if you want to start from scratch, without transferring in any money.

Transferring frozen schemes

You can transfer in frozen schemes. You have to chase up the company the schemes are lodged with as they need to send you forms (yawn!). You fill them out and return them – the company should then release the money to your trustee.

It can take time and you need to keep hassling them . The other issue is that it can be difficult to transfer in a *final salary scheme*. Some trustees won't let you because final salary schemes are supposed to be the bee's knees, and it could be argued you don't need a SIPP because the final salary schemes are excellent payers. This is something you will have to look at closely. These days there are hardly any final salary schemes around; most have been closed.

Anyway, all the hassle is worth it in the end. It's a great feeling to be in charge of your own destiny.

You can carry on trading your SIPP till you're 75, at which point the government reckons you'll be too ga-ga to trade any more. From 2015, you'll no longer have to buy an annuity with the money. Rules around taking the money out are being relaxed and you'll be able to access the entirety of it at any time after age 55 – but you'll have to pay income tax at marginal rates on three-quarters of the money. The other 25% is tax-free.

There are various other methods of 'drawdown' and other options you can look at but this is getting above my pay grade and I would suggest you check this sort of thing with someone in a suit. Or on the internet. And of course, laws could have changed by the time you read this.

Trading in a SIPP

Trading in a SIPP is exactly the same as trading your shares normally. You buy and sell shares as per usual just like in a normal account, except of course you can't get your hands on the money!

Once you have your SIPP, what sort of shares SHOULD you deal in?

You really ought to be sensible. You probably have many years to go before you want to cash it in. Don't go crazy – buy some decent, sensible shares with good yields. You're looking for a decent lift for the fund over time. You have time, and do not have to worry so much about the ebb and flow of the market, and can look longer-term.

Look for shares you'd be happy to hold for a while and follow the practices I've already outlined in this book.

Aim for growth of around 10–20% a year – the fund will soon grow nicely at this rate. Don't take too many risks, as you may be relying on this money in the future.

You could do some shorting in your SIPP by using an ETF that specialises in it, or a covered warrant. One or two providers allow you to trade part of your pension using CFDs where you could also short.

For example, when the market headed near a high recently I bought a few FTSE put covered warrants. This meant if the market tanked short term I would make quite a lot. This would help to cover any losses in the longs.

Just recently, I have been using my SIPP to buy high-risk AIM stocks, which has worked quite well for me. However, it is easy for me to do this because I have built up tons of money within my ISA which I can take at any time and I have decided to try and grow my pension money more quickly as I can afford to take the risk.

So all in all, why not give it a try? Just think: you can be your own fund manager!

And unlike the fund manager, who handles billions, you can nimbly get in and out of shares. They can't do that so easily! Give it a bash and good luck!

Summary

- You can run your own pension fund.
- You can make contributions and transfer in frozen pensions.
- You need a stockbroker and a pension trustee.
- It can take time to transfer in funds.
- Buy any shares you like, including AIM.
- You can short shares using covered warrants and maybe CFDs.
- Be cautious with your fund – you may need the money.

PART VI
Stories and Rules
for the Road

Traders' Tales

ere are some real-life traders' tales. These are real stories sent to me by real people (though names have been changed to protect the guilty!). I think they are an important read because they summarise a lot of the things that newcomers to the market can go through.

Perhaps you will find stories that mirror your own experiences. There's a lot to be learned from them! And I've made comments on each of the stories too.

Stop panicking, Corporal Jones!

Thomas's tale:

"I started trading shares on a whim last year and soon found myself losing money, mainly due to panicking and selling as soon as they dropped, thinking I'd make the money back elsewhere.

I then noticed that shares I had sold had eventually returned to a higher price than I had paid for them – so I should have kept hold of them!

After this experience, I lurched in the other direction. I bought shares in a small gold miner with no stop loss and watched them gradually depreciate in value while all along telling myself they would come back up. I eventually sold them at a 35% loss. I was finally persuaded to by the example in your book of an investor losing money while all along convincing himself it would come good. It's exactly what I was doing.

Although I lost a fair bit of money, there was a strong sense of relief once I had cut my losses. Much like the feeling one experiences when, having watched a faithful family pet's health gradually deteriorate, the decision is made to have it put to sleep.

In many ways I feel there is also a lot to be said for losing money as a learning experience. It certainly acts as a strong reminder of mistakes you have made in the past.

I have now invested in a company after doing a lot of research, primarily based on the research points in your book. It ticks every box and as a result I felt confident when clicking the buy button. If it doesn't work out, then I have set a sensible 15% stop loss – an amount I could easily build back up in my account with a couple of months' savings.

It would have been nice to have done it this way from the start, but at the same time I believe I will be a better investor because of the mistakes I have made."

NT comments: While losing money is always rubbish, it's great that you learned from the experience. Panicking is an easy thing to do; lots of us have a bit of Corporal Jones in our make-up. Selling up the instant a share drops can eat away at your money, but buying a small miner without an exit strategy is the way to the poor house. Now you're being sensible, with an exit strategy in place, I can only say: *well done!*

Range out of control

Harry's tale:

> "I really need some help. I am invested in Range Resources ... yes, yes, one of those AIM oil companies you warn about.
>
> I bought in at about 18p in 2011 ... a month later it jumped to 24p.
>
> But then it gradually plummeted; the price is now 3.335p (a loss of 78%).
>
> The company seems to have a number of decent assets and great plans. Just last week it announced a 19.9% stake in Citation Resources.
>
> I wouldn't normally email you for advice here – I know time is precious – but I am at my wit's end ... I keep thinking something will come of this share soon. Range Resources has great potential across all the regions it operates in and I can't afford to take the hit of a 78% loss."

NT comments: Oh dear, oh dear. This trader's story really is a cautionary tale for everyone and anyone. Notice the confirmation bias? This trader is determined the share will come good, come what may, and is not interested in any negatives *despite a massive loss*.

He didn't set any stop loss and let it carry on down, convinced with each down move that it would come back.

Worse, he says he can't afford to take the loss. In other words, he is not willing to admit a mistake by crystallising his losses. Trust me, this just leads to bigger losses. As I write, the shares are just over a penny! He's now lost more than 90%.

Let's look at the chart. It's a real picture of woe, the kind of situation you should always want to get away from *bloody quickly*:

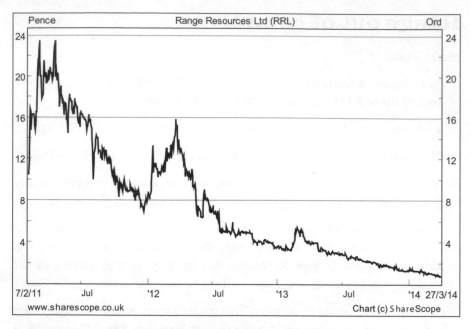

Range Resources (February 2011–March 2014)

The moral of the story? Set a stop, remember confirmation bias, small oil stocks can be a killer and get rid of anything losing more than 20%.

Lost a heap on pennies

Eliza's tale:

> "I am currently re-reading your book because, as I survey my trading account and both ISAs – all containing little more than the burned-out remnants of stupid little penny shares – there could only be one conclusion:
>
> YOU WERE RIGHT. STICK TO THE PROPER SHARES.
>
> I now have the job of rebuilding my portfolios, having learned the hard and expensive error of my ways.
>
> If you should at any time like to send me the most insulting email you can think of, using any expletives you like, just to remind me not to make the same stupid mistake again, I will gladly print it, frame it and hang it just above my screen as a reminder in case I am ever tempted to repeat the same cock-up."

NT comments: Well, okay, you *did* ask! You are a ***** **** idiot. You ignored everything I wrote in the book, you *****! Thought you'd get rich quick, you dozy **** ****** ... Hang on, I am enjoying this too much and that can't be good.

More seriously, don't fall for the penny shares! I suspect some of the bad trades you made involved being taken in by some penny share pump and dumps. Stick to decent companies that make real profits you can value properly.

Never trust tipsters

Norm's tale:

> "Where to start with my story? The worst trade I've made was Yell/Hibu – I lost 95% on that one. Various small cap gold miners have also proved nasty. I've made an average loss of 50% on them.
>
> So, somewhat expensively, I've finally learned to do my own research, use my own judgement, never ever trust tipsters and to not listen to idiots on the internet.
>
> I've also learned something specific about myself that I think should help my trading in future.
>
> I used to quite often jump into reckless/spontaneous trades as a result of irresistible newspaper or magazine articles, blather on the boards or sage online recommendations from 'those who know'.
>
> This has cost me a lot of money and eventually I have recognised it to be a disastrously bad habit. I have all but stopped. The warning sign I now recognise is the 'buy button adrenaline rush'. If I feel this when I'm trading (or about to), I know I'm trading too quickly and probably for the wrong reason, so I make myself turn off the computer, walk away and do not purchase anything until I have done some proper research.
>
> I still do slip – but not often.
>
> Unfortunately I still hold a few of my early calamity stocks. I know I ought to get rid of them all – there are quite a few. But the thought of crystallising such big losses is quite upsetting, so I hang on to them and hope against hope (I know, I know ...). I have got rid of a lot of real

bad-uns, and my approach since then is that when I have a new winner, I get rid of one of the rubbish stocks. It makes it a bit less painful."

NT comments: If you remember the stuff about tipsters earlier in the book, you won't be surprised to see what happened to this trader. Articles and recommendations can be interesting, but only as a first stage – you always need to do your own research, in depth, afterwards, and then you absolutely must wait to trade to avoid the market makers screwing you on the prices.

Tips are alluring. We get scared that other people know more about the markets than we do – that we're really no good, or they've seen something we haven't, or we've got no way of knowing if they're right or wrong and we don't want to be left out. Also, sometimes we're a bit lazy and think it's the easiest way to find good shares to buy (or sell).

Guess what?

It's complete rubbish. Some tipsters are good – but literally only a handful. And you still need to do your own research and wait before making your move.

Also, I completely understand the idea of dumping a loser when you get a new winner. But it's a terrible idea. What's the point of waiting? The losses aren't going to get any smaller. ALL the rubbish ones should be binned RIGHT NOW! Do not hesitate, get rid and use the money in proper stocks.

This trader made a really interesting point about the adrenaline rush. It is never a good thing to be pressing the trade button when excited. You are probably trying to gamble with a total stinker.

Played with money I didn't have

Aidan's tale:

"I had more money than I could afford to lose invested in FTSE 100 companies with high dividends. When the banking crisis came I didn't sell them. I just watched them lose value. In the end I sold at the worst possible time because I just couldn't afford to lose any more money.

All I can say to other readers is, don't over-expose yourself, don't invest money you can't afford to lose, sell when they have lost 20% of their value – regardless of anything! I do sell them earlier than this now, but that would be my absolute final figure! If things get too serious I make poor decisions and my judgement goes to pieces."

NT comments: Absolutely never play with money you can't afford to lose. It makes you a bad trader. As does not using stops. This trader thought he would be okay because he was in 'safe' FTSE companies paying high dividends. But if the markets smash down, they take everything with them and no stock is safe!

Spent loads on tuition and still losing

Kayley's tale:

> "I have read just about everything that's out there on trading. I've attended training sessions, bought DVDs on momentum trading and swing trading, gone on candlestick courses, travelled back and forth to seminars in London (from Oxford) every week – and yet I still can't consistently make any money. There is something that I am not learning and I want to know what it is.
>
> I think that I must have spent close to £5,000 on all this stuff and I am still missing the point. If I had spent the same amount of time and money learning how to play an electric guitar, I would be able to put Eric Clapton to shame!
>
> Of late, I think I have made some progress. But I'm not sure. I have been placing buy orders just above the first bullish candlestick after a pullback on the weekly chart, provided the 10 weekly MA is above the 20 MA, and this is above the 50 MA, when the MACD is rising on the monthly chart. The strategy has some merit. Additionally, in a similar vein, I am buying on the daily MACD cross of its signal line on the daily chart when the weekly and monthly MACDs are positive and preferably above the zero line. What do you think?"

NT comments: I think you have spent way too much! It's a bit tricky for me to blanket condemn seminars, of course, as I run seminars myself – but they are based on simple lines. Not secret principles or magical over-complicated nonsense. It's no wonder you haven't made money. You've been overcomplicating things by going on courses that blind you with loads of mumbo jumbo. And now you're talking mumbo jumbo!

I have no idea at all what you are on about with the last paragraph … but it might explain why you are not making money.

Over-trading like crazy

Edward's tale:

> "I started trading about six months ago and have made some losses (around £20,000) despite the market doing quite well during this period. It's not been fun.

> So over the last few days I decided to analyse where I've gone wrong and punched every transaction into a spreadsheet, over 80 in total (I have been over-trading ...). I thought you might be interested in the results.

> Of my losses (61), 36 ran over 10%. And when I cap these at 10% in the spreadsheet I make a profit of over £6,000 instead of a £20,000 loss – a sore lesson!

> So a ruthless 10% policy (with some adjustment for support/volatility) really would have served me well."

NT comments: Like I said earlier in the book: trade less, make more! Over-trading nearly always leads to losses as your 14% loss in a bull market shows. And as your research shows, if you had had stops in place you would have made a profit. There's a real lesson there!

Buying a big faller that ... fell more

Dom's tale:

> "I bought a share that had released a slightly negative statement which had caused the price to fall 70% or so. I concluded that it was definitely oversold and reassured myself with lots of indicators.

> After I bought it, it drifted slowly south towards where I had set a 'mental' stop loss (I no longer felt the need for automatic stop losses). Last week it dipped below this stop loss – but then rose again several times. I decided I should just hold on a little longer and give it one last chance.

> Alas, on Friday it plunged 11% and when the market opened again this Monday some more news was released that sent it falling like a stone.

> I got out at 8.01am on Monday for a total loss of 33% and a cost of about a month's living. Ouch."

NT comments: A few things went wrong here.

A lot of people like to buy shares that have fallen a lot as they think they are getting a bargain. But they use confirmation bias to talk themselves into thinking the share is oversold. Often such fallers end up falling a lot more as problems mount up.

No surprise the 'mental' stop didn't work. It should have been set in stone with a broker. Mental stops are fine for really experienced traders who know they'll be watching the markets should anything bad happen. I have started to use them. But they're really, really bad news for beginners.

And finally, you used 'indicators' – but as you were biased towards buying, I bet you only looked at the indicators in such a way that they came out positive!

Conned out of thousands

Tim's tale:

> "I've always been interested in working from home as I have two young children, so when I received a mail shot through the post advertising a trading system that would make me lots of money, I rang the company up immediately.
>
> The salesman was so good on the phone – he convinced me that I would make money from the system. It would cost £5,000 and even that was a special offer price, "for one day only". I paid with my credit card and the guy said I would be making money straightaway and would be able to clear my cards in no time.
>
> I think you probably know what happened next. I bought the shares the system told me to buy and they just went down and down.
>
> I 'invested' £3,000. I knew nothing about stop losses or researching a stock. I assumed what goes down must come back up.
>
> It never did.
>
> I have about £200 of the original £3,000 I invested. So, all in all, I lost about £8,000."

NT comments: Thanks for sharing this tale. There are so many conmen out there. Here's a useful blanket rule for dealing with them: if you get called by anyone offering cheap shares or systems or anything like that, put the phone down. (Swear at them first and demand they delete your number if you like.)

If anyone is cold-calling you, believe me, you do not need them or their products!

I'm afraid I have heard a lot of similar tales, including those conned by boiler rooms selling worthless shares. In the markets you should always be suspicious until you have proof to the contrary.

Spread betting losses

Rebecca's tale:

> "I have made many mistakes spread betting, with the worst being when I lost £14,000 in a day on a number of spread bets that went against me.
>
> I put several big bets on the Dow Jones and then I went out. I was totally shocked when I got home to see minus £14,000 and I was getting calls and emails from the firm asking for money to keep the bet open.
>
> That luckily made me close the bet. If I hadn't, two days later I would have been down £25,000."

NT comments: This is a real lesson on the dangers of spead betting – the kind of stuff highlighted earlier. It's also a lesson in the dangers of trading indices. An amazing 95% of people lose trading them. What you are really doing is entering a crazy casino, and casinos are great at taking money off you.

If you ever have a big bet open, use a guaranteed stop so know your maximum loss – and if you don't … do not go out!

A terrible time with Brent Crude

Andy's tale:

> "I had been playing with a spread bet demo account and was doing quite well, so I decided to do a bigger longer-term trade on Brent Crude [Basically the price of oil. – Robbie], over a few days. I went long and decided not to put on a stop as I have been closed down several times with spikes.
>
> Needless to say, the market fell. It almost wiped me out.

Lessons: (1) If I'm going to lose big, make sure it's a demo! (2) Brent crude is very volatile. (3) Higher positions lose money exponentially and if the market moves quickly, very fast. (4) Place stops and get annoyed when they get spiked out (it's cheaper). (5) Be much more thoughtful about each trade – I'd had a few good runs and felt I had found a licence to print money.

After reading your book, I started off by looking at fundamentals – then began to get into chart analysis, and this is where the trouble started."

NT comments: Well, at least it was a demo account. Demo accounts are a good idea, but they are *not* the same as real trading. Errors in demo accounts can get worse in real ones. Something happens to you when you're playing with real money. It does things, even if you think you're a pretty cool customer. So watch out!

The major moral of this tale is probably that nearly everyone loses trying to play commodities. You will get eaten alive by the very few pros who make money at it. Just don't go near it! I know the trader above read my book but it wasn't exciting enough for him, so instead he went out and found an exciting way to lose money. Don't look for excitement!

Don't trust the boards

Delia's tale:

"Don't trust bulletin boards, especially busy ones. I got conned into buying subprime lender Cattles by the idiots on the BBs.

It looked like a good company in a niche market and everyone on the boards said they were doing well and it was easy money.

Then shares were suddenly suspended and financial irregularities announced.

I decided I needed to learn more – I still couldn't work out what I should have done differently – so I went out and bought your book.

Hopefully I won't have another tale like this to share next time."

NT comments: Well, there are two things you did wrong. Firstly, believing what you read on the BBs. And secondly, you did not look at the net debt of the company. As I covered earlier, net debt is such an important thing to check.

All you had to do was take one look at the monster debt of the company and you would never have touched it.

Drugs disaster

Emma's tale:

> "I bought loads of a small drugs company called Renovo and I lost approximately £8,000. I got in with a holding that was worth roughly £10,2000 and got out when the same holding was worth roughly £2,200.
>
> The problem was I had taken the success of its clinical trials for granted. I should have assessed things when it seemed to peak and sold before it crashed.
>
> My first ever trade!"

NT comments: Not the greatest of first buys. But that is the problem with drugs stocks. You can get really stung if they don't get the approval they need. In this case it was such a risky stock you would have been saved by placing a guaranteed stop with a spread betting firm – then you wouldn't have lost so much money when it dropped rapidly.

I nearly lost everything

Robin's tale:

> "I had been buying shares/tracker funds for years and thought I could walk on water. I had made more per year through the late 90s than I could have earned as a wage. I had a good share portfolio and was doing very well indeed.
>
> But I wanted more, so much more, driven by the fact that I wished to retire at 50.
>
> So I got into CFDs without knowing what on earth they really were. I bought 1,500 contracts in one share at around 380. It went up, so I bought 5,000 more on the profit (still holding the initial 1,500). At around 430, I bought 5,000 more. Soon it was up to 501 and I was making a killing! So I bought 5,000 more at 510.

I was now holding 16,500 contracts. The share went all the way up to 586. I was so happy – on paper I had made a huge profit. I was invincible and a super trader! So very confident.

Meanwhile, I made a loss of £2,000 in another CFD position but learnt nothing from it. What was £2k when I was so far up on this one share?

I was paying around £300–£350 a month in interest on my big successful trade, but the paper profits meant this was nothing ... I never bothered looking at the global meltdown around me. And then the price started to fall.

I was too ignorant to act swiftly.

But it kept falling and falling. By the time I realised what was going on, I was way over my head but managed to close out the first two trades. I was left with an average purchase price of 505. The share fell down to around 108 that day. I was in trouble.

In this period, the broker moved the margin to 30% from 10% and placed a huge call and gave me until the end of the day for the funds. I borrowed on credit cards. I could not afford to lose; I had already sold every share I had to shore these contracts up. I borrowed from family, too. I actually had a wedding looming and my job was looking shaky. The next task was to borrow against the house.

I never told my family why I asked for funds, though they helped me all the same. Meanwhile I married my beautiful wife (a wedding which I paid for with a bank loan) who knew I was in trouble but was not in a position to help. I was so close to a complete nervous breakdown. Friends and family were growing concerned.

Soon we had a baby on the way and a car that was on its last legs. Miraculously I managed to get a better-paid job a little closer to home, which helped with the funds. It was just enough to keep me going.

My health had suffered greatly, though, and when I hurt my back I was off work for weeks. It would have been easy to hit the bottle but I had a good upbringing whereby you face what you have done and sort it out.

The share has only just (January 2011) gone above the price at which I originally bought in. Now I am in profit and going on your course (and reading the book). I have set my stop losses and will now make a few quid on the buy price (ignore the thousands of pounds in interest I have paid). I have become quite hardy, although I am not sure why I did not have a complete nervous breakdown.

The moral of this story for me is: don't play with more than you can afford to lose, don't be a 'cocky sod' (that's over-confident in Northern speak), and ensure you understand what the hell you are doing and the risks involved. If you don't get it, then don't do it.

Before your readers start to slash their wrists, I have managed to re-build my portfolio and managed to make a good amount (for me) to the point where I've been able to make myself mortgage-free. Good things can happen, eventually."

NT comments: Quite a dramatic story, and a serious warning, I think: never, ever, *ever* play with more money than you can completely, comfortably, safely afford to lose. And do not buy derivatives if you don't understand them. And always use at least some kind of stop loss!

You ought to never get in such a position. I hope this story might just save one of you out there that might be about to go down the same route. While you might note the story had a kind of happy ending, he knows he was really lucky. The share in question could have gone bust.

He is right, do not be cocky or smug.

I may have made a lot of money but I could easily lose a lot of it again. My way round this is to only add the ISA allowance in every year and trade with that. But to be honest, yes, I have on occasions felt cocky myself. And that is just when the market will come and kick you where it hurts.

Always treat it unemotionally, as a business.

The Naked Trader Rules

I debated whether to bother with some rules in this edition. After all, I feel I'm a rebel so my initial thought is "Rules? Screw 'em!"

Then I read though the rules in the third edition. They all stood the test of time. In fact, most of these rules will probably still be applicable in 50 years. So I guess they should run again.

You're not going to lose everything you have if you don't follow them. But after you finish reading this book and it's tossed on top of a lot of other books … and you come back to it one day … these rules are a pretty good summary of what I've been banging on about.

They are in no particular order. In other words, number 1 has no more importance than number 30. Because they're all equally important!

The rules

1. Only play with money you can really afford to lose. Be honest with yourself.

2. Get the whole story about a company before you buy. Learn everything about it.

3. Don't rush into anything or chase a share price. There's always another share coming along in a minute.

4. Be wary of buying into systems promising you thousands of pounds for no work. If it's too good to be true, it probably is.

5. Don't buy a share because someone on a bulletin board says it's going to double.

6. Cut your losses fast if you've bought a share and it's tanking.

7. Don't take profits too quickly. If you've got a good share and it's slowly heading up, stick with it. Run your winners.

8. Don't be panicked out of a good share if it goes down for a day. The market makers may be trying to get your shares cheaply.

9. Beware of buying a share just because a director bought some. They can get it wrong. Some shares have gone bust two weeks after a director buy.

10. If you are buying more than £3,000 of a small share, check its exchange market size. If the EMS is below £1,000 of shares, you may have trouble when it comes to selling them.

11. Never catch a falling knife. That means: don't buy a share because it's gone down a lot. Better to buy shares that are going up. That falling share may be a bargain – but end up even cheaper first. Or it may be a stinker that doesn't stop stinking.

12. In a general market downturn, think about using a FTSE short.

13. Don't buy a share after a profit warning (like London buses, profit warnings often come in threes, so the first may not be the last).

14. Check the spread between the buying and selling prices. If it's more than 5%, the share could be far too risky.

15. Beware of buying before 9am – the spreads can be at their widest. Don't be suckered into buying a share at a silly price early on.

16. Don't buy and sell indices like the FTSE 100 or the Dow, especially if you are a new investor. It's just gambling.

17. Be careful with mining and oil exploration stocks. One bad report can see these shares tumble. They are impossible to value properly. You don't have to entirely avoid them, but caution should be your watchword.

18. Don't buy companies that are making a loss. You're gambling they'll make a profit one day. It may never happen.

19. Think about buying after a black swan event.

20. Use stop losses. Set them around 10% away from your buying price (checking support and resistance levels to adjust if necessary). Monitor to avoid getting stopped out in the morning.

21. Try to have a plan with every share. Think about what your exit price will be.

22. Shares are for buying and selling. Do run profits but also sell by topslicing and moving stops up to lock in profits.

23. Don't get involved with things you don't understand. So don't buy CFDs or covered warrants if you don't fully understand them.

24. Beware of trading too much on margin. Using money that isn't yours may feel clever, right up until the point where you start losing money that isn't yours. Think about what your losses could be and whether you can afford to cover them.

25. If you're losing heavily it may be best to cut all your positions and come back to the market another time.

26. Don't over-trade. Keep to about eight or ten open positions. Any more and you are going to have trouble keeping on top of them.

27. Beware of overconfidence. If you're on a winning run don't start increasing the size of your positions.

28. Don't only go long; think about shorting stocks. This is not for beginners, though.

29. Be careful about relying on one method of stock-picking. Cover all the angles.

30. Don't lose control of your investments. Stay calm.

31. Always check your ex-dividend dates. Your share will fall on this date by the amount of the dividend, so don't worry when that happens.

32. Open more than one broking account. Then you can compare their services and systems.

33. Don't rely solely on charts, but certainly use them – along with other tools – to help your trading decisions.

34. Read the financial press – some of it is rubbish but you must keep in touch with what's going on.

35. Remember the sound advice of Corporal Jones in Dad's Army: "Don't panic!"

Trading FAQs

I often get emails from people asking me questions that were answered somewhere in the book. Maybe they missed it – I can understand, it is a big book! So here is a collection of answers to the most common questions.

Q. Using a spread betting or CFD account is it a valid strategy to short a share on ex-dividend day on the basis that it can be expected to go down in price?

A. No. Spread firms and CFD accounts all take into account the ex-dividend drop and it's either in the price or the dividend is deducted – no free lunch!

Q. I want to work in the City/get a job as a trader. Can you help? How do you do it?

A. Afraid I have no idea! I was a journalist. I've never worked in the City and don't have any contacts there. I know that becoming a trader is quite difficult. From books I've read it can be a horrible, stressful occupation, with long hours!

Q. I am thinking of buying/selling a certain share. What is your opinion on it?

A. As I'm unregulated I simply can't discuss individual shares with you one-on-one, as it could constitute advice. Sorry! And I think that even if I was regulated I wouldn't want to discuss specific shares like this as I'd hate to influence anyone into buying or selling something that then goes horribly wrong.

Q. When I look at net debt on ADVFN financials it always seems really high.

A. For net debt, profits, etc. don't look at ADVFN financials or rely on any other site like that. *Always go to the last company statement or report and find it there.* It is the safest way of doing it. The figures in ADVFN financials and similar are often out of date.

Q. I can't get your traffic lights system to work.

A. You're probably trying to download a company report! The traffic light system doesn't work on downloads. Once you have set up the system, click 'Quote' on any company on ADVFN and then press news. Then click on the full-year or interim reports and it will work! (Also, make sure you are logged in!)

Q. Do you think the FTSE will go down/up? Or what's your view on the economy?

A. I have no idea! I follow the market rather than trying to guess where it's going next. And in fact I don't really have a view on the economy at all. Markets overshoot and undershoot. Having a rock-solid idea of where the economy is going may not have any relevance to where markets actually go at all. It's best not to try and get too far ahead of the markets: all that money can blow you away, even if you're right in theory.

Q. I noticed that on your list of buys and sells, a share went below your stop loss yet you held onto it. What gives?

A. Sometimes that happens because I don't use automatic stops; I use the order book to make a final judgement on whether to kick a share out or not.

Q. Help, I'm losing money! What should I do? Should I sell X? Buy Y? Do Z?

A. Again, I can't really help, except to say you need to revise your strategies and maybe even come out of the markets for a bit. This is something you have to learn for yourself over time.

Q. I added up your trades list and it doesn't match the total profits given on your website. How come?

A. The total profit figures are from when the website started back in 2000. The trade history only goes back about three years, as that's about as much as the site will handle!

Q. I've designed a spreadsheet that takes everything from your book/analyses your trades/makes tea. Can you look at it and see what you think?

A. Please don't send me spreadsheets of any kind. Honestly, I'm just not a spreadsheet kinda guy and I won't look at it.

Q. You do well at trading but you could do better if you [*insert peculiar theory, strange invention, bee in bonnet here*]. Will you give it a go?

A. There is no point trying to teach an old dog new tricks!

Q. Do you trade currencies or metals. If so, can you help me with a problem I've been having?

A. Afraid not!

Q. Are the trades listed on your website the only ones you make?

A. No – I do a lot more spread betting but don't have the time/strength/will to list all these! The website trades are real at the real prices but I will often buy more/top up etc. without declaring it – again due to time/workload.

Q. I'm a complete beginner. Is it too early to come to one of your seminars?

A. They are designed for beginners and improvers – the only real stipulation is that you should have read the book before coming! I can send you the details of everything we'll cover and you can decide for yourself if it's for you!

Q. My share went down even though there were loads of buys – how is that possible? [And vice versa with shares going up despite lots of sells.]

A. Don't believe what you see if you press 'Trades' on ADVFN or other services. The computer is guessing and usually the buy to sell ratios are totally wrong. In fact, they can be ignored.

Many trades done via the order book are actually buys *and* sells! That's because someone is selling but someone else is buying and they are matched. Also, trades done through market makers can be delayed if they are bigger than the normal size, so buys can be disguised as sells and vice versa. Do not be fooled.

Q. I know you go over Level 2 at your seminars but can you suggest any books that explain it?

A. There aren't any that I know of and I'm not surprised: the nature of Level 2 is that it only really makes sense when explained live, with a feed in front of you and hours to spare. I suppose you could gain something from a book but it would be very, very difficult to read (and even more difficult to write!). Much simpler to watch it in action. And even then Level 2 is open to different interpretations!

Q. Why not film your seminars and provide DVDs or even do them online?

A. I'm afraid this is not something I am ever going to consider, as I don't want to become a DVD producer or turn the seminars into some kind of big business. Plus people in the audience often tell quite personal stories and the days can be ten hours or more. And I prefer to teach people for real, in the flesh.

In the end I want them to remain private to those who come. I also don't want to be an 'online teacher' of any kind. So thank you to everyone who writes in wanting to direct and produce my DVDs, but it's not for me!

Q. What makes you decide whether to take out a spread bet instead of just buying the shares?

A. I use spread bets for three things, basically. Firstly, for shorting (i.e. betting on a share to go down). Secondly if, say, I am fully invested in my ISA, or want to top up current holdings in my ISA. Thirdly, if a share is moving fast it can be easier and quicker to get a spread bet on than to try and get the shares at the price I want.

Q. How do I find out if a share is moving from AIM to the main one?

A. I find out simply by reading news reports every morning using the ADVFN news service – usually it is stated in either a company's full-year or interim report that they intend to move. Then you need to keep an eye on the date it's going to happen.

Q. How do I know if a share is AIM listed or on the main market?

A. Click 'Financials' on ADVFN for the share you are interested in. If under 'Market sector/segment' the first letter is an 'A' it is an AIM share – anything else and it's main. You can also use the London Stock Exchange website.

Q. How do you maintain your wonderful hairstyle?

A. I shave every other day to maintain its gleaming streamlined look – so hygienic too!

Q. I bought a share because you bought it and it's going down now – help! Should I sell it or not?

A. A few points here. The trades I list online or mention in my diary are not ones I recommend you copy! *Especially as the share price can already have gone higher.*

And you should never follow anyone into a trade, anyway, whether it's me or a newspaper, a magazine or a bulletin board *unless* you have done your own research, sorted the right timing and planned the trade properly.

The only answer I can give you is: you bought it, you sort it! And in any event I can't give you advice on what to do, and even if I could, I wouldn't! You must learn to take responsibility for your own trading and only you should decide when to take a profit or loss.

Q. I only have a small amount to trade with (£500 to £1,000 or so), so is it worth me investing in the stock market? If so, how many shares should I buy?

A. This is a tricky question to answer. And my answer is only my opinion. But here it is.

Honestly, I don't think it is enough. First of all, commissions and stamp duty will eat into any profit. Secondly, with a small amount it's impossible to buy enough shares to have a balanced portfolio and with maybe only one or two shares if one goes badly you could easily lose a lot of capital.

I would say wait till you have at least £3,000 because then it is possible to get around £500-worth of six shares. In the meantime, you could paper-trade to see how you get on.

I do think with a small amount of money, unless you are very lucky, it probably isn't worth it. However, this is only my personal opinion!

Q. I don't really understand ISAs – I read some people have made a million or more out of theirs and you have made a lot. Can I keep on buying and selling and really building up profits tax-free? Could I start with £10k and just keep building it from there?

A. Yes! There is no limit to the amount of money you can make or the amount of trades you can undertake in an ISA. The only rule is: you can only add in a certain amount of extra cash from outside each year. The broker's sites will tell you the latest figure. It tends to go up each year.

So if you take any profits out, they are not taxed but you can't just stick them back in. They'll count as new cash, and there is an annual limit on how much of that you can add.

You can trade as much as you want, though – and when you sell something you can immediately buy something else and build your profit just like in a normal trading account. And all the thousands (or millions) you make are completely tax-free.

Q. I'm a student and want to get into shares but am not sure how to do it. I wonder if you need an intern/help/dogsbody at your trading desk?

A. Trust me, you really would not want to see me in my pyjama bottoms at 10am. But it might be worth ringing round brokers/spread firms to see if one will kindly let you make coffee for a couple of days.

Q. What happens if I am short of a share with a spread bet and it goes bust?

A. Generally you should get paid out! However, you may find your bet is suspended for a while until the company is officially deemed to be a bust or has gone into administration. Spread firms are usually sensible and will pay you out at zero or a penny once it is obvious it is a gonner. Of course, spread firms do vary so it might just be worth asking your particular firm.

Q. What happens when a share I'm in gets bid for?

A. The price of a share usually goes close to the bid price. If it goes higher, the market thinks there might be a competing bid. If the bid goes through you can either sell at under the bid price to the market or else wait one or two months for the full bid price to be paid into your account.

But remember, there is no guarantee a bid will go through till it is confirmed. If it doesn't get confirmed then the share price could revert to what it was before the bid.

Q. I saw you bought a new issue but where do you find out about new issues?

A. There is no one place, unfortunately. The best way and the way I use is to check the news at 7ish every morning – you can then look for 'intention to list' in the headlines. Companies intending to list usually release this fact at 7am so it should be quite easy to find. I usually check every day. Also I find the *Times* and *Sunday Times* pretty good at mentioning new issues on the way. In the end, you just have to keep your eyes open!

Q. How do you decide when to sell a share? Are there any signals you use?

A. Well, I try and hold onto good ones for as long as I can. However, if I have made 20% plus on something I will often sell part of the stake, maybe a quarter, and bank it. Another thing I do is pretend I never saw the share before and look at it again. Would I still buy it now? I also use trailing stop losses. And it's worth looking at a chart. Does the share keep knocking up against the same price but fail to go through? It might be time to bank some of the profit. Remember, you don't have to sell *all* of your holding!

Q. Do you trade American/Australian shares? If not, why not?

A. No, I only trade UK shares on the whole. Why? Because I like to be finished at 4.30pm – I don't want to be looking at live shares at 8 in the evening! Also, I don't really know either market and prefer to concentrate on an area I know well. I really have no need to trade stocks in either country. So unfortunately I can't help you with any ideas about trading either country, or any country outside the UK, and have no idea whether my methods work outside the UK or not.

Q. Are you on Twitter or Facebook. If so, how do I sign up/follow you?

A. I'm not on either. I'm just not interested in social media, nor do I want to get into sticking trades on Twitter to be followed blindly, as it's pointless and dishonest. So if you see anyone called Robbie Burns or Naked Trader on any social network it isn't me – just some sad person pretending to be me. My site and the books are it!

Useful Information Sources

Worthwhile websites

There are tons of financial websites out there, and most of them, today, are actually very good. That's partly because the useless sites that got set up in the dot-com boom have disappeared. But it's also because the people that set today's sites up enjoy finance and shares and that tends to come across.

Most good websites provide a decent amount of free information, then you pay a bit extra for premium information such as always-on access to real-time share prices. For example, once you've had some experience you may want to access Level 2 services, which will cost something like £40–£50 a month.

The sites tend to offer premium material all priced around the same level, but you may want to shop around. The best thing is to experiment. You'll probably end up using two or three sites.

For brand-new starters you probably only need the free stuff to begin with. As you get more experienced, you may need to start paying for decent access to real-time information.

ADVFN

www.advfn.com

ADVFN is possibly the number-one site. I've mentioned it a lot in this book, and I use it all the time. Live prices and great research tools. Just use the free stuff to begin with.

> I've negotiated a deal with ADVFN so you can get access to their premium lists and bulletin board for £41 a year instead of £60. Those are the great lists where you can find eye-catching shares. You also get access to my *Naked Trader* discussion forum, where you can chat to some very decent traders. Email me for details at **robbiethetrader@aol.com** with 'Bronze' in the subject line.

Digital Look

www.digitallook.com

A decent source of information with a good diary of ex-dividend dates and company reports.

MoneyAM

www.moneyam.com

A similar site to ADVFN. It also contains real-time prices, but its bulletin boards don't have as many contributors. Handy as an alternative to ADVFN and I use it as a back-up should ADVFN go down.

Morningstar

www.morningstar.co.uk

Worth a look. Plenty of good research material here and a bulletin board worth dipping into from time to time.

Motley Fool

www.fool.co.uk

Despite its title, quite a serious site. Think pipe and slippers. Some interesting articles; worth a good gander.

Naked Trader

www.nakedtrader.co.uk

Er, my website. Bloody good if you ask me.

Proactive Investors

www.proactiveinvestors.co.uk

This site has got bigger and bigger and keeps on improving. It features news and well-researched articles on companies. The site also hosts presentation evenings where you can meet the bosses of companies. And it's free! What's interesting is that it researches the companies no one else does – especially smaller ones – and comes up with some gems.

Books

Read. Read. And read some more. I know this book is superb, but you should be reading others too.

There are many trading and investing books out there and I've read a whole load of them. I've never regretted buying a single one because, generally, there's always a gem or two inside to think about. Such books typically don't cost more than £20, and invariably help traders make much more than that in return, so it's a good investment.

So here are a few I very strongly recommend. They are in no particular order. They are all excellent reads for stock market beginners and old hands alike.

- *The Disciplined Trader* by Mark Douglas

  An excellent look at good trading practices, including a look at why what's in your mind can affect your trading. There are also some tips on how to become a profitable trader.

- *Your Money and Your Brain* by Jason Zweig

  This is a great one. It is all about psychology and how your brain affects every move you make in the stock market. Feel the need to conquer fear and greed? This is the book for you!

- *The Naked Trader's Guide to Spread Betting* by Robbie Burns

  Just who does this guy think he is? Yes, this is my book on spread betting. If you decide you want to take spread betting further then I hope this book will help you! It's not a rehash of stuff in here – it's brand new material that explores spread betting in depth.

- *High-Probability Trading* by Marcel Link

This book tries to teach the mindset of a successful trader – what you should think about before you reach for the buy button. No complex material, just good common sense.

- *Financial Times Guide to Selecting Shares That Perform* by Richard Koch and Leo Gough

This book uncovers ten ways to beat the market, and there are some very good ideas here. A good broad discussion of methods you can use to try and outperform the indices. I learned a number of excellent tips and I agree with pretty much everything the authors say.

- *Come into My Trading Room* by Alexander Elder

This one is the book I've read and re-read the most. Entering Elder's trading room is a very interesting experience. His years of profitable trading show through the pages and many of his warnings regarding some of the pitfalls of trading are excellent. I think this one is an especially good read if you have never traded before. There is also plenty of market psychology discussed – one of my favourite topics. And talking of psychology …

- *Investment Madness* by John R. Nofsinger

Subtitled: 'How psychology affects your investing and what to do about it'. This is one of the must reads! It is highly amusing but also very sharp. You may recognise your own character traits in the book – and once you recognise them, you can learn how to stop bad sides to your character ruining your trades. Topics include the problems of overconfidence, social aspects of investing, the 'double or nothing' mentality, seeking pride and avoiding regret.

- *Investor's Guide to Charting* by Alistair Blair

For those of you who decide charting is the way to work out which shares to buy and sell, this is the easiest read. Blair explains the art of a chart and what it's all about. Find out what all the chart jargon means, like 'double tops', and whether charting is suitable for you. What's really good is the discussion of how much of chart theory and practice should be taken with a pinch of salt.

- *The Investor's Toolbox* by Peter Temple

  Everything you need to know about spread betting, CFDs, covered warrants, options – all the funnies – to help boost your returns. The book goes through all the tools you need for successful investing. If there's any question on basic derivatives you need to know the answer to, it'll be here.

- *The Harriman Book of Investing Rules*

  Collected wisdom from the world's top 150 investors. Tons of unmissable rules from the greatest traders ever. Read and learn! It's one of those books you can keep in the bathroom because you can pick it up anytime and have a great read. A brilliant book of wisdom to keep dipping into.

- *The Investor's Guide To Understanding Accounts* by Robert Leach

  This may sound like a really boring one, but Leach has turned what could be a very unexciting subject into an interesting one. Ever wondered how to look at a set of accounts and know whether it's all good or there is trouble ahead? Are they cooking the books? There's also an excellent ten-point summary which will point you in the right direction.

The Naked Trader

The Naked Trader quiz

Here's a fun quiz to test your skills as a potential investor. Answer all the questions honestly. Do not cheat and look up the answers.

Pick only one answer for each question. Note down the question number and which letter you picked. If you did badly on the quiz in previous editions, I hope you do better now!

Questions

> ### 1. What's the best chart breakout?

a. When it goes up three years in a row

b. 52-week

c. Whatever is number one in the charts

d. Support and resistance

e. Nikki Minaj

2. What is the term for being blindly positive about a share?

a. Totally biased

b. Strong breakout

c. Total breakdown

d. Confirmation bias

e. A total idiot who is going to lose money

3. Someone calls you and offers you a cheap share or commodity. Do you:

a. Invite him round for a chat as *EastEnders* isn't on tonight

b. Hang up

c. Say "How much can I put in?"

d. Say "I've seen *Wolf of Wall Street*, no thanks"

e. Tell him to f*** right off

4. Which are the best shares for long-term gains?

a. Ones that raise their dividends every year

b. Ones where the charts have gone down a lot as there's plenty of room for them to rise

c. I ask my mate who's really good at shares to tell me

d. Ones with charts that just keep going up

e. Boring companies with rising profits

5. When researching a share, it's best to look at it from the point of view of:

a. Private Fraser

b. Gordon Brown

c. Mr Spock

d. Kesha

e. Corporal Jones

6. What's the best way to test demand for a share?

a. Use Level 2

b. Ask mates if they are buying it

c. See how many you can buy before the 15-second countdown stops coming up

d. Buy loads, then there will be more demand

e. Give the company a ring and ask

7. What's the best way to make money?

a. Trade forex – so easy to make money fast

b. Buy strong companies and average up

c. Buy strong companies and average down

d. Trade the Dow Jones on spread bets

e. Rob a bank (remember to wear a mask)

8. A guy on the bulletin boards tells you to buy a share that is about to rocket. Do you:

a. Warn others about rampers

b. Buy lots of it right away

c. Research it properly then make a decision

d. Buy it, then tell all your mates in order to get the price up

e. Get some. After all, it's only 2p. What could go wrong?

9. What's the way to ensure you can't lose more than 20% on a trade?

a. Use a stop loss

b. Use a guaranteed stop loss with a broker

c. Use a guaranteed stop with a spread bet firm

d. Keep an eye on it all the time

e. Don't put more than £20 on it

> ## 10. What can you use to make money when the market goes down?

a. CFDs

b. Flog your wedding ring at the pawnbrokers

c. Spread bets

d. Sell the *Big Issue*

e. Covered warrants

> ## 11. You've read The Naked Trader. Do you think the writer is:

a. Probably a genius

b. The best thing since the iPad Air 2/3/4/5/6/7 (delete as appropriate depending on when you read this)

c. Too good-looking to write books on money

d. A total tosser

e. Has completely lost the plot

Now look at the answers and add up the numbers.

Scores

1. a-0 b-5 c-0 d-0 e-0

2. a-1 b-0 c-0 d-5 e-1

3. a-0 b-5 c-0 d-4 e-5

4. a-5 b-0 c-0 d-4 e-5

5. a-0 b-0 c-5 d-0 e-0

6. a-5 b-0 c-4 d-0 e-1

7. a-0 b-5 c-0 d-0 e-0

8. a-5 b-0 c-4 d-0 e-0

9. a-0 b-0 c-5 d-2 e-0

10. a-5 b-1 c-5 d-0 e-5

11. a-2 b-2 c-1 d-100 e-100

(Anyone answering d or e to question 11 is disqualified from the quiz.)

Add up all your scores for your final total.

Analysis

40 or more: Master investor!

You have every chance of success in the stock market. Your approach to shares looks to be solid and I have every confidence that you will soon be in profit.

30-39: Good potential

You have the makings of a good investor, but you must be careful not to blow it by taking too many risks. Take it easy.

25–29: A lot of work to do

You are too liable to take major risks and you're likely to make losses unless you temper your gambling instincts.

Under 25

Oh dear! Did you really read the book? You need to get right back to basics before you lose all your money!

The best and the worst moments of life at NakedTrader.co.uk

You can catch up with my trading adventures at my website, **www.nakedtrader.co.uk**.

My email address is **robbiethetrader@aol.com**. I'm happy to answer emails but one thing I can't do is offer any advice as to whether you should buy, sell or hold anything!

Also, I do get a *lot* of emails so please be kind and stick to 150 words or fewer – no life stories! And do check the FAQs on my website or in this book, as the answer you could be seeking might already be there.

Here's a little compilation of some of the best (and worst) moments from my online diary over the last couple of years. Hey, it's fine if you skip it – I understand. Maybe it's a bit like looking at someone else's holiday snaps …

THE SCRUFFY ENCLOSURE

This Friday we paid a visit to the Ascot races, and got to watch from a nice box courtesy of Spreadex. Ascot is a lovely course and it's better to go when it's a low-profile day: you don't have to wear a top hat and stuff and it's not that busy, which makes it more enjoyable.

Amazingly, I wasn't the most scruffily dressed in the box – I was well beaten on that score. Though I *was* the second-worst dressed.

At one point I was accosted by a bloke in a pinstripe suit who told me I must be rich as I was badly dressed.

"I happen to notice," he said, "that all the really wealthy people are scruffy."

"Well," I said. "I must introduce you to shops like Primark and Mr Pound…"

I lost £100 trying to back 8–1 shots, while all the odds-on favourites went in. Never mind, it was all good fun.

It actually gave me a great idea for any spread bet company.

Rent a box at the races. Invite 30 of your worst losers/addicted gamblers, take all their bets on the day. Assume they lose an average of £300 each. That's £9,000 turnover, after say two-grand in costs – leaving a profit of £7,000.

Now do that six days a week and that's £42,000 profit a week, or over £2m a year. Neat idea, huh?

MY LUXURY ITEM

Ed Milliband's music choices for *Desert Island Discs* pretty much sum him up (though one has the suspicion that there was a massive Labour Party meeting to decide what the best choices would be).

So, he went for: Neil Diamond's 'Sweet Caroline' (!), Aha's 'Take On Me', and Robbie Williams' 'Angels'.

If I was on a desert island and had to put up with those three bits of music non-stop my luxury item would be a gun so I could shoot myself.

GIVE ME THE TOP OR BOTTOM

I've decided I'm just not a mid-market guy, I hate middle anything. Give me top end or bottom end (just like in bed ...).

I was thinking about this at the cinema the other day.

I like watching films either at an amazing top-end cinema such as the Electric in Notting Hill or the new fab one that's opened in Barnes. Both offer amazing seats, excellent food and a great experience. Home-made ice cream? Yes please!

But I also like a real old Cineworld fleapit in Hammersmith. Hardly anyone goes, you have the place to yourself, can stretch out and relax – but mind the fleas. And Tuesdays? Just £7.

I really hate the mid-market ones that everyone goes to. They're full, expensive and rotten. Mid-market people rustle and chatter and play on their phones. The places smell of a mix of farts and aftershave.

It's the same for me with shops. I'm either in Poundland, Primark or Pringle.

You wouldn't find me in Next. It is just so MIDDLE. Middling clothing, middling service (but a great business for traders, of course).

The pound shops are great. I could be in there for hours. It's fascinating what you can buy. And I always enjoy hearing someone ask the cashier: "How much is this?"

In the park, I'd rather mix with what you might call the 'rough' kids and parents. They're fun and open and talkable. Even though last night the rough lady with the massive Alsatian kindly advised me not to kick the football or her dog would " 'ave it".

The middles are awful. So stuck up. "Pomegranate, Xavier ... come away from those horrid rough kids now!"

You can't get a conversation going with them. They look at you like you're something nasty the cat dragged in.

I love the uppers, though. So jolly and fun. And lovely and posh and comforting, and again easy to talk to.

Hotels? Travelodge or Ritz Carlton. Hate the middles and the 'boutiques'.

Restaurants? You'll either find me in the local café with a bacon sandwich or at the top places eating lovely food. I hate the middle ones. Those chains serving up horrible middle food at middle prices. With middle flavours.

Taxes – either go for it left-wingers and tax at 70% if you think that works (but see how well France is doing with that). Or tax us at 30%.

I realise I am also either bottom at something or top. I never manage the middle of anything. At school I was in the top 2% for English and the bottom 2% for science.

One school report I got said: "Robbie is one of the most backward pupils I have ever taught."

So if you want to find me, look somewhere near the top ... or near the bottom.

EXCUSE THEIR FRENCH

Christopher is now into chart music which does bring the odd problem. French radio stations don't know the English bad words, so they tend to play the bad versions of songs instead of the watered-down ones.

So there we were on holiday in France listening to Icona Pop's 'I Love It' on French radio. The watered-down lyrics go: "You're from the 70s but I'm a 90s chick".

The real lyrics as played in France go: "I'm a 90s bitch".

Cue: "What's a bitch?"

"A female dog," is the best reply we could come up with. He wasn't buying it. Kids can always tell when a word is dodgy. "So it's okay if I say bitch, then?"

He's also noticed that every song I like appears to have the word 'sexy' in it. And he's right. What can I do? I'm just too sexy for my shirt.

Coming back from the France trip we arrived at border control. The control man passed Mrs NT and Christopher but then looked two or three times at my photo and frowned.

Oh no, I thought. *What's up? Did I do something bad and forget about it?*

The chap looked back at me and said, "Are you the Naked Trader?"

Goodness me, that was funny. "Yes," I said. "How are your trades going?"

"Rubbish," he said.

I hastily departed.

HERE TO HELP

So *there I was in Sainsbury's* minding my own business when a sweet old lady bustled up.

"Are you staff?" she enquired.

I wasn't sure whether to be flattered or offended. Perhaps what I thought of as a trendy Timberland jacket actually resembled the Sainsbury's uniform.

Either way, I decided to help.

"How can I help you madam?" I replied.

It turned out she couldn't find the condensed milk (whatever condensed milk is – milk that's been edited down?).

Lucky for me, I spotted it quickly.

"Thanks for being so helpful," she said. I realised I was doing wonders for Sainsbury's. I was even tempted to get a badge printed up. *'I'm Robbie, how can I help?'* Just imagine the share price after a few weeks of that.

To be honest, I'm not sure if I'd go long or stick on a short …

ALL I CAN REMEMBER OF SCHOOL

My son Christopher needed some help with his homework recently, so I patronisingly offered to help him. Easy stuff for me, obviously.

"Right," I said confidently, turning to the first item. I read the title: '*Personification*'. I gulped.

What the hell is that? I couldn't remember. I read the next bit. '*Metaphors*'. I gulped again. I could only remember similes (like it was yesterday).

'*What is being personified in this sentence?*' said the homework.

"It's the wind," said Christopher.

"Yes, correct son, well done," I bluffed.

Next: '*What does the sentence mean?*'

What do they mean what does the sentence mean? I totally froze. I crashed and burned. Well, what does it mean? I went blank.

"Erm, let's ask mum when she comes home," I said.

Look, she used to be a teacher. I had no idea what we were supposed to put. A sentence means, well, what it means – doesn't it?

We moved onto maths. *Right*, I thought, *I'm quite good at maths.*

"What does 'perpendicular' mean?" asked Christopher.

"I *think* it means it stands up on its own or something. Let's Google it." Thank God for Google. It was tough in my day: no Google at all. And if you want to know what that was like, you could probably Google it.

"What's an equilateral triangle?"

"Hang on, let me get online. Actually ... even better ... let's play football and mum will help you with your homework later."

And this was just at eight years old. What's going to happen next year? I am going to have to do some serious revision.

I can remember almost nothing at all from school. This is all I can remember:

Shakespeare wrote in iambic pentameter, Peter the Great was weird and had a bushy beard, I can for some strange reason recite a Browning poem, and I know the French for knackered is *epuise* and the capital of Denmark is Copenhagen (tricky one that).

And that is the lot. And a fat lot of good any of the above has done me. Well, I guess I can read and write, so that must be something.

Anyway, who cares? I must have done something right – at least ten people a day want to link with me on LinkedIn, so there! (Please don't ask to link to me!)

WOULD YOU LIKE A SMILE WITH THAT?

A coffee shop in France charges €7 if you don't say please.

€4.25 if you say please.

€1.40 if you say "Good morning, a coffee please".

I'd be happy to pay €50 to say: "Get me a ******* coffee you ****!"

Ooh la la!

BIG ALAN

Wow, thanks Alan Sugar!

Lord A has done a deal with Tesco. His new advertising screen will scan you to decide what kind of advert is going to be blasted at you when you fill up with petrol.

Our thanks to the gracious baron for making the world a better place. The system will scan you for age and gender. Hmmm, I wonder which age group will be targeted with which ad and what new Lord A products might be advertised to you.

20s: Am App: Some crap phone app you pay £2 for and only use once.

30s: Am Dum Dum: Lord A's new baby dummy emergency replacement service – can't find that precious dummy? Call us!

40s: Am Affair: Need help with that midlife crisis?

50s: Am Sack: You've been fired and will never work again info pack.

60s: Am Latte: All you'll be able to buy with your pension payout.

70s: Am Lift: A nice sparkling stairlift for your home, with free wi-fi built in.

80s: Am Nearly Dead: A discount for a designer coffin (no wi-fi included).

90s+: An Amstrad E-m@iler: Only way to get rid of the rest of the stock. At least these people can't say no.

FIGHTING CRIME WITH SIR CLIFF

Cliff Richard has just completed his 100th album.

With 15 tracks on each one it must mean he has recorded 1,500 tracks.

So I have an idea: instead of filling up our prisons with minor criminals, instead force them to spend a week listening to every single Cliff track. Say, roughly 200 songs a day full-time.

I guarantee you: these criminals will never reoffend again and taxpayers will save a fortune, especially since if they reoffend next time they will have to listen to every track recorded by Blue, Westlife and One Direction.

"Let me outta here, I promise I will never commit a crime ever again … pleassseeeee!"

HAIRY BUMS

Some gossip: apparently Luisa from 2013's *Apprentice* has taken part in orgies. Oooh.

An orgy? Please, no, can I just be on my own with a cup of tea and some carrot cake? Thanks.

I always thought orgies usually only involved extremely fat people with hairy bums? (That's all there were at the ones I went to anyway … and you should have seen the blokes too!)

DRAGON'S DONE

I'm not surprised Duncan Bannatyne says he is not going to date anyone else after various failed relationships.

It's hardly surprising he had trouble with the women in his life. After all, if you're in bed you simply can't keep a running commentary on things:

"I'm in … I'm out … I'm in … I'm out … I'm in … I'm out … "

NAKED TRADER'S FAVOURITE TV SHOWS!

1. Breaking Bad

2. The Sopranos

3. Curb Your Enthusiasm

4. Seinfeld

5. House of Cards

6. Mad Men

7. Girls

8. The Apprentice

9. Dragons' Den

10. Air Crash Investigation

Seminars

If you enjoyed the book and want to bring it to life, why not come to one of my seminars? You get to meet me (you lucky thing!) and we spend the whole day together looking at live markets. There's plenty of drinks in the bar afterwards too! I hold the seminars roughly five times a year, always close to London.

The seminars are for beginners and intermediates and you don't need to know anything about the markets before coming – although it would be handy if you have read the book! The seminars are held in a pleasant, relaxing and informal setting.

A three-course lunch, coffees, snacks and, of course, loads of chunky KitKats and fruit gums are included in the price. For the current price please check my website. Best time to book is early because that's when I give out massive early-booking discounts!

The idea behind the seminar is *simplicity*. I don't use jargon or fancy words – everything is in *plain English!* The idea is for you to come away from the event a wiser and better investor with lots of new ideas.

The subjects covered in the seminar include:

- how to find value shares
- Level 2: how to use it to grab great-timed buys and sells
- how to beat the market makers
- how to spot tree shakes and use them in your favour
- how to get a market edge when timing trades
- how to tell when *not* to buy a share
- spread betting – how to do it and why it's a good thing
- how to short shares
- the best ways to buy and sell shares
- how to become a confident investor
- charts: how I use them
- profit target and stop loss setting
- how to plan share trades: exits, entries and timescales
- how to research shares simply and effectively
- how to spot an undervalued share
- what to do when shares crash suddenly
- avoiding stock market sharks and tipsters
- how to handle market volatility
- direct market access.

Phew!

I give tons of live examples all day of how to research shares quickly, easily and effectively. We'll watch how shares move live on screen. And we'll look at *why* shares move and how you can use the two effective tools I employ to produce a powerful buy or sell signal.

Not forgetting plenty of questions and answers – all the things that bug you about the market but you were too afraid to ask about!

So if you feel you are interested in a seminar, email me for details at **robbiethetrader@aol.com**. Please put 'Seminar interested' in the subject line. I will then send you full details and you can decide if you fancy coming.

The seminars are usually held at a hotel close to Heathrow airport in London, so if you live up north, in Ireland or further afield you can easily fly in. Maybe I'll see you soon!

Finally ...

I'm almost off – this book is nearly over. In fact I'm about to shout for joy, given I don't find writing that easy and it's all been a right pain in the neck – though it wasn't quite as hard as edition three, given some of that stood the test of time

Tipping point

Well, the tipping point is now. So you can tip me if you like for all the valuable information you've got from this book. It's worth a lot more than £14.99, so I suggest a tip of about a tenner will do. Please put your tip in an envelope and send it to me. Much appreciated. Thank you, guv'nor!

Oh all right, I guess that ruse won't work. So what is a tipping point in reality, and how does it affect trading?

A *tipping point* in gambling, investing or trading circles is the point where you 'lose it'. Instead of making money you have a mental crisis – you go bananas and start throwing money away and losing heavily.

A tipping point is basically a small thing that tips you over from being a sensible investor or trader into a complete and utter nutter.

It's something every trader will come close to now and then, especially in their early days, so I didn't want to leave you without telling you to watch out. You should be excited about trading now – but you still need to be careful.

A tipping point could be something simple like: you started out doing really well but one stock lets you down, even though you *know* it's really a good one. So you throw more money at it. You get annoyed and take out some spread bets for it too. Suddenly the share lurches down more and you're losing capital hand over fist. But you buy more of the stock, as you're sure it's a good purchase.

Soon you're out of capital, so you get credit and invest all that into the stock too.

And then – the market tumbles.

You are showing huge losses. But you're now utterly beholden to the share and leveraged up to the gills to keep with its fall.

All of a sudden, from a reasonably good investor, you've become a crazed gambler. And all because one stock tripped you up.

The tipping point can be anything. In fact, usually – from a longer-term perspective – it's actually just a small issue. Maybe you had a good run, showing a profit of £20,000 in your spread betting account. A couple of bad market days later you're back down to only break-even. You're determined to show a profit so take out more bets than you should, and now you're in a loss. You've tipped over.

You have to learn to stop before the tipping point catches you out.

What's the solution if you recognise you've reached a tipping point?

Cut your stakes dramatically. Or get out completely. Get rid of whatever it was that began to tip you over.

How do you recognise a tipping point?

You start to feel out of control of everything and lose command of your investments. You begin to over-trade – anything to start winning again. Symptoms may even include feelings of excitement; though perhaps more common are irritation and bad moods that are seemingly only alleviated (briefly) by a trade.

So one day, when something tips you over, remember what you read here and do something about it before your brain and bank account take a hammering.

And if all the above isn't a good tip, I don't know what else is.

Final thoughts

An accountant came to one of my seminars. After I covered some basic analysis of various companies, he piped up:

"But don't you look at acid test ratios? And what about the PEG value versus historic P/E?"

And various other things. As an honest(ish) person I replied:

"No, in fact I don't really know anything about them. But do you think all these measures are relevant?"

He then went on to describe how he analyses accounts in the minutest detail. He carried on for ten minutes, leaving me and the audience a bit bemused. We didn't understand much of what he was on about, but I certainly wouldn't dismiss it as I don't mind learning something new.

And I did wonder: am I too basic? Should I be looking at a whole host of financial data? Should I try to understand everything in the accounts?

I had a chat with him in the bar later. He said:

"Actually, I think I maybe overanalyse. The fact is I can't bring myself to buy many shares because there's always one figure I don't like. I've hardly been able to trade because I get scared after all the analysis."

He realised there and then that overdoing the analysis had actually cost him a lot of money.

So, my parting shot to you is: *don't overdo it.* You don't have to analyse everything to the *n*th degree. My simple methods outlined in this book should work. And you will, in time, work out your own parameters. Simple can be best. Ask the best chefs. It's the same with shares.

I really hope you enjoyed the book. I hope you got something out of it and at least a few ideas of how and what to trade.

However, I do realise some of you will read it and take no notice at all of anything I've written. Which brings me to this email I got from a reader of the last edition.

"First of all, as I'm sure you never hear – what a fantastic book!

"Have you any thoughts about this amazing small miner? Reading your book it breaks a lot of the basic rules you speak about in your book such as spread and debt-to-net-profit ratio (with is four times greater).

"However I am attracted to this AIM-listed share because of the promise of diamonds. The company seems to be on the way to concluding a seven-year journey locating diamonds in Finland and although the company doesn't look good on paper the RNS [Regulatory News Service] announcements recently are promising. I've also researched diamond exploration in general and this one appears to be nearing the end of the journey – and the CEO recently purchased loads of shares, so a good sign of confidence. The BBs are buzzing for the shares!

"Very interested in your thoughts on whether you think I should stick with my gut instinct or listen to my head?"

So there we have it. He thinks this is a great book but the first share he bought breaks nearly every rule I banged on about throughout the whole thing.

I said:

- Avoid commodity companies.
- Don't buy something because you saw it on a bulletin board.
- Don't buy penny shares.
- Don't buy tiny market caps. If anything happens, they are impossible to sell.
- Don't buy just because a director bought.
- Don't be greedy and think you are going to make a fortune on a tiny prospecting share.
- Never use gut instinct.
- Don't buy companies with big debt.
- Don't buy shares with big spreads.
- Beware of penny share pump and dumps.

So there you are, some of the major rules of the book neatly broken by someone who just read it.

I guess that sums up nicely what not to do. Which probably won't stop you.

But, hey ... I did try!

I wish you the best of luck and hope you make a fortune. Just make sure you do it over time and don't try and make your millions in a week. So long, and pick some good ones!

And don't forget you can catch me at my website **www.naked trader.co.uk** – see you there...

"The thing that most affects the stock market is everything."

– James Playsted Wood

Index